THE MANY AND THE FEW

MARK JURDJEVIC

The Many and the Few

Machiavelli's and Guicciardini's Critique of Aristocratic Regimes

UNIVERSITY OF TORONTO PRESS
Toronto Buffalo London

Toronto Buffalo London
utppublishing.com
Printed in Canada

ISBN 978-1-4875-6686-9 (cloth)
ISBN 978-1-4875-6691-3 (EPUB)
ISBN 978-1-4875-6690-6 (PDF)

Toronto Italian Studies

Library and Archives Canada Cataloguing in Publication

Title: The many and the few : Machiavelli's and Guicciardini's critique of aristocratic regimes / Mark Jurdjevic.
Other titles: Machiavelli's and Guicciardini's critique of aristocratic regimes
Names: Jurdjevic, Mark, author
Series: Toronto Italian studies.
Description: Series statement: Toronto Italian studies | Includes bibliographical references and index.
Identifiers: Canadiana (print) 20250304295 | Canadiana (ebook) 20250304449 | ISBN 9781487566869 (cloth) | ISBN 9781487566913 (EPUB) | ISBN 9781487566906 (PDF)
Subjects: LCSH: Guicciardini, Francesco, 1483–1540—Criticism and interpretation. | LCSH: Machiavelli, Niccolò, 1469–1527—Criticism and interpretation. | LCSH: Aristocracy (Social class) | LCSH: Populism. | LCSH: Florence (Italy)—History—1421–1737.
Classification: LCC DG738.14.G9 J87 2026 | DDC 945/.060922—dc23

Cover design: Will Brown
Cover image: Imagedoc/Alamy.com

We wish to acknowledge the land on which the University of Toronto Press operates. This land is the traditional territory of the Wendat, the Anishnaabeg, the Haudenosaunee, the Métis, and the Mississaugas of the Credit First Nation.

This book has been published with the help of a grant from the Federation for the Humanities and Social Sciences, through the Awards to Scholarly Publications Program, using funds provided by the Social Sciences and Humanities Research Council of Canada.

University of Toronto Press acknowledges the financial support of the Government of Canada, the Canada Council for the Arts, and the Ontario Arts Council, an agency of the Government of Ontario, for its publishing activities.

Canada Council for the Arts
Conseil des Arts du Canada

Funded by the Government of Canada
Financé par le gouvernement du Canada

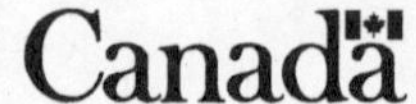

To Oliver, a fellow historian

Contents

Acknowledgments

It is a pleasure to acknowledge the numerous sources of support and encouragement from which I have benefited while writing this book. Thanks to the John Simon Guggenheim Memorial Foundation for a fellowship in 2019–20 and to the Social Sciences and Humanities Research Council of Canada for an Insight Grant from 2020 to 2025. I am grateful to my colleagues in the Renaissance Society of America and the American Political Science Association who provided valuable feedback on first drafts of chapters at the society's annual conferences in San Juan, Boston, Dublin, Montreal, Toronto, and Philadelphia. Thanks also go to a particularly warm community of fellow travellers who made writing this book a pleasure, particularly Natasha Piano, Sean Irwin, James Hankins, Katie Robiadek, Giulia Belloluogo, Milos Mitrovic, and Yves Winter. At University of Toronto Press, I would like to thank Suzanne Rancourt, the two anonymous readers who provided expert feedback, and Angela Wingfield for her superlative copy-editing. I owe a special debt of gratitude to John McCormick, who organized a symposium dedicated to Francesco Guicciardini at the University of Chicago in 2018. John is the embodiment of everything that is good about the academy. For years he has been unstintingly generous as a scholar, mentor, and friend and a source of intellectual and professional inspiration. I know that I speak for so many other people when I say, "John, thank you! You're the best."

THE MANY AND THE FEW

Introduction: The Politics of the Few and the Many in the Political Thought of Machiavelli and Guicciardini

This book examines the improbable friendship between Francesco Guicciardini and Niccolò Machiavelli and its impact on Guicciardini's political thought and interpretation of Florentine history. In the literature on these two pioneering thinkers of the late Renaissance they are almost always presented in terms of dramatic contrasts. Machiavelli's family had been persecuted by the Medici in the fifteenth century, and as a result Machiavelli grew up in a politically alienated family of modest means.[1] In his first political career in the republican government led by Piero Soderini, Machiavelli had to navigate sustained *ottimati* opposition to his various initiatives, such as the militia project, and in the end, owing to their resentment, he relived the fate of his persecuted ancestor Girolamo after the Medici restoration of 1512.[2] Machiavelli was imprisoned, tortured, and spent the remainder of the decade in impoverished political isolation. Guicciardini's family, by contrast, were exceptionally high-ranking and influential lieutenants of Cosimo and Lorenzo de' Medici throughout the fifteenth century, as Guicciardini proudly related in his *History of Florence.* With only a few brief exceptions, Guicciardini operated at the centre of Florentine politics throughout his adult life and, as president of the Romagna and a prince in his own right, dramatically exceeded his ancestors in the acquisition and display of power and wealth.

In terms of political preferences, Guicciardini championed aristocratic government – he was its most "unrepentant defender," in Quentin Skinner's words – whereas Machiavelli displayed a pugnacious anti-elitist populism in his two most celebrated works of political thought.[3] The Guicciardini was one of Florence's most distinguished and powerful houses, always close to power, whereas the Machiavelli family, though established, occupied a considerably lower rung on the city's social ladder and was alienated from the regime during Machiavelli's youth. As

Roberto Ridolfi observed, they also differed in innately psychological terms, one cold, austere, and aristocratic, and the other effusive, indulgent, and egalitarian.[4] As John Najemy put it, they are the "two most celebrated political thinkers of the Florentine Renaissance, so close in their origins and culture, yet so distant in their political experiences, loyalties, and inner convictions."[5] Despite their contrasting world views and class solidarities, however, they became good friends who promoted each other's interests: Guicciardini was instrumental in the first staging of Machiavelli's play *Mandragola*, before a papal audience, and Machiavelli was Guicciardini's agent and advocate in the complex marriage negotiations for Guicciardini's daughter. In the final years of Machiavelli's life they became political allies and close collaborators as papal employees tasked with defending Florence from an imminent and potentially catastrophic invasion by Charles V.

Counter-intuitively, I did not set out to write about Guicciardini. The book began as an investigation into Machiavelli's political thought. Following comparative lines of inquiry about the relative merits of aristocratic and popular politics that I had hitherto assumed were uniquely Machiavellian, I wound up inadvertently writing a book about Guicciardini's lifelong scrutiny of the same questions and his unexpectedly common conclusions.

I initially intended to revisit arguments I made in *A Great and Wretched City* about the way in which Machiavelli's convictions changed as his focus shifted from ancient Rome to Renaissance Florence.[6] Focusing on his last and longest text, *Florentine Histories*, I traced there the new themes in his writing that had emerged uniquely as a product of reflection on Florentine history and political culture. Most significantly, I stressed the degree to which the *Histories* demonstrated a reconsideration of his characterization of elite and popular politics. In his two early major works of political theory, *The Prince* and *The Discourses on Livy*, Machiavelli characterized all political culture, ancient and modern, as driven by conflict between elites and people, each group permanently disposed towards certain types of behaviour because of their innate and timeless dispositions. Everywhere and always, elites aspire to domination, treat abusively those below them, and engage in destabilizing internecine factional quarrels. They therefore pose a permanent threat to a stable political order. Everywhere and always, the people aspire merely to live unmolested in the enjoyment of their material goods and display moderate political ambition but, because of their superior numbers, always possess the ability to subdue violently the elites who rule in their name when elite abuse becomes excessive. They therefore possess uniquely effective constraints on the dangers implicit in the ubiquitous elite domination of political life. Machiavelli constructed all his early political theory upon that conviction about the contrasting natures of elites and people.

Although the Florentine experience always informed Machiavelli's thinking, he found much of his evidence and inspiration for his binary view of nobles and people in a broad reading of ancient history and most especially the Roman republic. After 1520, when he emerged from a painful period of political ostracization, he benefited from two requests from the Medici family that caused him to focus exclusively on Florentine politics and history: the first, a request for his view on how best to reform the city's constitution to stabilize Medici power; and the second, the commission, theoretically from the Florentine Studio but following the instructions of Cardinal Giulio de' Medici, to write a history of Florence. I argued in *A Great and Wretched City* that Machiavelli recognized that the social fluidity of a mercantile city with a robust industrial and banking economy simply could not fit into his earlier binary theory, which had been inspired in large part by reflection on the agrarian slave economy of ancient Rome. When meditating upon Livy's Rome or contemporary Venice, he could meaningfully analyse political conflict in terms of patricians and plebeians, but he recognized that in Florence there were many more categories: the Medici family, who exercised de facto princely power; the *ottimati* class, a broad middle class spanning the *popolo grasso* (wealthy merchants) and the *popolo minuto* (shopkeepers and artisans); and a dispossessed industrial proletariat (such as the *sottoposti* of the Wool Guild). In addition to the city's social complexity, individuals and families were not permanently tied to legal classes with corresponding political rights. Social status was a function of wealth, and in Florence's proto-capitalist banking economy, family fortunes were frequently in a continuous cycle of being amassed and lost. Yesterday's plutocrat could and did become today's impoverished debtor and vice versa. Compounding the natural vicissitudes of economic life was the city's political culture in which triumphant factions routinely bankrupted their foes with punitive taxation and impoverishing, forced loans.

A Great and Wretched City focused on novel arguments about elite and popular culture in Machiavelli's *Florentine Histories*. Although he continued to make excoriating remarks about elite conduct throughout the text, he also made striking, new, positive claims about the Florentine elite. Most significantly, he attributed Florence's present vulnerability to its corrupt military culture of dependence on fickle mercenaries, and that in turn he attributed at the end of book 2 to the city's class wars, the people's definitive defeat of the city's elite, and the consequent transformation of the latter from an armed warrior culture to an unarmed merchant culture. Although most of his *Histories* condemned the corruption and weakness of Florentine culture, his early chapters chronicled the achievements of the *primo popolo*; chief among them were the city's fearsome and muscular native military forces. Those forces disappeared after the people aggressively disarmed the vanquished nobility. However tragic the loss of the city's military self-sufficiency, one would expect at least that the people's triumph would have resolved the problem of the violence and factional strife caused by elite misconduct. But the remainder of the *Histories* continued to trace the relentless persistence of internal strife. In explaining the persistence of the civil discord, Machiavelli for the first time began to display the dismissive and critical views of the people that were typical of the humanist political culture that surrounded him and of the entire political canon against which he had formerly been the only dissenting voice. In Machiavelli's narrative, once triumphant, the people acted on the same bellicose, monopolistic instincts that were typical of elites, creating anew the very problems they had intended to solve by disarming the nobility. For the first time in his oeuvre, Machiavelli began to characterize the people as immoderate, inconstant, and unjust.

Machiavelli's surprising new utterances were not limited to historical reflections on Florence's early class wars. When the Medici solicited Machiavelli's opinion on how best to stabilize their power in the city, he drafted a constitutional proposal that reflected these new assumptions, assumptions that were not evident in his earlier theory derived from Roman culture. *A Great and Wretched City* concluded by analysing the ways in which Machiavelli's republican theory from the 1520s abandoned his earlier binary axioms in favour of a tripartite analysis of the city's social groups: elite, middle ranks, and people. Contrary to earlier convictions that nobles always posed a major threat to the rule of law and robust, accountable, public-facing institutions, he now conceded that any stable regime would have to grant the city's elite a conspicuous leadership role that affirmed their high self-regard. The people, too, no longer appeared to be content simply to live unmolested in the secure enjoyment of their property and possessions; they, too, required class-specific councils in the regime for the expression of their political ambitions and identity. Machiavelli also signalled overtly that his vision for Florence was not based on the Roman model; he announced at the outset that the circumstances faced by the city required the consideration of new types of government. His proposal never invoked Roman example, never referred to Livy, or to any Roman statesman or jurist whatsoever. To the extent that his model reflected other existing regimes, it bore some similarities to the Venetian constitution and what J.G.A. Pocock famously called the "mechanized virtue" of the city's complex, interlocking councils.

A Great and Wretched City thus became part of a larger debate about whether Machiavelli's later writings reflected an aristocratic or conservative departure from the radical populism of *The Prince* and *The Discourses.*[7] Immersed as I was in a close reading of the *Florentine Histories,* I understood that transformation as a purely internal product of Machiavelli's reading of his city's past and its painful history of vicious factional conflict.

Robert Black's recent studies of Machiavelli, however, suggest instead that the changes in Machiavelli's later political and historical work were less the product of his engagement with Florentine history and more the result of Machiavelli's improved social circumstances. In Black's view, the angry and uniquely populist content of Machiavelli's early political thought reflected his middling social status, resentment at the *ottimati* that had caused his political ruin, and contempt for the aristocratic pieties of the Florentine republican establishment whose myriad flaws had led the republic inexorably into the hands of the princely Medici. After 1520, he regained the trust of the Medici family and joined the aristocratic circle upon whom the family relied for counsel. He had finally returned to the life of politics that he had declared many times mattered more to him than anything else. Owing to the exceptional success of his play *Mandragola,* he was also widely and highly regarded as a literary talent. In Black's summation, "In his last great political and historical work, Machiavelli becomes the voice of the status quo and of compromise: in his ideal Florence there was room for the Medici (at least until the death of the pope, of course lacking direct legitimate male heirs), for the people, and for the aristocracy – in other words, a mixed constitution ... At the end of his life, Machiavelli was moving towards a political conservatism that recalls the greatest Florentine champion of the mixed constitution, Machiavelli's intimate friend and admirer of Venice, Francesco Guicciardini."[8]

Reflection on that sentence was the first step in Guicciardini's displacing of Machiavelli in this book for centre stage.[9] Given that Guicciardini was Machiavelli's closest friend and most voluminous correspondent during the years that related to his new embrace of the mixed constitution long cherished by Florentine aristocrats, it seems possible that those new Machiavellian arguments might have been the result of his sustained correspondence with Guicciardini. John Najemy has already shown the considerable degree to which *The Prince* reflected issues and themes that Machiavelli had debated extensively in his earlier correspondence with another powerful Florentine aristocrat, Francesco Vettori. Perhaps those new perspectives were less the result of reflection on Florentine history and less the result of Machiavelli's newly elevated social position and literary success, but rather the result of sustained persuasion by one of Machiavelli's few (arguably only) intellectual equals.

Accordingly, I turned to the Machiavelli-Guicciardini correspondence to consider its content and themes. Machiavelli certainly engaged Guicciardini in his letters, much as he had done earlier with Vettori, advancing arguments from his political writings. For example, in his letter of 15 March 1526, defending his plan to muster a native militia, Machiavelli defended popular rationality and judgment: "You know – and anyone who knows how to reason about this world knows it too – that the people are fickle and foolish; nevertheless, as fickle and foolish as they are, what ought to be done is frequently what they say to do."[10] Just as he rhetorically urged the Medici to capitalize on an auspicious moment to liberate Italy from the barbarians, he urged Guicciardini to do the same, with a similar rhetorical flourish: "You are aware of how many opportunities have been lost: do not lose this one or, putting yourself in the hands of Fortune and Time, put your trust in having it again, because Time does not always bring identical circumstances and Fortune is not always identical. Were I talking to a man who was ignorant of secrecy or who was unaware of the world, I should discourse longer. Free Italy from long-lasting anxiety; eradicate those savage brutes, which have nothing human about them save their faces and voices."[11] But Guicciardini typically restricted himself to discussion of the immediate political questions related to their missions and rarely engaged Machiavelli's conversational lures, leading Robert Black to conclude that "most of the significant political ideas there came from Machiavelli, with whom Guicciardini did not trouble to disagree, and so their correspondence – lively and significant as it was – did not rise to the overarching unity and profound dialogue characteristic of the earlier Machiavelli-Vettori correspondence."[12] In terms of political content, their exchange of letters was more Machiavellian monologue than dialogue.

If their correspondence did not display the give and take that was characteristic of Machiavelli's debates with Vettori, it certainly affirmed active discussion between them during and about the composition of the *Florentine Histories.* Following Machiavelli's commission, Guicciardini wrote to him:

> You see that, with only the faces of the men and extrinsic colours changed, all the very same things return; and we do not see any incident that has not been seen in other times. But changing the names and forms of things means that only the prudent recognize them; therefore history is good and useful, because it sets before you and makes you recognize and see again what you have never known or seen. There follows from this a brotherly

syllogism: that he who gave you the task of writing annals is greatly to be commended; and you are to be exhorted to carry out the charge given to you with diligence.[13]

In 1524, towards the completion of the *Histories*, Machiavelli wrote to Guicciardini: "Here in the country I have been applying myself, and continue to do so, to writing the history, and I would pay ten soldi – but no more – to have you by my side so that I might show you where I am, because, since I am about to come to certain details, I would need to learn from you whether or not I am being too offensive in my exaggerating or understating of the facts."[14] In 1525 Machiavelli wrote Guicciardini again, to report that "I am just now beginning to write again, and I vent my feelings by accusing the princes who have all done everything they can to bring us to this situation."[15] The two were evidently alert to each other's points of view.

Further, in spite of Black's claim that Guicciardini was disinclined to engage with Machiavelli's political ideas, their correspondence clearly reveals his familiarity with Machiavelli's corpus and respect for his opinion. Guicciardini must have read Machiavelli's *Discourses on Livy* by 1521, judging from his likely allusion to that text when he wrote, regarding Machiavelli's mission to the chapter-general meeting of the Minorite Friars, "I believe this legation will not be completely useless for that, because in these three days' idleness you will have imbibed the entire Republic of Clogs and you will make use of that model for some purpose, comparing it or measuring it against some of those forms of yours."[16] In a subsequent letter Guicciardini addresses Machiavelli as "you who have read and written so many histories and seen so much of the world" and concludes by explaining that he holds Machiavelli to a higher standard owing to Machiavelli's talents: "Many excuses are admissible in others that cannot be accepted in one of your wisdom and experience."[17] In 1525 they exchanged a series of letters in which Machiavelli responded to Guicciardini's reading of Machiavelli's *Mandragola*, which Guicciardini was arranging to be performed before a papal audience.[18] In one of their last exchanges Guicciardini declared that "your advice carries so much weight with me that it has no need of others' authority."[19]

I became curious about the extent to which Guicciardini's numerous allusions to Machiavelli's political thought reflected significant engagement with those writings. Owing to Guicciardini's sustained refutation of the value of Roman institutions and customs in his *Considerations on the "Discourses" of Machiavelli* and book 2 of the *Dialogue on the Government of Florence*, the literature overwhelmingly stresses the adversarial nature of Guicciardini's response to Machiavelli's political thought, their evident mutual esteem notwithstanding.[20] Although Guicciardini's impact on Machiavelli remains an open question, I discovered that Machiavelli's impact on Guicciardini was substantial. In my rereading of Guicciardini from the vantage point of his relationship with Machiavelli, it became clear that Guicciardini did indeed engage in meaningful dialogue with Machiavelli – but more so in his political writings from this period than in the correspondence. Guicciardini was never overt – either to us or to Machiavelli – about his adaptation to Machiavelli's challenges and provocations; they are embedded and camouflaged within larger elaborations of Guicciardini's ideal senatorial political order. In this respect the hidden nature of Guicciardini's dialogue with Machiavelli is consistent with Guicciardini's generally more elusive and prudential prose style. As Gennaro Sasso observed in his seminal analysis of the two thinkers, Guicciardini always displayed a tendency, in stark contrast to Machiavelli, to obscure his genuine thoughts and convictions. Machiavelli had an irrepressibly confessional prose style – he almost always spoke and wrote directly, not infrequently at considerable cost.[21] Guicciardini's obsession with honour, reputation, and prudence resulted in a deliberately ambiguous mode of reasoning and arguing that revolved around cautious contrasting and weighing of pros and cons, thesis and antithesis.[22]

On a prima facie reading of Guicciardini's constitutional proposals, his political preferences are unambiguous. He consistently upholds the aristocratic mixed constitution praised by ancient luminaries such as Aristotle and Cicero and long championed by the Florentine *ottimati*, gazing admiringly at the stability of aristocratic rule in Venice, who saw in it the best path to avoid the popular challenges to their hegemony from below and the autocratic challenges by the Medici above them. Implicitly in his *History of Florence* and explicitly in the *Discorso di Logrogno* and book 2 (but only book 2; see chapter 4 for anticipatory subversions in book 1) in the *Dialogue on the Government of Florence*, Guicciardini defines his ideal political order as a mixed regime in which a prudential few, conspicuous for their excellence, carried out all the most important aspects of statecraft.[23] The *Discorso* in particular contains the most Platonic ideal opposite form of Machiavelli's view of elite rule as synonymous with abusive misconduct. Having advocated in that text for a lifetime gonfalonier, he acknowledges that the extreme term length would discourage many from applying. But he defended that as a strength rather than a weakness: "And even if this is a prospect likely to inspire only a few men, this stimulus is not therefore worthless, because in every well-ordered republic it is obvious that it is always a few able and virtuous citizens who exercise control: glorious deeds and great achievements have always been initiated and performed by a few men, because to be in charge of great enterprises and to be heads of government in free cities, great and varied talents and virtues are required, and these are to be found in very few men."[24] Relative to the precedent of previous Florentine regimes, with their complex and sometimes even competing councils, Guicciardini's model situates important decision-making power in a powerful and restricted senate, "in which all the wise and prudent men will sit ... all the most important work of governing will really be carried out by very few men, which is what always happens in republics, in both ancient and modern times."[25] These utterances drive the vast majority of interpretations of Guicciardini's political thought.

A more sustained reading of the Guicciardinian corpus, however, reveals a vastly more complex thinker who subverts his own aristocratic ideals to devastating scrutiny, on a par with and occasionally exceeding Machiavelli's critiques. From his very first to very last texts, Guicciardini consistently embeds an alternate narrative in which he thoroughly embraces, and arguably exceeds, Machiavelli's view of the innately positive qualities of the people and the innately destructive qualities of the elites. This aspect of his thought is substantially under-appreciated in scholarship on Guicciardini and Renaissance political thought. Gennaro Sasso identified aspects of it in a 1984 essay comparing the two thinkers, still the most sustained consideration of their points of convergence and divergence. Sasso's assessment, however, considerably understated the scale and complexity of Guicciardini's doubts about the virtues of rule by the prudential few. He ultimately placed Guicciardini, contra Machiavelli, squarely in the tradition of Florentine civic humanism and, like most scholars, identified him as a supporter of the consensus politics championed by the Florentine establishment even while recognizing that he frequently expressed frustration at the corruption and short-sighted policies of various oligarchic regimes. For Sasso, Guicciardini's occasionally conflicting utterances on elite rule reflected a corresponding contradiction between his general preference for aristocratic rule – rooted in an idealism, pride in his own achievements, and his family's station – and his acute and substantial familiarity with the chronic shortcomings of the actual Florentine elite, who never (how could they?) lived up to his ideals.

A fair point, to be sure, but defining Guicciardini's political vision as largely in keeping with the pieties of civic humanism, albeit with some historical reservations about elite conduct, understates the scale of Guicciardini's common ground with Machiavelli, for three reasons. First, Guicciardini not only frequently criticizes the self-serving corruption and incompetence of the Florentine aristocracy at crucial moments in the city's history but also condemns elite rule *in general* as systemically prone to self-serving, violent, corrupt, and incompetent politics. Guicciardini's ambivalence is not merely a conflict between historical reality and abstract principle but rather a conflict with elite rule at all levels – historically, in terms of actual practice, and at a theoretical level, in terms of innately problematic consequences of wealth, pride, and entitlement. Second, interpreting Guicciardini as a civic humanist altogether omits any mention of Guicciardini's corresponding acknowledgment of the rationality and moderation inherent in popular politics. In several texts Guicciardini implicitly concedes that the people make good judges of character, are instinctively inclined to share power reasonably with others, and take up arms only when compelled by extreme abuse from their betters – just as Machiavelli argued. Third, Guicciardini entirely shared Machiavelli's provocative ethical revolution expressed in the *Prince*, making his way of thinking fundamentally incompatible with the dominant virtue politics of their contemporaries; further still, his defence of that ethical revolution justified itself in ways that echoed Machiavelli's axioms about elites and people.

A few disclaimers at the outset are warranted. This book does not engage the question of whether Machiavelli's political thought changed over time and, if it did, whether he embraced a more conservative political outlook during his years of friendship with Guicciardini. I agree with Robert Black and others that it did, but I remain unconvinced that he embraced or championed the conventional, establishment views of the Medici circle and, less still, the virtue politics of Florentine humanism. For the purposes of this book, however, the issue is not relevant. Machiavelli remains a central figure and appears on virtually every page, but he is less the object of analysis than a device through which to excavate and appreciate Guicciardini's sustained acknowledgment of the virtue of populist politics, to allude to John McCormick's recent book with which this study substantially engages. In my frequent invocations and summaries of Machiavelli's political thought I limit myself to his first two major works of political theory, *The Prince* and *The Discourses on Livy*, both of which, in my view inarguably, advance a muscular and radical populism.

Nor does this book dispute conventional wisdom regarding Guicciardini's political preferences. Guicciardini tells us many times that he desires for Florence a mixed constitution anchored upon a narrow, aristocratic senate in which the city's excellent few govern with wisdom and prudence. I see no grounds for (and little merit in) speculating otherwise. I similarly see little merit in questioning Machiavelli's equally frequent advocacy for regimes empowering the people, whether in princely or in republican contexts. Although there is a school of thought, in Machiavelli scholarship at least, cautioning against purely surface readings, I agree entirely with McCormick that when surface readings harmoniously dovetail with every biographical and contextual detail regarding an author's life, they must be correct.[26] Texts may express hidden agendas, but few people take the trouble to advance a complex, camouflaged political agenda only tirelessly to work against it in practice over the course of their lives. Machiavelli's and Guicciardini's personalities, careers, and private utterances are entirely consistent with surface readings of their political thought. In any case, as the scholarship on both sides of the question robustly demonstrates, there is ample and important material for debate irrespective of one's reading methodology.

If we shift the focus from Guicciardini's preferences to his method of analysis and argumentation, as this book does, we see first and foremost that Machiavelli was not, in fact, alone when he attempted to defend the wisdom of the multitude, as he declared in *discorso* 1.58: "I do not know whether I am undertaking a task so hard and full of difficulties that I shall be forced to give up in disgrace or to continue with reproach when I try to defend something that, as I have said, has been condemned by all the writers." Irrespective of whether one reads exoterically or esoterically, there is a consensus that, as Leo Strauss put it, Machiavelli at least appeared to be "the first philosopher who questioned in the name of the multitude or of democracy the aristocratic prejudice or the aristocratic premise which informed classical philosophy."[27]

Machiavelli was neither alone nor the first. Guicciardini subjected the aristocratic pieties in Florentine political thought to searing critique, every bit as thoroughly and at times more sharply as did Machiavelli. He began doing so before Machiavelli's downfall transformed him from civil servant to political philosopher, so he arrived at his acknowledgment of the people's political merits on his own terms. Even if his defence of popular rationality and moderation was merely his reflexive lawyer's habit of examining every issue *in utraquem parte*, the depth and thoroughness of his defence is equal in sophistication to any of Machiavelli's arguments and every bit as persuasive. As his political writings began to reflect his friendship with Machiavelli and familiarity with his writings, Guicciardini continued to critique the viability of oligarchy but began to incorporate Machiavelli's vocabulary and historical perspective. The accumulated effect of his frequent concessions in favour of popular politics and against elite rule is evident in the only work that he wrote formally dedicated to Machiavelli's republican thought, his *Considerations on the "Discourses" of Machiavelli.* Even when explicitly attempting to refute Machiavelli's populism, Guicciardini could not repress his tacit, sustained acknowledgment of their substantial agreement on the vicious conduct of Roman patricians and virtuous conduct of Roman plebeians.

The remainder of this book demonstrates these claims in detail. Chapter 1 provides character sketches, biographical details, and a summary of the transformation in their relationship from adversaries to friends that give the historical context for the dense textual analysis that follows. Even if the main contours of Machiavelli's life and professional career are relatively well known, even outside of specialist circles, I include a brief overview of his political service to the republic and to the Medici family to highlight the contrast in social standing and influence between him and the younger, but vastly more influential, Guicciardini. Even to readers familiar with Renaissance political thought, Guicciardini's biography is less well known and his writings considerably less widely read. Accordingly, the chapter devotes more attention to a summary of Guicciardini's political career and principal texts. Chapters 2 to 6 focus chronologically on Guicciardini's counter-arguments to his own stated preference for aristocratic oligarchy.

Chapter 2 focuses on one of Guicciardini's earliest works of technocratic political analysis, *On the Method of Electing Offices in the Great Council* (1512), a text that anticipated the heart of Machiavelli's radical populism. Reflecting on the republic in the year of its downfall to the Medici, Guicciardini considers the advantages and drawbacks of two electoral methods proposed by the architects of the renewed republic in 1494. Just as Machiavelli would assert at a universal, theoretical level the following year in *The Prince*, Guicciardini's analysis asserts that Florentine politics consists of permanent competition between nobles and people whose contrasting goals and behaviour preclude civic unity and the pursuit of any collective, common good. Guicciardini's reasoning displays a remarkable affinity for the core convictions that would later become the essence of Machiavelli's political thought. He acknowledges the rationality of the multitude, repeatedly stresses the inherent moderation of the people, and concludes with a sustained deconstruction of the concept of nobility itself, arguing that – far from reflecting a superior capacity for judgment and prudence – it derives from a conspicuous capacity for criminality and abusive behaviour.

Chapter 3 shifts the focus from constitutional issues to political ethics. Given that the two Guicciardinian texts that explicitly invoke Machiavelli critiqued his *Discourses on Livy*, scholarship largely focuses on the two thinkers' contrasting republican theories. Beyond acknowledging that Machiavelli and Guicciardini initiated the realist turn in early modern political thought, scholarship rarely considers Machiavelli's *Prince* when comparing their political thought. Chapter 3 demonstrates that Guicciardini's *Ricordi* advanced similar arguments to those of Machiavelli's *Prince*, made similarly provocative challenges to the ethical assumptions of prevailing political thought, and defended those provocations with characterizations of nobles and people proximate to consistent with Machiavelli's political thought. The chapter focuses on the false virtue of generosity, the value of cruelty well used, the tactical superiority of fear over affection, the value of calculated deceit, the degree to which traditional virtues functioned as vices in many contexts, and the church's role in the peninsula's political servitude. It concludes that portrayals of the two as advocates of rival republican political theories miss a much more profound common intellectual agenda. Guicciardini fully shared Machiavelli's revolutionary reappraisal of ethics in political life, a point of considerably more intellectual significance, given the impact of their assault on virtue politics on subsequent political thought, than their class-specific contrasting republican theories.

Chapter 4 turns to Guicciardini's *Dialogue on the Government of Florence*, his most extensive analysis of Florentine political culture and the first text that he wrote during his years of friendship with Machiavelli. It considers in particular Guicciardini's contrasting comments about the Albizzi oligarchy that had ruled Florence from 1393 to 1434 and about aristocratic oligarchy in general in three texts: *The History of Florence*, begun in 1508; the so-called *Discorso di Logrogno*, written in 1512; and the *Dialogue on the Government of Florence*, written sometime between 1521 and 1524. In the two early texts Guicciardini praised the politics of the few, in general abstract terms and in historical terms with specific reference to the Albizzi regime. In the *Dialogue*, however, Guicciardini quarrelled at length with his earlier self, revisiting those early statements only to subject them to sustained scrutiny, revision, and at times outright rejection. The *Dialogue* condemned the Albizzi oligarchy as a corrupt faction that had caused considerable violence and discord and excluded the people from an appropriate role in politics. Nor did he limit his argument to the specifics of the Albizzean context: he argued at a theoretical level that such sins were an inevitable result whenever government was in the hands of the few. In doing so, Guicciardini literally deploys Machiavellian criticism and language – the very same critique that Machiavelli made in contemporaneous texts, the *Florentine Histories* and the *Discourse on Florentine Affairs after the Death of Lorenzo*. In the *Dialogue* we see that Guicciardini began to employ Machiavelli – his populism, his political vocabulary, and his interpretation of Florentine history – as his intellectual foil, an equally formidable intellect (we might say greater, even if Guicciardini did not) against which Guicciardini would have to measure the viability of his aristocratic preferences. Guicciardini's dramatic reversal of opinion regarding the virtues of the Albizzi oligarchy reveals the degree to which Machiavelli expanded and sharpened Guicciardini's style of adversarial reasoning.

Chapter 6 considers Guicciardini's *Considerations on the "Discourses of Machiavelli,"* the text most routinely invoked to demonstrate Guicciardini's rejection of Machiavellian political thought. Guicciardini's overall intent, without a doubt, is systematic rejection of Machiavelli's account of Roman history and the abstract principles that he derives from it. The *Considerations* intends to draw sharp lines of division between Guicciardini's esteem for aristocratic prudence and Machiavelli's contrasting populism, which Guicciardini argues is rooted in a flawed reading of Roman history and a blinkered perception of populist politics in general. To refute Machiavelli, Guicciardini engages in a sustained dissenting reading of Roman history. He also combines his considerable experience as a ruler and the supporting authority of tradition to portray Machiavelli's populism as both an isolated case and confused. But Guicciardini's reasoning in each of those three categories of analysis betrays the same doubts about the merits of aristocratic rule and the same reluctant acknowledgment of popular rationality and moderation that we witnessed more overtly in his earlier texts. Whereas most scholars point to the *Considerations* as definitive proof of Guicciardini's anti-Machiavellian sentiments, the fact that Guicciardini continued to exhibit those same doubts even while attempting a systematic refutation suggests instead that the *Considerations* is the best evidence that Guicciardini's characteristic equivocation about his preferences was not a rhetorical strategy but rather a genuine, sustained acknowledgment of common ground with Machiavelli's political thought, even if he was reluctant to admit it.

Chapter 6 shifts the focus to Machiavelli and the question of whether to read *The Prince* exoterically or esoterically. In particular, it focuses on his portrait of Cesare Borgia in chapter 7 of *The Prince*. Borgia "the Valentino" is unique in Machiavelli's and Guicciardini's histories and political thought – the only prince who they declared was admired by his subjects. Guicciardini's treatment of Cesare in *The History of Florence* and *History of Italy* coincides strikingly with Machiavelli's praise of Cesare's good government in the Romagna in ways that shed new light on a long-standing controversy over the meaning of Machiavelli's enigmatic utterances on Borgia. Machiavelli scholarship has long been and remains divided on how to interpret the meaning of the seventh chapter of *The Prince*. Machiavelli claims to idealize Cesare Borgia as a model new prince, but his narrative also appears to contradict that positive verdict. If Machiavelli's habitually playful and ironic prose voice creates interpretive ambiguity, the same cannot be said for Francesco Guicciardini, who reiterated every aspect of Machiavelli's claims for Borgia's good government. My chapter first revisits Machiavelli's portrait of Cesare, arguing that Machiavelli's estimation of his good foundations was primarily a reference to Cesare's conception of government rather than to his military self-sufficiency. Shifting the focus from Cesare's military accomplishments to the nature of the regime he built in the Romagna resolves most of the chapter's alleged contradictions in favour of the literal reading – Machiavelli clearly esteemed Borgia's political accomplishments. It then contests the claims, frequently made in satirical readings of *The Prince*'s chapter 7, that no evidence exists for Machiavelli's claim that the Romagnol people embraced Cesare's rule. In addition to evidence from Machiavelli's writings, it analyses Guicciardini's assessments of Cesare's government in his *History of Florence* and *History of Italy*, demonstrating that he confirmed virtually every aspect of Borgia's government praised by Machiavelli. Further, Guicciardini's high estimation of Cesare's regime consisted, much as it did for Machiavelli, in his protection of the Romagnol people from their rapacious nobility. The case study of Borgia affirms the proximity of Guicciardini's historical outlook to Machiavelli's view of nobles and people. The conclusion situates Machiavelli and Guicciardini in the subsequent political tradition.

Chapter One

Machiavelli and Guicciardini: Background and Relationship

Machiavelli's major writings and political career are relatively well known, but Guicciardini's are much less so. For basic orientation to readers unfamiliar with Machiavelli's powerful friend and intellectual sparring partner, this brief opening chapter provides character sketches and political biographies of the book's two protagonists, as well as a summary of their relationship, which was adversarial at first but subsequently warmly intimate. Its summary of Guicciardini's career also contextually situates each of the major Guicciardinian texts that feature in the rest of the book: his *On the Method of Electing Offices in the Great Council, Ricordi, Dialogue on the Government of Florence, Considerations on the "Discourses" of Machiavelli,* and Guicciardini's portraits of Cesare Borgia in his *History of Florence* and *History of Italy.*

The earliest texts by both thinkers reveal a sharp contrast in status and entitlement and prefigure what would become enduring patterns in their basic outlooks and relationships with Florentine society and politics. In Machiavelli's case, the first two letters in his hand yield an early glimpse of his instinct to view the world in terms of unequal conflict between the rich and powerful and those further down the social ladder. We also see an early manifestation of his irrepressible pride, defiance, and angry refusal to accept that inequality, a recurring aspect of all his writings. Guicciardini's diary, by contrast, reveals the upbringing of a consummate insider, a scion of one of the city's most powerful families who expected much and to whom much was given. Guicciardini also reveals an irrepressible pride, but whereas Machiavelli's was adversarial, Guicciardini's pride reflected the calm and certain assurance that the powers that be would naturally welcome and reward – as they did – his talent and undeniable precocity.

The first two letters in Machiavelli's hand deal with a property dispute in Fagna between the Machiavelli family and the Pazzi family, another wealthy patrician family on a par with the Guicciardini in terms of status and power. The details are fragmentary but revolve around church territory over which the Machiavelli formerly had patronage rights and that was subsequently transferred to the Pazzi family by Cardinal Giovanni Lopez via a pontifical annulment.[1] In the first letter Machiavelli seeks intervention on his family's behalf from an unnamed and presumably powerful intercessor. His request for assistance implicitly acknowledges the necessity of extraordinary assistance when conflicts between the powerful and the powerless render basic issues of justice irrelevant. It also reveals his instinct for confrontation and for unwillingness to show deference, even if doing so results in inevitable defeat:

> Toward this end I ask that you show your might, and use all your might; for if we, mere pygmies, are attacking giants, a much greater victory is in store for us than for them. For them, inasmuch as it is base to compete, so it will be a very base thing for them to give in; we, on the other hand, shall consider it not so ignominious a thing to be beaten, as it is honourable to have competed, especially having a competitor at whose nod everything is done immediately. Wherefore, whatever Fortune may reserve for us, we shall not regret having failed in such endeavours.[2]

The next day Machiavelli wrote directly to Cardinal Lopez to plead his family's case. That letter also reveals the first brushstrokes of a recurring self-portrait of someone who resented the inherent corruption implicit in social status (as did also Guicciardini at times – considered in detail in the following chapter) and who refused to accept subordinate status. Although the Machiavelli were a relatively prosperous middle-class family (even if the father was impoverished, by their standards), they were nowhere close to the Pazzi family in terms of status, connections, wealth, and power. But Machiavelli deployed a humanist conception of nobility of character rather than blood to insist on the superiority of the Machiavelli: "Whoever might wish to weigh our house with the house of the Pazzi on an accurate scale, if he determined the two to be equal in everything else, will determine ours far superior in generosity and *virtù* of spirit."[3] The self-portrait expressed in these first two documents – outsider, proud, defiant, adversarial – persisted throughout his life and writings. It is evident in his ambassadorial dispatches to his superiors in Florence, which were frequently written in curt and dismissive tones. It is evident in the violent populism of his political theory. He continued to display it even during the height of his literary success. In the conclusion of the prologue to his satirical play *Mandragola* he cautions his audience: "Yet, if anyone believes that by speaking ill he can grab the author by the hair and frighten him or make him withdraw to the side, I warn him, and say to such a one that the author knows how to speak ill, too, and that this was his earliest art; and that, in every part of the world where *sì* is heard, he stands in awe of no one, though he might bow to those who can wear a better cloak than he."[4]

Guicciardini was similarly proud, but born to an insider's world of privilege and connections, his pride reflected a seamless integration with the city's political culture. His diary entries show constant interaction with and support by the city's most powerful families – the Strozzi, Salviati, Capponi, Soderini, and Medici, among others – all of whom brokered clients for young Guicciardini's law practice from the churches and towns of the Florentine territorial state and arranged positions in the Florentine government that would culminate in his first major appointment as ambassador to the Spanish court in 1511. Every year multiple doors opened for Guicciardini. In 1506 he was elected advocate for the commune of Fivizzano; in 1507 he was sent thrice to greet inbound ambassadors and escort them to the Signoria and was elected consul for the merchants' guild, advocate for the podesteria of Chianti, and assessor in the merchants' guild; in 1508 he was elected captain of the hospital of Ceppo; in 1509 he was summoned by the Signoria to provide counsel on the Pisan campaign, elected advocate of the Florentine cathedral, and chosen by the Signoria to chaperone Emperor Maximilian's envoys to the city; in 1510 he became advocate to the company of weavers; in 1511 he was appointed advocate of the tower and of the Bigallo and elected ambassador to Spain; in 1513 he was appointed advocate of the friars of the abbey of Florence, advocate of the friars of Settimo and Cestello, advocate for consuls of the guild of exchange, advocate for Castelnuovo di Val di Cecina, and advocate for the new congregation of the hermitage of Camaldoli and appointed by Lorenzo de' Medici as one of the seventeen reformers of the Monte. In 1514 he became advocate for Volterra, the hospital of San Paolo, and the Otto di balìa.[5] By contrast, Machiavelli gained his first appointment and entered the historical record (apart from a handful of letters) at the age of twenty-nine.

As Guicciardini itemized the steady stream of appointments in his diary, he frequently noted the prestige of the circles in which he moved, the swift ascent of his reputation, and the degree to which he was accumulating positions at an unprecedently young age. For example, when he opened his law practice at the age of twenty-two, he recorded: "I had greater reputation in comparison with other young lawyers than could have been expected, taking into account my age, and the numbers practising in Florence, and the few lawsuits because of the unsettled times."[6] His explanation for why he chose Maria Salviati as his wife, in spite of his father's objections, reveals his ambition and precocious appreciation of the degree to which social capital had greater political potential than did wealth. His father objected to the alliance because Piero Soderini, the city's lifetime gonfalonier, was hostile to the Salviati and because of Maria's relatively modest dowry. Nevertheless, "I determined to take her, because at that time Alamanno and Iacopo were far greater in family connections, wealth, reputation, and popularity than any other private citizens in Florence. I set great store by such things and therefore wanted their alliance at all costs."[7] In 1508, recording the first time that the Otto di guardia, the city's magistracy for political crimes, summoned him for legal counsel, he noted: "I was called to council with a number of other doctors and many of the former citizens of Florence among whom was also my father, and none of them was less than ten years older than me."[8] In the same year, after Guicciardini had been elected as one of twelve lifetime captains of the hospital of Ceppo, he noted: "This election – although the office was of small importance – was honourable with regard to the standing of the men in whose company I was to serve: Domenico Mazzinghi, Pietro Lenzi, Giovacchino Guasconi, Niccolò del Nero, Alessandro Mannelli, Bartolommeo Benci, Giovan Battista Bartolini, and Alamanno Salviati, who were all present at the election."[9] When the republic elected him ambassador to King Ferdinand of Spain in 1511, he recorded: "It seemed an excursion from which I would not profit, and would harm my law practise in which I was very well advanced for my age ... still, on the advice of Piero my father ... I accepted. For he felt it to be a great honour, as the embassy was most distinguished because of the importance of that monarch, and particularly at my age, as no one in Florence could remember when so young a man had been appointed alone to any similar embassy."[10] When Guicciardini was elected one of two advocates for Santa Maria del Fiore, the Florentine cathedral, he noted: "It was an affair without any money in it, but very honourable for me because of the prestige of the place and because the foremost doctors of Florence had always held the position."[11] Little wonder, then, that his classmates called him Alcibiades on account of his "restlessness and ambition."[12]

Until 1512 it appeared that Machiavelli was on track for a long and promising political career (if on a different scale than Guicciardini was) in the Florentine republic. Machiavelli won his first appointment as the second chancellor in 1498, responsible for correspondence with the subject towns of the Florentine territorial state. Shortly after his appointment as chancellor, he was appointed as secretary to the Ten of War, the government's powerful war council. Both positions involved managing communications with foreign powers, such that Machiavelli also became a de facto ambassador (though without the formal title because he lacked the social status – unlike Guicciardini, who, as we saw, became ambassador to Spain at a remarkably young age) and undertook several significant diplomatic missions to the courts of the warring parties in Italy, France, and Germany. The government sent him, among other missions, to the French court in 1500–1 to discuss Pisa's revolt from Florentine rule, to Cesare Borgia in 1502–3 to discuss a revolt in Arezzo and Cesare's threatening demand for a Florentine alliance, to Rome in 1503 to report on the papal election that elevated Giuliano della Rovere as pope Julius II (on which see chapter 7), and to the court of Louis XII to discuss the recent Spanish military victory. In the middle years of the decade Machiavelli devoted considerable energy to mustering and training a civic militia recruited from the Florentine *distretto*, a project that reflected both his long-standing aversion to mercenary warfare and the close working relationship he enjoyed with Piero Soderini, the city's lifetime gonfalonier. In 1507–8 the republic sent Machiavelli to the court of Emperor Maximilian I, who had entered the peninsular conflict hitherto dominated by France and Spain. The remainder of his diplomatic career was largely spent navigating the challenges posed by the Florence's stubborn alliance with France while Julius II was assembling the Holy League, an alliance with Venice and Spain to expel Louis XII from Italy.[13]

Even though Machiavelli had numerous enemies amongst the city's *ottimati* class, had the Florentine republic survived, it is likely that he would have continued to play a significant role in the city's politics, given the respect that Soderini had for him. But when Spanish forces allied with the Medici sacked Prato, and a Medici coup toppled the republic in 1512, Machiavelli experienced a dramatic reversal of fortune. With an anti-Soderini faction triumphant and with Soderini in exile, Machiavelli lost the protection of his powerful patron and became politically exposed to the many *ottimati* whom he had alienated with his often curt, dismissive, and superior letters to the aristocrats on the war council. The new regime dismissed him from his post, forbade him entry to the Palazzo della Signoria for a year, scrutinized his militia payments (powerful *ottimati*, including Guicciardini, had vocally opposed the militia project), and confined him to Florentine territory. Stubborn and defiant by nature, in spite of the regime's evident hostility to him, he continued to push away former allies by openly highlighting what he saw as the Medici regime's weakness, thereby developing a politically compromised reputation.[14] In 1513 two anti-Medici conspirators, Pietropaolo Boscoli and Agostino Capponi, drew up a list of potential allies that included Machiavelli – based likely on his reputation rather than on his actual involvement – for a coup against the regime. After the Medici discovered the plot, they had Machiavelli arrested and tortured. Shortly thereafter, Cardinal Giovanni de' Medici won papal election and, as Leo X, controlled both Rome and Florence, leading the family to declare a general amnesty for all political prisoners. Suddenly released from prison, Machiavelli nevertheless left the city a political pariah and settled at his family's farm in Sant'Andrea in Percussina to immerse himself in writing the transformative works of political theory for which he is famous.

If 1512 marked a swift and tragic end to Machiavelli's political career, it marked for Guicciardini an equally swift elevation to major player in the republican regime. In that year he completed his *History of Florence* that analysed the fifteenth-century Medicean, Savonarolan, and Soderinian regimes and was sent as ambassador to the court of Ferdinand of Aragon. Given the perilous times and the high status required to hold the title of ambassador, his appointment reflected the ruling group's respect for Guicciardini (the logical culmination of the many lesser appointments itemized in his diary) and the continuation of his family's long-standing history of involvement at the highest levels of government. From Spain he began writing the first of two technocratic constitutional analyses of the republican regime – the *Discorso di Logrogno* – and *On the Method of Electing Offices in the Great Council* (the subject of chapter 2). He also began the first draft of his *Ricordi* (the subject of chapter 3), his collection of political maxims and familial advice that he would continue to expand and revise for eighteen years. Shortly afterwards, Spanish and papal forces reinstalled the Medici to Florence, who then recalled Guicciardini to Florence, first appointing him to significant committees in the new regime and, upon gaining the papacy, to major posts in the papal administration.[15] Given Guicciardini's evident talent and his family's history as major allies of the fifteenth-century Medici, rumours circulated in Florence that he must have known of the plans for a Spanish-backed Medici restoration while he was at Ferdinand's court, and withheld them.[16] When the tides turned against the Medici in 1527 and Guicciardini found himself facing investigation by a reinvigorated republican regime, the latter put that accusation to him directly.[17] Whatever the case may have been, the fact that the triumphant Medici relied extensively upon Guicciardini and eventually elevated him to the status of a major prince of north central Italy suggests that they never once doubted Guicciardini's willingness to serve them with loyalty and characteristic competence.

The end of 1514 marked the transition for Guicciardini from Florentine to papal administrator. Leo X appointed him a consistorial advocate in December, papal governor of Modena in 1516, and papal governor of Reggio in 1517.[18] The alliance between the Medici and Spain forged in 1512 (that would ultimately result after 1559 in complete Spanish control of the peninsula until the Napoleonic era) resulted in Guicciardini's appointment in 1521 as commissary-general of papal forces, allied with Charles V of Spain to drive the French out of the peninsula. In that year he began writing his major assessment of Medici power in Florence, the *Dialogue on the Government of Florence*, the subject of chapter 4, and a second draft of his *Ricordi.* Guicciardini was entrusted with yet greater responsibilities upon Leo's death and the election of his cousin, Giulio, as Pope Clement VII, who appointed Guicciardini president of the Romagna in 1524 (on which see chapter 7). After the French king, Francis I, was imprisoned by Charles V after the Spanish victory at the Battle of Pavia and the peninsula consequently faced the spectre of total Habsburg domination, Guicciardini was entrusted by Clement with the position of lieutenant-general of papal forces and became the architect of a new papal alliance with Venice, France, and England to reverse imperial fortunes in Italy. Those efforts led to catastrophe for the anti-imperial cause and the Medici – and for Guicciardini at a personal level, giving him his first taste of the kind of political ostracization that plagued Machiavelli after 1512. Charles V's unpaid army, consisting of many German Lutheran conscripts, invaded and sacked Rome in 1527. With Clement imprisoned in Castel Sant'Angelo, a Savonarolan-inspired uprising in Florence overthrew the Medici regime and restored the Florentine republic.[19] Viewed with suspicion owing to his service to the Medici popes, Guicciardini retreated to his villa in the countryside. As conditions in Florence became more desperate and more extreme following the emperor's decision to restore the Medici in 1529, the besieged republican regime summoned Guicciardini to answer charges for his conduct. Although he had been acting as a kind of diplomatic courier between Clement and the republicans, they viewed him as actively conspiring to undermine the republic. Punished with high taxes and threatened with imprisonment, Guicciardini left Tuscany for Rome, leading to charges of contumacy and exile. As he fled for papal protection in Rome, he began his polemic against Machiavelli's republican theory, the *Considerations on the "Discourses" of Machiavelli,* the subject of chapter 5, and the final draft of his *Ricordi.*

After the republic collapsed, following a long and brutal siege by papal and imperial forces, Guicciardini returned to Florence as one of Clement's lieutenants entrusted with re-establishing Medici power and exacting vengeance on the previous regime's leadership (a task that he carried out with ruthless zeal, as detailed in chapter 6). In spite of his long-standing republican sympathies and his advice to the Medici in constitutional proposals from 1530 to 1532 not to establish a principate, he nevertheless played a crucial role in assisting the family in the abolition of the republic and its reinvention as a ducal state under Medici princes.[20] Between 1532 and 1537 Guicciardini helped Alessandro de' Medici transform the family into dukes of Florence and was one of Alessandro's principal advisers.[21] Alessandro's assassination in 1537 caused a succession crisis because his only son was four years old and illegitimate. Guicciardini joined a group of *ottimati* to engineer the accession of Cosimo de' Medici, a descendant of the cadet branch of the family, son of the *condottiere* Giovanni delle Bande Nere, and grandson of Caterina Sforza. As Cosimo had lived most of his life in the relative obscurity of the Florentine countryside, the party orchestrating his accession believed he might function as a figurehead through which it could establish oligarchic rule (as Guicciardini's constitutional proposals all generally favoured). To help attain this goal, the party included a condition for its support by which Cosimo agreed to transfer considerable power to a new council of forty-eight members. Cosimo soon outmanoeuvred his supporters, dismissed many of them, and – ignoring the conciliar cause – proceeded to build the foundations of a strong authoritarian state. Disillusioned, Guicciardini retired to spend his final years writing his *History of Italy*, which would contain the portrait of Cesare Borgia that is the subject of chapter 6 herein.

In 1520 Machiavelli managed to return to the good graces of the Medici family and go back to active political service (through the intervention of friends close Giovanni and Giulio de' Medici, likely including Guicciardini). The Medici initially enlisted Machiavelli for a series of relatively minor missions and, more substantially, solicited his opinion (among that of others) for a constitutional proposal on how best to stabilize Medici power in the city; they also commissioned him to write a history of Florence, thereby indicating his elevation to the status of establishment intellectual.[22] In 1525 Machiavelli managed to persuade an impoverished Clement VII to muster a native militia in the Romagna instead of raising funds for costly mercenary forces, a plan that sent Machiavelli, as stage two, to persuade Guicciardini, Clement's ruler in the Romagna (on which see chapter 7). Although since 1520 they had become good friends with considerable mutual intellectual respect, Guicciardini rejected the project as unfeasible, and Machiavelli was sent to Venice shortly thereafter by the Wool Guild to represent Florentine merchants whose goods had been seized by the Venetian government. More significant missions in 1526 again brought Machiavelli into contact with Guicciardini, first to advise on military matters in Lombardy at the camp of the League of Cognac, the pope's anti-imperial alliance, and then to Modena to discuss with Guicciardini the imminent threat to Florence posed by Spanish and imperial forces in northern Italy. Machiavelli was also sent to inspect and repair Florentine fortresses, an assignment that again intersected with his missions to Guicciardini and that earned him yet more of Guicciardini's respect. After one visit Guicciardini wrote to his brother: "Machiavelli has left here with the orders for the supplies and officers to be carried out, people are to start the fortifications in the way that you will learn from him ... Machiavelli was the man who fostered this plan, hence please be obliged to treat him well during his stay and in the other matters that may be required because he has earned his share full well."[23] In 1527 the Medici sent him again to discuss and relay information between them and Guicciardini, who was on the move throughout Emilia-Romagna – Parma, Forlì, Bologna – to navigate the impending crisis of the imperial march southward. Machiavelli died that year, shortly after the Florentine republic had been reinstated following the sack of Rome.[24]

At a personal level, Machiavelli was involved with the Guicciardini family long before he and Francesco became close friends in the 1520s. Guicciardini's father, Piero, knew and respected Machiavelli, as we see from his letter to Machiavelli in 1502 discussing the prospect of an alliance with Cesare Borgia, in which he wrote, "[C]oncerning the affairs down there, I have nothing else to tell you except for you to continue as you have done up to now, since it seems to me you are giving satisfaction to everyone."[25] Machiavelli socialized with Francesco and his brothers Luigi and Jacopo as part of a common social circle as early as 1509 (and was therefore in contact with him during the composition of Guicciardini's *History of Florence*). In a letter of 1509 to Luigi – to whom Machiavelli also wrote his Boccaccian account of a sexual encounter gone comically wrong – Machiavelli closed, "If you write your Messer Francesco, tell him that I send the gang my regards."[26] In both letters he implies friendship with Jacopo: "Your letter ... distressed me ... since I learned that Jacopo had again caught a bit of fever," and "greetings to Jacopo and give him my regards."[27] A letter from Roberto Acciaiuoli in October 1510 also implies an intimate social circle shared by Machiavelli and Luigi Guicciardini. Acciaiuoli wrote to Machiavelli: "I seem to see Casa and Francesco and Luigi coming to drag you from your house after your arrival and taking you to a sunny place or to Santa Maria del Fiore to consecrate you and to hear about everything over here."[28] Machiavelli was friends with the Guicciardini outside of Florence as well. In the famous Vettori letter of 10 December 1513 Machiavelli alludes to playing cards in one of the Guicciardini country homes near his farmhouse: "Frosino da Panzano ... wanted to withhold ten lire that he said he won off me four years ago at Antonio Guicciardini's house." Among Machiavelli's customers for firewood was Battista Guicciardini, with whom he exchanged jokes about politics and his meagre circumstances.[29] Correspondence within the Guicciardini family discussing Biagio Buonaccorsi and Machiavelli's dismissal from office in 1512 indicates that the family was alert to Machiavelli's role in Florentine politics.[30]

In spite of these moments of apparently friendly interaction, during the second republic Machiavelli and Guicciardini were publicly and visibly members of opposing parties.[31] Soderini relied on Machiavelli extensively for chancery work, diplomatic missions, and an attempt to create a citizen militia, all of which were noted and resented by Soderini's *ottimati* opponents. Through his marriage to Maria Salviati, Guicciardini became a member of the Salviati network that functioned, in Roslyn Pesman's words, as a "kind of constitutional opposition" to Soderini. For them, Machiavelli was merely one example of a larger pattern of Soderini's deliberately excluding the *ottimati* to boost his power, relying instead on less powerful members of the middle ranks who were easier to manipulate – "men of lesser mind and quality," as Guicciardini put it.[32]

Although Machiavelli did not write anything specifically about Guicciardini during the years of his service to the Florentine republic, the memorandum to the Medici that he wrote in the wake of the collapse of the Soderini regime demonstrates harsh criticism of the aristocrats associated with the Salviati circle who had been instrumental in toppling the Soderini regime and reintegrating the Medici into the city. He explained that aristocratic efforts to secure public condemnation of Soderini were a veiled attempt to shore up their own power at the expense of the Medici. His language was typically direct: "If you look into who these people are, you will see that what I am saying is true. As they see it, their having been enemies of Soderini, their faction will have drawn the hatred of the populace upon themselves unless they can now prove that he was evil and deserved their enmity. The reason that they want to free themselves of the populace's hatred is so that they can promote their own interests, not those of the Medici."[33] As the husband of Alamanno's daughter Maria, Guicciardini was an important and highly visible member of the Salviati faction, along with Jacopo Salviati, Giovanbattista Ridolfi, and Lanfredino Lanfredini.[34]

The social and psychological distance between the two men, and Guicciardini's marriage to Maria Salviati, no doubt played a role in Guicciardini's first and influential negative assessment of Machiavelli's character and role in Florentine politics. Along with the historian Bartolomeo Cerretani, who famously indicted Machiavelli as Soderini's puppet, Guicciardini is one of the major sources of evidence for the sinister factional interpretation of Machiavelli and Soderini's relationship and their covert agenda for the fledgling militia program.[35] Much like in his criticism of Cosimo and Lorenzo de' Medici, Guicciardini clearly resented the degree to which Piero Soderini had obstructed the venerable Florentine *ottimati* families from exercising the control over Florentine policy to which he felt they were entitled and uniquely competent to administer. Further, he viewed the gonfalonier's conspicuous reliance on Machiavelli as one of his primary methods of such obstruction, strategically deploying him to pursue the gonfalonier's private agenda in issues usually limited to Machiavelli's social betters. In this respect, Guicciardini shared the widespread and well-documented prejudices of the *ottimati* class against Soderini and Machiavelli.[36]

Machiavelli first enters Guicciardini's narrative in 1505 during a complicated moment in in which Guicciardini portrays Soderini as manipulating the hiring of Florence's mercenary captains to increase the power of his brother, Cardinal Francesco, in Rome. In the wake of the sudden and unexpected failure of the republic to hire the Marquis of Mantua as its *condottiere*, "great differences of opinion" arose on whether to hire Marcantonio and Muzio Colonna. "The gonfalonier pushed it [hiring the Colonna] to please the cardinal [his brother Francesco in Rome] who, it was said, had promised it to the Colonna and had already begun to pay them."[37] In retrospect, Guicciardini adds, people began to suspect that Soderini had obstructed the Marquis of Mantua's hire for the express purpose of hiring the Colonna. Led by Alamanno Salviati – Guicciardini's powerful father-in-law – the Council of Ten opposed Soderini's plan (later in the narrative, the Council of Eighty would also order Alamanno and Jacopo Salviati to take over Machiavelli's responsibilities as overseer of the city's forces besieging Pisa).[38] As part of a counter-plan the Ten sent Roberto Acciaiuoli to the commander of Spanish forces, Gonzalo Fernández de Córdoba. Guicciardini here introduces Machiavelli and implies that he was an agent of Soderinian, rather than Florentine, interests: "The Ten sent Acciaiuoli as emissary to him. (That had proved difficult to do because the gonfalonier opposed it; he would have preferred to send one of his intimates, Niccolò Machiavelli, chancellor of the Ten, whom he trusted completely.)"[39]

Guicciardini next turns to Soderini and Machiavelli's questionable but nevertheless effective methods in their attempt to establish a militia in spite of *ottimati* opposition, including Guicciardini's father, Piero, a committed opponent of the militia.[40] Having in mind the Spanish mercenary Don Micheletto Corella as the eventual militia leader, Soderini, as his first step, hired Don Micheletto as *bargello del contado*. Suspecting that the Ten would oppose his plan, he "first had the chancellor Machiavelli very subtly sound out the state of mind of messer Francesco Gualterotti, Giovan Battista Ridolfi, Piero Guicciardini, and some other leading citizens."[41] Learning of their opposition through Machiavelli, Soderini did not submit Micheletto's commission to discussion by the Ten, as Guicciardini implies he should have, but rather introduced it directly to the Council of Eighty for voting, where it passed. Shortly thereafter, Machiavelli persuaded Soderini to allow him to undertake a more ambitious variation on the citizen militia, a plan that went forward for the second time without consultation because Soderini "rightly feared that the leading citizens would advise against it."[42] Seeing that their input had been carefully and successfully avoided, the leading citizens viewed Soderini's intentions with considerable suspicion, intimating that he and Machiavelli were building a private army: "The leading citizens were very disturbed because they feared that his desire to have Don Michele might bespeak some evil design: such a man might help him to bring about a tyranny; or, if the gonfalonier were in some difficulty, he might use such a man to get rid of his enemies."[43]

Guicciardini's third major acknowledgment of Machiavelli in his *History of Florence* deals with the republic's choice of ambassadors to the imperial court and hews closely to the earlier interpretations of Machiavelli as a compromised figure overly beholden to Soderini's private interests. Alarmed by Emperor Maximilian I's sudden declaration in 1507 to march on Italy, the government determined to send an ambassador. According to Guicciardini, "the gonfalonier, who wanted someone he could trust, saw to it that Machiavelli was chosen."[44] Influential *ottimati* opposed Machiavelli's selection and compelled Soderini to send Francesco Vettori in his place.[45] A few pages later, however, Guicciardini reveals that Soderini nonetheless managed to secure Machiavelli's participation: "But the gonfalonier, who wanted to have a trusted agent there to look out for his interests as well as those of the city, suggested to the Ten that it might be better to send someone to speak in person, since letters might go astray. When no one opposed this suggestion, he succeeded in getting Machiavelli sent."[46]

Contact between Machiavelli and the Guicciardini largely vanished during Machiavelli's pariah years after 1512. By 1521, however and despite their earlier political divide, they began an extensive correspondence demonstrating close friendship and mutual intellectual respect. The first collection of letters deals with Machiavelli's mission to the Franciscan chapter-general meeting of the Minorite Friars in Carpi, where Giulio de' Medici and the government had sent Machiavelli to persuade the friars to separate themselves from the other convents in Tuscany (part of a larger attempt to centralize political control over Florentine ecclesiastical institutions). The government assigned him, once there, the additional task of recruiting one of their preachers for the Lenten service in Florence.[47] The warmth, humour, and familiarity of Guicciardini's first letter to Machiavelli reveals that their friendship was already fully formed. Reflecting on the irony of assigning irreligious Machiavelli the task of selecting a preacher, Guicciardini wrote: "My very dear Machiavelli. It was certainly good judgment on the part of our reverend consuls of the Wool Guild to have entrusted you with the duty of selecting a preacher ... I believe you will serve them according to the expectations they have of you and as is required by your honour, which would be stained if at this age you started to think about your soul, because, since you have always lived in a contrary belief, it would be attributed rather to senility than to goodness."[48]

This collection of letters also reveals Guicciardini's capacity for humour (he was otherwise famously austere), an aspect of his personality that – from a textual basis at least – he displays only with Machiavelli. Guicciardini hatched a plot to improve Machiavelli's standing with his host, Sigismondo Santi, the chancellor of the city's bishop, and thereby to improve the food, drink, and ceremony shown to Machiavelli. Guicciardini, then governor of nearby Modena and right hand to the pope, sent numerous couriers in extreme haste to Machiavelli, armed with mysterious documents and dispatches, to give the impression that Machiavelli was evidently on a covert mission for the pope that had considerably greater significance than his actual mission, which Guicciardini conspired to present as misdirection camouflage.

> I am sending you posthaste the present crossbowman, whom I have ordered to come with the greatest dispatch, since this is a most important matter, so that he has come with his shirt flying behind his hips. I do not doubt that, between his racing and what will be said by him to those present, it will be believed by everyone that you are an important personage and that your business has to do with more than just friars ... I wrote to M. Gismondo yesterday that you were a very exceptional person. He answered me, begging me to inform him as to what this exceptionalness of yours consisted of. I did not feel I should answer him, so that he may be kept in suspense and have reason to show you full respect.[49]

Machiavelli's equally humorous and mocking letters in response demonstrate reciprocal warmth and implicit recognition of their intellectual superiority.

The next collection of letters dates from 1525 and 1526 and again reveals the degree to which Machiavelli brought out Guicciardini's sense of humour. Guicciardini had purchased two unseen properties and asked Machiavelli to visit them for an assessment, signing the letters "as a brother." Machiavelli itemized numerous shortcomings of the first property, dubbed Finocchieto: situated in a desolate environment, small and dark rooms, stunted meadow, and poor soil. Guicciardini wrote his reply in the voice of the spurned house, his one and only instance of literary playfulness, accusing Machiavelli of rash judgment and lack of vision: "It was rash of you to make a judgment in one moment ... things are to be judged not by their surface but by their substance" – perhaps an invocation of the injudicious multitude whom Machiavelli faulted in chapter 18 of *The Prince* for judging more with their eyes than their hands. Other letters from that year include Machiavelli's frequent assistance in arranging marriages for Guicciardini's daughters, and discussion of peninsular politics. The 1526 letters alternate between discussion of productions of *Mandragola* and big-picture analysis of breaking political developments, in which both Guicciardini and Machiavelli played a role. As the chief advocate of Clement's anti-imperial policy, Guicciardini played a major role in forming the League of Cognac that united the papacy, France, Milan, and Venice against Charles V. Machiavelli frequently intersected with Guicciardini that year while the latter coordinated Clement's anti-imperial policy and, as overseer of Florentine fortresses for Clement VII, wrote to him extensively about his work: "I have not written you since I left there [Florence] because my head is so full of ramparts that nothing else could enter it."[50]

The Florentine government sent Machiavelli to join Guicciardini and the papal army in Parma in February 1527 and to apprise him of the increasingly desperate situation in Florence. Machiavelli remained with Guicciardini (hence the absence of correspondence) and travelled with the army until his return to Florence in April, where Machiavelli died two months later. Guicciardini would of course continue his "dialogue" with Machiavelli after the latter's death, after his own persecution by the republican regime of 1527–30, composing his *Considerations on the "Discourses of Machiavelli"* as he, a temporary pariah in Florentine political life, travelled to Rome. The sudden parallel between his fate and that of Machiavelli in 1512, both ostracized politically and both certain of the injustice in that ostracization, did not incline Guicciardini to acknowledging the merits of Machiavelli's republican theory, but as the remainder of this book shows, and particularly chapter 6, he conceded its legitimacy even while trying to condemn it.

Chapter Two

Populist Perspectives in Guicciardini's *On the Method of Electing Offices in the Great Council*

Scholarship on the presence of Machiavellian themes in Guicciardini's writing generally follows Gennaro Sasso, who limited them to an exceptionally brief, early period in which Guicciardini displayed a shared affinity for several causes at the heart of Machiavelli's political vision and career in Florentine government. The key text for Sasso was Guicciardini's first formal constitutional text, *Discorso di Logrogno*, in which he endorsed a citizen militia, the Great Council, and the office of Standard-Bearer for Life. After that early text, however, Sasso concluded that the remainder of Guicciardini's constitutional writings charted an increasingly anti-Machiavellian course that championed traditional values at the heart of virtue politics.[1]

There are strong textual grounds for this general interpretation of Guicciardini's thought. Even in that early text and more thoroughly in his *Dialogue on the Government of Florence*, he advocated for an elitist regime in which executive power was concentrated in a narrow senatorial order composed of the city's most virtuous few. Guicciardini excluded the broad ranks of the people from participating in decision making on the grounds that, in every polity and at every moment in history, only a few possessed the requisite judgment to formulate policy on important questions of war, peace, diplomacy, and economic policy. Guicciardini integrated the people in his system in a purely electoral capacity – he entrusted the multitude with determining who merited election to higher office. He defended the system as free and open, rather than overtly oligarchic, on the grounds of its "virtue egalitarianism," to use James Hankins's recent term.[2] Guicciardini condemned formal oligarchies, in which power was monopolized by a closed, legal caste, stressing instead the degree to which his system embraced an open nobility of virtue rather than a narrow nobility of blood. As the acquisition and display of virtue was equally open to all, every citizen was potentially equally eligible to serve in the senate. For Guicciardini, this equality of opportunity ensured that everyone had a stake in the regime and thereby created auspicious foundations for unity and consensus, the primary ideals of the Florentine humanist tradition. If the system tended repeatedly to return the same few to office, so much the better because excellence was by definition a trait that many people could not possess – only the exceptionally talented and virtuous few. As Guicciardini saw it, an oligarchy of the conspicuously virtuous was the best regime because it benefited from rule by the best and yet was also open and free, since the oligarchy was put in place by the free will of the people rather than imposed on them by a restrictive legal caste system.

Machiavelli famously disputed the assumptions on which this political vision and its *quattrocento* predecessors relied. First and foremost, he rejected as a myth the very possibility of unity. Machiavelli portrayed politics in terms of inherently and inevitably antagonistic social groups for which no common good existed – unlike the humanist virtue politics and Guicciardini's idealized senatorial order that defined legitimate regimes in terms of their ability to suppress conflict in favour of consensus and the pursuit of the common good. Machiavelli defended his conviction by equally rejecting the possibility of an "equality of virtue." A sound political system could not possibly consist of the popular identification of an excellent, exceptionally virtuous few who were entrusted wisely to rule over all, because Machiavelli disputed that individuals were capable of improving their moral character. Instead, he posited that all politics, whether in Florence or in ancient Rome, consisted in irrepressible conflict between two social groups – the people and the nobles – who shared no common goals and no political values. Like Guicciardini, who defined the elite not in terms of closed blood caste but rather in terms of individual excellence, Machiavelli also viewed the elite not as a closed blood caste but rather as those with disproportionate wealth and power at any given moment. The nobles and people could never transcend conflict, because their desires were fundamentally incompatible: the people desired merely to live unmolested and secure in the enjoyment of their material possessions, whereas the nobility desired to oppress and bully those around them. In Machiavelli's vision, elite culture and its innate desire for oppression was the major potential problem of political life, and popular culture and its innate moderation was the major potential solution to that problem. With diametrically opposed ends, no political system could possibly integrate the two social groups harmoniously.

As we will see in this chapter, however, which focuses on Guicciardini's earliest technocratic text, *On the Method of Electing Offices in the Great Council* (1512), Guicciardini strikingly anticipated these axioms at the heart of

Machiavelli's radical populism. In this text, largely overlooked by Sasso, Guicciardini considers the relative advantages and drawbacks of two electoral methods that were under consideration during the early years of the renewed Florentine republic (1494–5). Surprisingly, he portrays the principal engine of Florentine political conflict as an irresolvable competition between nobles and people whose contrasting natures precluded any possible common good. Guicciardini's reasoning displays a remarkable affinity for the core convictions that would later become the essence of Machiavelli's political thought. He acknowledges the rationality of the multitude, repeatedly stresses the inherent moderation of the people, and concludes with a sustained deconstruction of the concept of nobility itself, arguing that – far from reflecting a superior capacity for judgment and prudence – it derives from a conspicuous capacity for criminality and abusive behaviour.

Following the structure of Guicciardini's text, the first section of this chapter considers his argument in favour of the majority vote system, demonstrating the degree to which it relied on the capacity of the many for superior judgment than of the few; the second section turns to his argument in favour of sortition, demonstrating the degree to which it relied on the inherent moderation of the people; the third and final section examines Guicciardini's critique of the concept of nobility and the degree to which he associated it with violent, abusive behaviour.

To be clear at the outset, this chapter does not argue that the pointed popular critique of Florentine noble culture in *On the Method of Electing Offices in the Great Council* necessarily reflects a truer or more sincere version of Guicciardini than he expressed in his more elitist and traditional utterances. Typical of many of his writings and a product of his legal training, Guicciardini's analysis of the Florentine electoral debate deploys *in utramque partem* reasoning, the first half adopting the position associated with the city's elite families and the second half adopting the popular counter-argument. Guicciardini frequently and by design obscured his own preferences within complex, multi-perspective considerations of any given question. Which voice in this text reflected Guicciardini's inner convictions, to the extent that they existed, I leave to the reader.

The point of this chapter is to highlight that Guicciardini displayed from his very first writings a precocious and systematic capacity for critiquing the idealized senatorial system that he appeared more straightforwardly to champion in other texts. If elsewhere he frequently contrasted the irrationality and fickleness of the people with the prudential excellence of the elite, he reveals here the degree to which he always understood that that contrast was more a piety of *ottimati* chauvinism than a concrete social reality. Before we conclude, as Sasso did, that "the ancient idea of Concord" was Guicciardini's metaphorical north star, we should recognize the magnitude of his doubts and the degree to which he shared Machiavelli's view that unity in practice consists of dominance by the wealthy. This chapter demonstrates that Machiavelli was less Guicciardini's adversary than the personification of one half of Guicciardini's psyche, the critic who laid bare the self-regarding pieties of the Florentine elite. In this respect we see here in Guicciardini's earliest writing what we will also see in his other texts examined in later chapters: Guicciardini's thinking was considerably more complex than the traditional portrait of a "Florentine patrician exhibiting the ... limitations of an outlook determined by class," as Felix Gilbert influentially expressed it.[3]

The Many Possess Superior Judgment to the Few

On the Method of Electing addresses debates surrounding the procedures (election or lottery) for appointing officials used by the Great Council, the central institution of the renewed Florentine republic established after the expulsion of the Medici in 1494. From the outset of the revived republic the city's factions fiercely contested the Council's composition and powers. Chief among them were the *ottimati* who had carried out the coup against Piero de' Medici and who envisioned the Council as the foundation of an oligarchic regime, much as Venice's Great Council had supported the city's closed aristocratic caste, and a popular faction, affiliated with Savonarola but also led by members of the Florentine elite, that wished to see the council as an anchor for a broader and more inclusive regime.

At issue was the relationship between the electoral procedures that the Council used to appoint offices and the social composition of the city's rulership. After the coup the government initially used a majority vote system, a process whereby offices were filled by those who had won the most votes in the council. Over time, however, the majority vote system tended to reward a small, recurring group of the city's wealthiest and most distinguished families, many of whom had belonged to Lorenzo de' Medici's inner circle. The narrowness of the results and the high representation among families who had enjoyed prominence in the previous regime created discontent in the broad ranks of the citizenry who assumed that the whole point of driving out the Medici family had been to expand the regime. Advocates of a broader regime therefore argued for the adoption of sortition, a process whereby the names of each person who received at least 50 per cent of the council's votes for any given position were placed in a pouch from which a triumphant winner was drawn randomly. Somewhat ironically, when the regime was squarely in the hands of the small group of aristocrats who had expelled Piero de' Medici, their first reform of 2 December 1494 that created the Great Council had used sortition. Agitation by a populist faction led by Savonarola pressured those *ottimati* to switch to majority vote elections, a system initially championed by Savonarola as vital for the preservation of the popular constitution. By 1495, however, election results had clearly favoured the city's elite (in keeping with the well-documented "aristocratic effect of elections"), such that the popular faction reversed course and insisted on random sortition as the best safeguard against the tyranny of the few.[4]

The conflict between these two groups – elite families advocating for the majority vote and a popular movement advocating for sortition – provided the young Guicciardini with an ideal opportunity to consider issues and questions that would remain at the heart of all his writings and much of his engagement with Machiavelli: how to construct a regime in which the best citizens – by definition a select few – could rule with unity and consent, the rationality of the people, and the relative merits of the prudential few.

Guicciardini opens his defence of the majority vote system by first outlining the central challenge for political reformers, in popular, republican contexts: "First, and most important, they must ensure that every single citizen is equal before the law. No distinction between rich and poor, nor between the powerful and the weak, can exist … The second end is that the benefits of the republic – that is, the offices and the public honors – are widely distributed so that as many citizens participate in government as possible."[5] Procedurally, the first goal is relatively easy to implement precisely because of its absoluteness – no exceptions should ever be permitted regarding the equality of all citizens under the law. The second goal, however, is procedurally more complex to implement because exceptions to that wide distribution of offices can and should be made on a regular basis. An optimal regime distributes offices as widely as possible *only among* a subset of citizens possessing the requisite competence, responsibility, and ambition necessary for the city's most important posts. The question then becomes how to ensure that the system generates competent candidates; as Guicciardini sees it, majority vote is the answer. These two principles – equality before the law and a culture of competition for office in which presumably the city's best citizens succeed and thrive – remained more or less at the heart of all of Guicciardini's formal constitutional writings that championed equality of opportunity over formally aristocratic caste systems.

Guicciardini's first defence of majority vote elections in the Great Council relied structurally on a thesis that Machiavelli would put to more radical ends – that the people collectively possess an effective capacity for political judgment, rational calculus, and the discernment of good character and competence. Guicciardini served two important ends by making appointment to all the city's important offices the result of majority election in a large representative body such as the Great Council. The first point was simply a basic observation on which all could agree in the immediate aftermath of a Medicean shadow government: by placing appointments in the hands of a large collective body, the system militated against the formation of private clientage networks under the control of a single family or a faction of aligned families. Given that Guicciardini's subsequent writings often decried the people as irrational, undiscriminating, and vengeful, we might expect him here to justify the people's participation not as an ideal but rather in pragmatic terms as the lesser of two evils. If entrusting the appointment process for key positions to the largest and most socially inclusive institution might yield haphazard and capricious results, living with that problem was superior to the alternative system, an appointment process controlled by fewer numbers that would make the regime vulnerable to tyranny – whether under a single family like the Medici or an oligarchic faction.

Guicciardini asserts, however, not only that the majority vote system obstructed the formation of powerful factions but also that it resulted in judicious, informed appointments – *precisely because* many people had weighed in: "Distributing office by election in the council created a well governed city because the magistrates were more discriminately chosen. If one hundred men judge whether a citizen is well suited to an office, the judgment will undoubtedly be more secure if sixty men agree, as opposed to merely fifty."[6]

Guicciardini then turns to critics of the majority election system, who complained that the process returned many of the same people to office on a recurring basis and excluded many deserving candidates (one variation on a more general phenomenon known as the "aristocratic effect" of elections). His first rebuttal is strictly procedural, merely observing that those who complain about the narrowness of election results are the very people empowered to cast the votes: "[B]ecause the people distribute the offices to whomever they want, however they want, there is really no wideness or narrowness to be spoken of except that which they make themselves."[7] The second and more ambitious stage of his rebuttal hinges on the inherent rationality of collective deliberation – the greater the number of voices, the greater the probability of a prudent choice. Anticipating Machiavelli's observation in the *Discourses* that the "few always behave in the mode of the few," Guicciardini defends the prevailing system by asserting that "the participation of a larger number renders the decision less likely to be corrupt than the decision of a smaller group."[8] Guicciardini effectively dismisses even the possibility that meritorious candidates could be excluded. By definition, meritorious status can only be conferred by the multitude: "if one merits office, he does not need the approval of individuals but of the whole people; the people judge better than anyone because the people are the prince who make decisions dispassionately ... If nothing else, we distribute offices only to those who seem to deserve them most."[9] A few years later Machiavelli would express a similar sentiment in *discorso* 1.47: "I believe also that we may grant that a prudent man need not avoid the popular judgment in particular things about the distribution of offices and dignities, because in this alone the people do not deceive themselves, and if sometimes they are deceived, this happens so seldom that more often a few men who have to make such distributions will be deceived."[10]

Having declared on general principles the unique capacity of a broad, collective assembly to correctly distinguish between competent, patriotic individuals and incompetent, self-serving individuals, Guicciardini then proceeds to analyse the Florentine context to illustrate an additional aspect of the people's rationality: the capacity for continual self-improvement. In the immediate aftermath of the anti-Medici coup, the Council made chronically poor appointments that Guicciardini attributed to ignorance and ideology. As the Medici had excluded such vast numbers of citizens from any meaningful role in their regime, the broad ranks of Florentines simply did not possess enough knowledge about their fellow citizens to distinguish between the deserving and the undeserving. And because so many had been excluded for so long, the newly empowered people felt both insecure and vengeful and therefore appointed candidates ideologically, which for Guicciardini meant promoting people who the Medici regime had excluded and excluding everyone to whom it had distributed offices or honours. In both cases, the Council's determinations were entirely irrespective of an individual's merit and evident capacity for office. In short order, however, the quality of election results improved, in part the result of the inherent rationality of collective deliberation outlined earlier but also in part the result of the people's capacity to improve their judgment. With each passing day and every subsequent election, the people gained additional experience and consequently honed their prudence, discretion, and judgment, qualities that Guicciardini typically reserves for the *uomini savi*: "individuals of the citizenry will become more studied and better known: one day actions of this one citizen will be witnessed and adjudicated, and tomorrow of this other fellow. The people ... will realize that this government really belongs to them. Consequently, they will put more thought into their judgments and better scrutinize the comportment and habits of their fellow citizens ... The populace will thus become an even better judge of which men merit office. Every day things become more clear, and they continually improve."[11]

Having established the people's good judgment and capacity for improvement, Guicciardini uses those attributes to portray sortition as precisely the kind of bullying tactic that Machiavelli would associate with the *grandi*. Advocates of sortition criticized the majority election system because it appeared to them as an instrument of oligarchy because it repeatedly returned the same small fraction of eligible candidates to office. *On the Method of Electing* effectively turned the tables on their criticism by adopting the perspective of the people and condemning sortition as both unjust (because it rejected majority will) and practically dangerous (because the entire city benefited from the majority will's ability to empower only the most competent people):

> If the offices are not held by as many people as they desire, this is not inconvenient because the people like it this way. The people do not deserve to be lacerated or criticized if they decide to place their affairs in the hands of those who are more often chosen, which actually can benefit everyone in the government of the city because it employs the most competent ministers possible ... If it seems strange to see someone who has been given offices or dignities many times, it does not seem odd to the people, who ultimately look for their city and dominion to be well governed.[12]

Guicciardini here implies (as he does elsewhere) the conviction that in any regime, irrespective of constitution or time period, experienced, ambitious, and wise citizens are rare and that the mark of any well-ordered regime is its capacity for constructively harnessing the talents of the virtuous few.[13] *On the Method of Electing*, however, is the only text in which Guicciardini infers that conclusion via the Florentine people's electoral wisdom rather than from personal experience or his reading of ancient history.

What Guicciardini only hints at here – that at least some advocates of sortition had self-serving motives and resented the influence conferred on the people by the majority vote system – he elaborated in greater detail in his *History of Florence*. His account of the city's electoral politics in the *History* portrays advocates of sortition as corrupt *ottimati* plotters knowingly sabotaging an effective system to sow discord and dysfunction. His *History of Florence* identifies a crucial aspect of the controversy omitted in the briefer *On the Method of Electing*: the degree to which conflict over electoral systems was actually a by-product of a larger quarrel between supporters of Savonarola and a group of his aristocratic opponents.

Consistent with his account in *On the Method of Electing*, Guicciardini explains in the *History* that in the early months of the Council's existence its elections empowered people with little experience or competence and systematically excluded most of the powerful aristocratic families that had prospered under the Medici. As post-coup passions cooled, however, the Council reversed its priorities and began favouring those households at the expense of middle- and lower-class candidates, much to the city's satisfaction: "In this respect the Council had improved a great deal, and it became clear that if elections by a simple majority continued, the government and its offices would remain in the hands of the few and the best qualified."[14] At this point, the Council was well on its way to creating Guicciardini's ideal regime of rule by the experienced and competent few, selected and empowered by the judicious many.

Given the aristocratic effect of elections in the Council's choice, we would expect the excluded middle- and lower-class candidates to make arguments for sortition. Contrary to expectation, however, the advocates of sortition were in fact a faction of disgruntled anti-Savonarolan aristocrats led by Bernardo del Nero (not himself an aristocrat). Their real objection to the majority vote system in the Council was that, owing to Savonarola's influence, elections tended to favour Piagnoni candidates at their expense. They could not point their fingers at the Savonarolan faction, however, and simply accuse them of exploiting their numerical advantage in the Council for self-serving mutual self-promotion, because, as Guicciardini explains, "in truth, except for Bernardo del Nero, messer Guidantonio [Vespucci], Bernardo Rucellai, and a few others like them, the friar's men were better qualified."[15] They had hoped via their cynical embrace of electoral sortition to unite the city's elite families against Savonarola but began to appreciate that the generally high quality of the Council's election results was slowly but surely winning over formerly disaffected aristocrats to the new Savonarolan regime: "It seemed to the enemies of the Council that the continued improvement in the quality of elections would cause many of the aristocrats to reconcile themselves to the present government, which would strengthen it."[16]

Guicciardini portrays this group as engaging in precisely the kind of entitled and destructive behaviour that Machiavelli attributed to elites in general. Their motives were purely self-serving and unconcerned with the common good: they began to lobby for sortition not because of flaws in the majority vote system but precisely because it was clearly producing good results and a competent regime. They believed that sortition would damage the regime by indiscriminately placing unworthy candidates in office (which Guicciardini evidently believed as well) and thereby generate aristocratic hostility that they could harness in their larger plot to overturn the Council, undermine Savonarola's influence, and "establish an oligarchy of aristocrats with Lorenzo and Giovanni di Pierfrancesco [de' Medici] as their leaders."[17] Since they recognized that their inferior numbers meant they could not succeed through proper deliberative channels – namely by persuading the Council to agree to its own undoing – they reverted to open sabotage: "They tried to do it by casting negative votes for all candidates running for an office abroad, so that if nobody won, other methods of election would have to used."[18] *The History of Florence*, much like *On the Method of Electing*, associates the majority vote system with popular virtue, and sortition with repressive and irresponsible aristocratic efforts to establish an oligarchy. As he concludes in *On the Method of Electing*, advocates of sortition "make a lot of noise, smearing the judgment of the people who currently enjoy liberty and security."[19]

On the Method of Electing also features one of Guicciardini's earliest uses of the "fruits of liberty," a term that he would regularly deploy, with varying and telling meanings, in all his major texts. Surprisingly, however, he does not use it here in his most frequent formulation advocating for the rule of a narrow, meritocratic elite, even though the aforementioned context is a perfect example. As he put in in his *Ricordi*, "It is not the fruit of our liberties nor the purpose for which they were founded, that everyone should govern, for only those should govern who are suitable and deserve to."[20] *On the Method of Electing* deploys the term in a sense that corresponds closely to Machiavelli's view of the nature and virtues of the people. While acknowledging the disapproval of disgruntled critics of majority elections – namely, that many citizens who had been excluded under the Medici remained excluded in the newly invigorated republic – Guicciardini argues that such criticism overlooks the far more substantial achievement of the Great Council: it had already and was continuing to deliver the far more important priorities of freedom from oppression and of security of one's property: "[R]ight now, every citizen enjoys the principal fruits of liberty: to not fear being oppressed beyond the dictates of the law; to have no one above the magistracies; to not need to show deference or submission to anyone; to distribute the honours and offices of the city; to have as much authority before the law as the richest and most powerful man."[21] In *The Prince* and the *Discourses* Machiavelli would describe the nature of the people in strikingly similar terms: whereas the *grandi* had an insatiable appetite to oppress and bully those beneath them, which explained their instinctively monopolistic desire to occupy the highest positions in government, the people merely wished to live free from arbitrary violence and humiliation and secure in the enjoyment of their property and possessions. In Machiavelli's republican theory the people's attributes were a means to an end: because the people hungered not for office and political power but rather only to enjoy what they already possessed, they became the optimal mechanism through which to safeguard republican liberty from aristocratic saboteurs.[22] What for Machiavelli were attributes of the people were for Guicciardini – at least in this text – the attributes of good republican government itself, and the Great Council's system of majority election was the safeguard.

However often Guicciardini would subsequently condemn the people as a generally ungrateful and fickle mob, the positive declarations of this brief technocratic text about the people's capacity for astute judgment implicitly recur in every one of his constitutional prescriptions for republican regimes led by a small circle of *uomini savi.* Scholarship generally portrays Guicciardini as a traditional aristocratic elitist who championed regimes of the few because he viewed the many as inherently irrational (and in one sense rightly so because his aristocratic chauvinism is undeniable). But it is also worth stressing the degree to which his conception of a natural elite that was distinguished by patriotic ambition, wisdom, and experience necessarily required an a priori conviction about the rationality and discretion of the multitude (whether Guicciardini fully recognized this relationship is another question – he nowhere declared it outright). In his idealistic moments, at least, Guicciardini insisted on the vital distinction between formal oligarchies or caste systems, in which certain families own elite status as transmissible property, which he consistently condemned as unjust and prone to tyranny, and regimes led by a small group of individuals conspicuous for their political virtue but only and crucially as identified by the people.

Guicciardini put this most clearly in his explication of the ideal configuration of optimate rule in the *Considerations*:

> [I]f they are optimates by birth and not by election, from prudent and good men at first, affairs soon fall into the hands of imprudent and wicked ones. In order to extract from this kind of government what is best and avoid what is worst, the optimates must not be drawn always from the same lines and families, but from the whole body of the city, from all who according to the law are qualified to take part in the magistrature, and a senate must be elected to deal with difficult matters, containing the flower of the prudent noble and rich men of the city ... The Spartans had optimates of this kind, drawn not from a special class of men but from the whole body of the city.[23]

Asserted in multiple texts but most clearly here, Guicciardini portrays elite status as open to all, the result of competition in a context of equality of opportunity rather than of rank, status, or wealth and in which the people collectively determine the results with discretion and perspicacity.

Without a rational, discerning multitude, there is no way to empower the meritorious few.

So far we have considered the ways in which Guicciardini's defence of the majority vote system relied on an affirmation of the people's capacity for circumspection, rationality, and discretion, articulated in ways that would subsequently echo in Machiavelli's political thought. One could argue, however, that Guicciardini's affirmation was merely a rhetorical strategy by which to champion covertly the rule of the few over the many in terms palatable to the many. The narrow focus of this text on electoral technology enabled Guicciardini to omit asserting the aristocratic conviction at the heart of the republican tradition that he subsequently made explicit in the *Discorso di Logrogno* and *Dialogue on the Government of Florence*: the people should always have the power to choose who rules over them and in their name but should never be entrusted with important policy decisions, be they in war, diplomacy, or domestic politics. Justifying the restriction of real decision making to a prudential few required another invocation of the collective psychology of the people, circumscribed, however, in ways that substantially undercut their putative rationality. Simply put, choosing officials required mental powers that were many orders of magnitude lower than those of devising policy. As he elaborated in the *Discorso*: "While the election of magistrates is indeed important, it is not all that difficult to judge: the people rely on the reputation and estimation of men, which is based on a broader popular conception, composed of many opinions, as opposed to the judgment of one particular person … This is not the case with legislation. Laws require the consideration of wise men (*uomini savi*), for when the laws are driven by the appetite of the multitude, they are clearly always harmful or useless."[24] If we situate *On the Method of Electing* within a broader reading of Guicciardini's writings, we see that, by insisting on the unique capacity of the people to judge character and competence and granting them complete freedom over the elections process, he effectively consigns them to a subordinate role of passive subjects rather than active citizens.

Sortition and the People's Inherent Moderation

Having considered Guicciardini's arguments in favour of majority vote, composed in an aristocratic voice, we now turn to the second half of *On the Method of Electing*, in which he argues in favour of sortition and adopts a populist perspective and voice. Since this text, as so many of his do, features his cautious tendency to compare and contrast different views on an issue without declaring an overt personal stance, we can only infer and interpret Guicciardini's own view on the electoral question. Given his other utterances in favour of majority election and his constitutional recommendations assigning the people a primary role in the appointments process but virtually no role in executive and legislative deliberation, I tend to infer Guicciardini's own preferences from the text's first half. Two points nevertheless merit emphasis. The first, intrinsic to Guicciardini as a thinker, is that however much he remained an aristocratic chauvinist at core, he was never a mere ideological, elitist shill. Here and elsewhere, his formidable intellect displays a considerable willingness and aptitude to view the world from other perspectives; to subject his own preferences to searching, dispassionate critique; and to have a precocious appreciation of the degree to which ostensibly objective truths are in fact powerfully conditioned by and relative to class, status, and wealth. Second and more importantly for the larger context of this book, we see that his critique of majority vote from a populist perspective introduced both concepts and language about nobles and people that Machiavelli would subsequently incorporate into his own political theory, albeit to different purposes. If their ends differed, their categories of analysis were strikingly similar.

In his persona of middle-class advocate of sortition, Guicciardini begins with relatively technocratic contrasts between the inherent unfairness of majority vote and the rationality of sortition. On the surface, majority vote seems just, since the many elect the person they judge most qualified. That favourable judgment, however, always reflects the person's reputation and experience, both of which are directly measured in terms of prior electoral successes. As a result, the system continually rewards the same small group of people – perceived as possessing a superior reputation – who gain elevated status by virtue of their disproportionate access to the offices that confer reputation. "If magistracies and government are always possessed by the same few, the others never participate, and who doubts that reputation and greatness would remain in those few office-holding hands? Precisely as a result of holding office, judges and magistrates generate such great respect that every subsequent election pits one category of reputable men against another sort that is perpetually at a great disadvantage [because he has not been able to accrue the honour and prestige that comes with office holding, thereby creating inequality]."[25] When one group of people is systematically excluded from gaining the experience upon which status depends, it exists in a state of de facto servitude while "the advantages and honours" of its opponents "become private possessions."[26]

Turning to the advantages of sortition, Guicciardini revisits his earlier axiom about the two ends of government, securing the equality of all citizens before the law and distributing offices as widely as possible. His defence of majority vote began with the distinction that whereas one should tolerate zero exceptions to the first end (equality), in practice one could and should tolerate some exceptions to the second (distribution) because excessive wideness leads to disorder. His defence of sortition opens by asserting the rigid interconnectedness of those two ends. Without equal access to offices, there can be no equality before the law. As for the concern that sortition would result in incompetent people being charged with important tasks, Guicciardini defends the system with similar arguments about the many expressed in the first half. As all candidates eligible for the sortition stage must have received at least 50 per cent of the Council's vote, the many still collectively assess candidates and will withhold votes from the truly incompetent: "It will never or rarely be the case that half of the council is deceived and judge someone adequate who is truly not, nor will enough private matters converge behind one candidate that he can have so much favour."[27] His defence of the collective scrutiny stage of the sortition process relies on a similar view of the people's rationality and respect for competence. In part 1, he concluded that Florentines generally appointed people who merited the office most; in part 2, he observes that "our peers generally make a profession of being governed and often voluntarily concede to one who supposedly knows more."[28]

The bulk of Guicciardini's consideration of the merits of sortition has less to do with technocratic observations about each system's probability of appointing competent officials, however, than it does with a contrasting assessment of nobles and people as collective groups in which the former pose a threat to a well-ordered regime and the latter provide a stable foundation for one. As we shall see in detail, Guicciardini portrayed noble culture as entitled and domineering by nature. and noble status itself as the product of transgression and criminality. The people, by contrast, he portrayed as reasonable, naturally respectful of the laws, and instinctively disinclined ever to leverage the superior power of their numbers to seize more than their share. Guicciardini's ideas and language in this short early text resurfaced so clearly and so precisely in Machiavelli's political thought that *On the Method of Electing* reads like a primer for understanding the stakes of Machiavellian democracy, in which elites and people are respectively threats to and safeguards of collective liberty.

In defending sortition, Guicciardini effectively portrayed the people, much as Machiavelli would make explicit in the *Discourses*, as the best guardians of liberty because they desired freedom from oppression rather than power over others. Contrary to the claims of advocates of majority vote who infer the rarity of patriotism and competence from the recurring election of a small inner circle, Guicciardini assures his audience that there are just as many "good, courageous" citizens among the city's middle and lower classes as among the upper. In fact, owing to the people's inherent moderation, he infers that there must be more qualified candidates among them than among the ranks of nobles: "There are just as many lovers of liberty among the lower stations; in fact, there are probably more among them than among the higher stations because we do not long for anything except a free way of life, while they hope to have a narrow state headed by tyrants, like they have had in the past."[29] Since excessive wealth almost always indicates greed, expropriation, and the primacy of self-interest over any other consideration, those lacking it possess a far greater probability of carrying out office in pursuit of its intended purpose and without regard for personal enrichment: "If your ancestors were modest citizens in their service [*uomini da bene*], and did not seek to make themselves great through these means (corrupt acquisition of wealth), this does not make you any lesser than them, nor does it mean that you should play a more minor role in this city. In fact, on the occasions when they have been given offices, your magistrates have done much good for the republic and not bad, like most of them [*uomini da bene*], who have been ministers of narrow states and are enriched through these [sinister] arts."[30] As the people's appetites are moderate and they prioritize humility over glory, they possess a naturally superior ability for collective governance: "If we take stock in he who has the greatest aptitude for government, then we demonstrate as much spirit, sentiment, and language as they do, and we exhibit less passion and desire, which ultimately corrupts their judgment."[31]

Guicciardini also observes, multiple times, another quality of the people that Machiavelli went on to elaborate at greater length: even when goaded into open conflict with elites, they never use their overwhelming numerical superiority to banish or suppress their opponents and claim the state for themselves. Even in charged, violently militant moments, the people generally limit their requests to an appropriate share in the regime and even agree to a settlement in which they remain disadvantaged, such as during the Ciompi revolt.[32] Guicciardini's people in *On the Method of Electing* are no different.

In his persona as voice of the multitude, Guicciardini opens with a frank statement of the inherent injustice that the debates about electoral systems hoped to resolve: namely that for most of the fifteenth century the Medici oligarchy had violently excluded most of the city from exercising any meaningful role in the governance of the city.[33] Given that the anti-Medici coup, at least notionally, was carried out with loud proclamations of the traditional republican slogan of *popolo e libertà*, the people were disillusioned to discover that, within a few months of the coup, the regime remained largely in the hands of the same families who had formed the inner circle of Medici lieutenants. A just settlement, Guicciardini observes, would result in the disproportionate inclusion of those who had been traditional excluded, at the direct expense of the oligarchy that had corruptly prospered under the Medici: "Theoretically it would be just not only that we now enjoy our share in government, but also that we participate more than the others in order to make up for lost time."[34]

Although he acknowledges that justice would require placing a majority of offices in the people's hands, he nevertheless pleads only for a modest popular presence in the regime, reflecting the people's general disinclination to pursue immoderate or exclusionary demands. Recognizing that an openly partisan approach would heighten tension and provoke factional discord, the people turned to the method of sortition, a system that, by its very randomized nature, could not address or reverse the historical ledger's one-sided imbalance. Sortition's virtue lies in obstructing monopoly, not replacing the monopoly of one group with another: "I suggest that you rest content, leave the memory of the past behind you, and demand only your share in government participation, which is in itself laudable and modest."[35] Guicciardini urges the people neither to litigate the past nor to deny their former oppressors seats at the table, only to request a few additional seats for themselves.

In a majority vote system, at least theoretically, the people possess a major advantage over the city's noble families via their considerable numerical superiority, a point used by Guicciardini in his text's first half to stress that any electoral outcome – even a narrow oligarchy – reflects popular will. But Guicciardini's discussion of the two groups' voting habits in the second half reveals why a numerical advantage alone cannot obstruct the aristocratic effect of elections. Rather than assessing a candidate by reputation, experience, or talent, the nobles judge fitness for office in terms of status. Since they conflate the dignity of public office with the dignity of household, they instinctively seek to exclude the middle and lower classes from high office. The nobles' innate sense of entitlement and conflation of the regime with their families leads them to think and act in concert, resulting in their voting as a unified bloc: "They hand out favours to each other and form coalitions when they vote (*quando vanno a partito*), and give us – those of the threes, twos, and aces – nothing but white beans."[36] In an open, unconstrained system, class solidarity conditioned by a naturally greater hunger to exercise power offsets the nobles' numerical inferiority. Guicciardini offers us here an example of what Machiavelli would later describe in *discorso* 1.7 as the "few behaving in the mode of the few."

The people possess no such calculating instincts. Within their own ranks they view each other as equally legitimate and equally entitled to office, which removes the need for strategic alliances. In stark contrast to the nobles, who openly consider those of lesser rank fundamentally unsuited to high office, the people, often awed by the status and wealth of the elite, just as often assume – frequently erroneously – that many nobles do indeed merit electoral success. "This is the real reason why, even though we can easily find someone among ourselves capable of any task, he can never earn the majority of the votes: the person who wins the most votes must necessarily win among the fours and above, who are always supported by their peers along with some of us; but we can at most achieve support only among ourselves, and they will give us only white beans."[37] In short, the noble's vote is always unified, and the people's vote is always split.

Guicciardini acknowledges that the people's fundamental decency and modesty prohibit them from emulating the self-serving tactics of their social betters, even while the people are aware not only of those tactics but also of the superior potential of their own power. Having assessed the structural problems evident in the current majority vote system, he offers two related solutions. The optimal solution would be for every citizen in the Council, irrespective of social station or wealth, to embody the selflessness championed by civic humanism and to vote for the most capable candidate. The majority vote system, in theory at least, was fundamentally predicated on the cherished humanist belief that people were capable of suppressing self-interest in favour of the common good. Guicciardini clearly recognizes here, however, that Florentine social reality renders this solution impossible: owing to their irrepressible aristocratic chauvinism, the Florentine nobles will always view their social inferiors as incapable of exercising office competently, irrespective of their individual merits.

The other, more muscular solution would be for the people to give the nobles a taste of their own medicine by coordinating the popular vote as a unified bloc, not with the intent of promoting the best candidates but with the far simpler task of systematically excluding the city's elite families: "It would be necessary … that those of us from the threes, twos, and aces act as they do and give our votes only to one of our own. Given that we are far more numerous, we can quickly make them realize what it means to only favour one's own and disfavour all the others."[38] As Guicciardini presents it, the people possess not only the power to deny the nobles access to office but also the awareness of that power and the ease with which they could deploy it: "We can address this only through violent and scandalous modes, which we could easily employ because we far outnumber them."[39] Their moderate nature, however, prevents them from pursuing that strategy, just as the nature of the nobles prevents them from abandoning their reflexive oligarchical clannishness. Their innate sense of decency shrinks from adopting openly partisan, extremist tactics: "The second [option] would be scandalous and divide the city."[40]

Rather than recommending an electoral uprising, a plan both simple and effective, Guicciardini's popular advocate instead champions sortition as a conciliatory third way, *even while acknowledging that sortition still tacitly privileges noble status.* As every sitting member of the Great Council was theoretically eligible to hold office, a true sortition system would simply draw names randomly from among the Council members. All agreed, however, that such a system was excessively indiscriminate and that, in practice, many Council members lacked the requisite skills for high office. As a result, the sortition proposal combined lottery and election. Stage one involved a nominations process; stage two involved voting on each nominated candidate; stage three involved a lottery in which office holders were drawn from the ranks of each candidate who received at least 50 per cent of the Council's vote. As a result, the psychological factors that biased outcomes in the majority vote system were mitigated but not removed altogether. Viewing the election of those outside their circle as a slight to their own status and pre-eminence, the nobles will continue to hold those of lesser station to an unreasonably high bar, such that all non-noble candidates will receive a bloc no vote "unless one of us achieves the status of an Aristotle or Solon."[41] Only the rare few people with an outstanding and impeccable reputation for competence and skill can hope to succeed. The nobles, on the other hand, can hope to succeed not only through recognition of their suitability for office but also as a result of the psychological influence exerted by excessive wealth, power, and status: "In fact, if a disadvantage exists [in the sortition system], it will be at our expense, because many of us let ourselves become dazzled by their condition more than we judge their aptitude for office, something that does not exist in the reverse situation: if they are not taken by our virtue, then they will never add us to the coalition."[42]

When their opponents confront them with false historical precedents in favour of the majority vote system, Guicciardini shows the people not only as superior readers of history, aware of their opponents' duplicity, but also as unwilling to capitalize on their superior knowledge because of the dissension it would cause. As he explains, the city's aristocratic champions of the majority vote invoke the august precedent of ancient Rome, which they declare always used the method of majority vote. Not true, declares Guicciardini's man of the people, who understands that his social betters "do not honestly explain what happened." [43] The Roman nobles initially held the entire state in their hands, a regime so clearly exclusionary that eventually "the people rebelled and raised themselves up against them." Far from adopting a majority vote system, the Roman nobles recognized that, owing to their numerical inferiority, such a system would dramatically undermine their control of the government. As a result they made a tactical concession: "They divided the city into two parties; in our terms, between the sixes, the fives, and the fours on one side, and the threes, the twos, and the aces on the other. Thus, the Romans ordered by law that the offices were divided – that is, each part of the city was entitled to half the magistracies."[44] By rightly calculating that the Roman plebeians would be content with half the magistracies, the Roman nobles managed, in spite of the uprising that their political monopoly had generated, to ensure their own survival and even to retain 50 per cent control of the regime. Guicciardini's popular leader thus recognizes that, in the Roman system championed as a worthy precedent by their opponents, the nobles had actually accepted an outcome that permitted the people a vastly larger role than the Florentine elite would tolerate.

> If we were to propose this method [i.e., to accept Roman precedent, but understood properly], you would all forget the Romans, who you use as example only when it is convenient, proclaiming that this policy is a mad and dishonest attempt to divide the city. You would never admit that the method of majority vote is far more dishonest because it removes any opportunity for those who merit office to obtain it, or that it divides the city more, because one part, placed outside the circle, so to speak, needs to despair more than when they are subjected to tyranny.[45]

Even though their opponents invite them to follow Roman precedent, the people decline to do so because they recognize that, irrespective of the relative justice of the Roman example, asking for half of the city's offices would generate excessive dissension and resentment.

Guicciardini outlines here the essential elements of Machiavelli's conception of the people's moderation. Even when knowingly in possession of the power to annihilate their opponents and in the face of their opponents' open, chauvinistic hostility towards them, they advocate only for modest gains and voluntarily participate in systems that continue to disadvantage them.[46] Guicciardini's summary of sortition's merits makes plain its modest scope and the continued deference to a status quo of elite-dominated government. "If this provision were to succeed, it could afford some of you the occasional opportunity to become a candidate, and perhaps even to be selected for office."[47] The vision expressed in

On the Method of Electing was of course hardly Guicciardini's final word on the nature of the people, and his final utterances on this topic years later in his *Considerations on the Discourses of Machiavelli* were diametrically opposed. There he defined the people as a dangerously fickle body in thrall to envy of noble pre-eminence: "As for envy it arises much more easily in men of the people for whom every kind of eminence of birth, riches, valour, or reputation, is usually unwelcome. There is nothing they dislike as much as seeing other citizens higher than themselves and they always want to pull them down."[48] In 1512, however, Guicciardini was at least open to viewing the people as inherently moderate and even constrained by their sense of decency from fully pursuing their self-interest or fully protecting themselves from noble entitlement. More significantly, one of the fundamental building blocks of his method of political inquiry – attributing a collective positive psychology to the people – would echo in substantial ways when Machiavelli himself turned to these questions.

Following the structure of Guicciardini's text, the first section of this chapter considers his argument in favour of the majority vote system, demonstrating the degree to which it relied on the capacity of the many for superior judgment than the few; the second section turns to his argument in favour of sortition, demonstrating the degree to which it relied on the inherent moderation of the people; the third and final section examines Guicciardini's critique of the concept of nobility and the degree to which he associated it with violent, abusive behaviour.

Sortition and the Nobles' Inherent Violence

Guicciardini's defence of sortition's merits also involved a scathing critique of the concept of nobility itself, another recurring theme in Machiavelli's political vision. Guicciardini introduces this theme with a specific phrase and acknowledgment that directly anticipates a similarly loaded phrase in Machiavelli's *Discourses on Livy*. As the outward displays of wealth and trappings of eminent status tend to create in equal parts awe and intimidation amongst those of lesser station, Guicciardini reasons, people do not appreciate the degree to which noble status is almost always the by-product of a disposition towards criminality. Given that ancient and Renaissance political thought generally condemned democracy as anarchic and privileged regimes of the virtuous few, Guicciardini's critique was highly provocative and he clearly recognized the novelty of his critique of aristocratic excellence. And because the culture of Renaissance Italy equated intellectual legitimacy with conformity to ancient authorities, Guicciardini had first to disclose to his readers his awareness that the realities of Florence's social context did not conform to the aristocratic pieties of the political tradition: "It seems timely for me to say something about this, *not in the way that many writers have spoken about the subject in the past*, but in our own terms and according to our way of life in this city."[49] A few years later, when Machiavelli wrote a similarly provocative defence of the people's superior capacity for wisdom than the princes', he acknowledged his departure from tradition in similar terms: "I do not know whether I am undertaking a task so hard and full of difficulties that I shall be forced to give up in disgrace or to continue with reproach *when I try to defend something that, as I have said, has been condemned by all the writers*."[50] Their departures from received wisdom mutually reinforced each other, Machiavelli's by praising the people and Guicciardini's by condemning the few.

Guicciardini asserts his general thesis using one of the most recurring terms in Machiavelli's lexicon – extraordinary (*istraordinaria*) – and uses it to convey precisely the same range of meanings that it performs in Machiavelli's writing. To see nobles for what they truly are, Guicciardini asserts, one must first recognize that "it was not virtue but extraordinary circumstances that hurled them [the *uomini da bene*] to such honourable status, and we must keep these circumstances in mind."[51] As the subsequent discussion will make clear, Guicciardini understood *extraordinary* to mean a wide range of illicit, corrupt, and self-interested practices.

Here we have another use of a distinctly Machiavellian term *avant la lettre* – the sense of corrupt practices taking place outside of existing and licit *ordini*. In both *The Discourses* and *Florentine Histories*, Machiavelli used the term *extraordinary* to describe the methods by which Cosimo de' Medici subverted the republic and established his family as de facto dynasts. As John Najemy put it, "Liberty, for Machiavelli, is ultimately a function of the laws and public institutions he called *ordini*: constitutional procedures capable of diverting political ambition away from private, factional interests toward the public good. The gravest danger to liberty and *ordini* is the power of ambitious and wealthy citizens with the resources to build factions that bypass, disrupt, and undermine laws, courts, and public restraints on their ambition. Subversion of the *ordini* is what Machiavelli called 'corruption.'"[52]

Guicciardini's elaboration of his thesis conforms in every respect to Najemy's account of Machiavelli's conception of extraordinary threats to liberty. As Guicciardini explains, unlike virtually everywhere else in Europe, a blood connection to a family possessing legal and political privileges in perpetuity does not define the Florentine nobility, the *uomini da bene*. Anywhere that feudalism prevailed in Europe, every aristocratic house could trace the origins of its status as a reward for military service, usually conferred in the wake of a specific battle (at least prior to the sale of venal office in the sixteenth and seventeenth centuries). The Florentine conception of nobility, however, was largely a social construction, a cluster of houses that had come to enjoy exalted status in the eyes of others. Considering the origins of that status, as Guicciardini sees it, the best-case scenario is luck: some people simply prospered "with fortune and the favour of the time."[53] For most of the *uomini da bene*, though, the origin of their status was almost always material wealth, and, further, the origin of that wealth was almost always corrupt and repressive political practices: "If they ever enjoyed success, it was ... because of tyrants, or because some wealthy man among them found a way to ennoble himself with his money. Some of them curried favour with the heads of state in ways too shameful to mention."[54] Their perceived nobility stems not from "their virtue, merit, or prudence, but in their fortune, favours, and illicit business practises (*guadagni*) ... There are those who enter this group through their wealth ... Many times, it is purchased through usury or other dishonest and viperous arts, and those who have unjustly gained titles of nobility (*la roba*) deserve to be punished."[55] The Florentine nobility, once one peers behind the curtain, are a de facto kleptocracy, perpetuated by the majority vote system and its veneer of popular empowerment. Much later in life, Guicciardini again hinted at this conclusion, in his *Ricordi*, when he acknowledged that malevolence was an intrinsic characteristic of wealthy people: "Among the poor, malevolence may easily be caused by accident; in the rich it is more often there by nature. And so ordinarily it is more reprehensible in the rich than in the poor."[56]

Since the Florentine *uomini da bene* enjoyed their pre-eminent status primarily as a reward for bad behaviour, they were hardly likely to become exemplars of wisdom and selfless leadership. The Florentine elite consistently conducted themselves oppressively and with a sneering, exclusionary sense of entitlement: "They call themselves good men (*uomini da bene*) [and] they have used this title to expropriate and oppress others."[57] Without that sense of entitlement, there would be no need for the sortition system because the nobles would vote as the people consistently do, for the person they deemed most competent and suited for office. Their entitlement, however, both prevents them from recognizing merit in those of lower station and normalizes their monopoly on higher offices and their potential for lucre: "There is one sort of men, those who are from the fours and up – those who are wealthier and considered more noble, or those who have enjoyed reputation from their fathers and ancestors – that think the state belongs to them, and that we – those of threes, twos, and aces – do not deserve dignities, but rather that we should be happy with a few petty offices, and have the rest of us carry all the burdens, like we have in the past."[58] The majority vote system cannot benefit the city because it rewards those who "appropriated the state to themselves based on the presumption and false opinion of their own self worth."[59] Further, the evident display of weakness signalled by reluctance to adopt the sortition system will only encourage yet more vicious behaviour: "It will augment their arrogance that they maintain through their families, and they will treat you in a way that will force you to desire a remedy at some point, but then it will be too late."[60]

Guicciardini deploys a combination of scathing, hyperbolic condemnation and stirring exhortation to shake his imagined popular audience out of their complacent attitude towards accepting less than their lot. Owing to their inherent modesty and decency, the people chronically fail to recognize that the external symbols of wealth and status of the few impose a condition of psychological slavery on the many that makes them willing collaborators in their own subordination: "They drown us in their nobility and reputation, which brings with it a certain splendour that continues to dazzle us … Those who are the worst are called good men … nevertheless, we are so thick (*grossi*) that we hold them in higher regard than we hold ourselves."[61] As a result of that successful social illusion enabling vice to appear virtue, the people become guilty of only one, defining, and artfully engineered excess: immoderate humility: "I would accuse you of governing yourselves too respectfully and with too much modesty. You behave like a man who has recently been introduced to liberty after a long period of servitude, and who consequently cannot shake his servitude. This submissive behaviour manifests itself in timid and abject actions that retain the memory and vestiges of your ancient servitude."[62] Guicciardini implores his readers to see that the stakes of the choice between sortition and majority vote are nothing less than freedom and slavery. Failure to adopt the sortition method will result in "not only danger, but also great shame … Your fate remains in your own hands, and you can either bring yourselves in practise and in name to a true state of liberty and to enjoy its fruits, or confine yourselves to liberty only in name – a false liberty that is really servitude."[63]

We have seen some ways in which the units and method of Guicciardini's political analysis – sharply foregrounding permanent and fixed psychological contrasts between nobles and people – recurred as Machiavelli's point of departure for the prescriptions he offered in *The Prince* and *The Discourses*. In those texts Machiavelli considered the *grandi* and the *popolo* in general, intermixing examples from Greek, Roman, and Persian antiquity with those from the present. When he later turned specifically to his own city's culture of divisions in his *Florentine Histories*, he included a strikingly similar passage, in terms of both methodology and content, in his account of the Ciompi revolt, another moment of popular contestation of an elite-dominated regime. In book 3, chapter 13, Machiavelli transports us into the deliberations of the Wool Guild's disenfranchised plebeians, the *sottoposti*, as they deliberate on how to proceed after having commenced their insurrection. Just as Guicciardini adopted the voice and perspective of a common citizen, exhorting the Council to adopt sortition, Machiavelli adopted the voice and perspective of an aggrieved and lowly woolworker, exhorting his fellow insurrectionaries not to lay down their arms. The woolworker's speech contains all the elements of Guicciardini's populist speech: the conviction that the social function of nobility is hardly a reward for excellence but rather a way to inculcate deference in those of lower station; the conviction that the origins of noble status are always violence and transgression; and the recognition that the people, owing to their inherent modesty, must be bluntly and provocatively shaken out of their submission:

> Do not let their antiquity of blood, with which they will reproach us, dismay you: all men, having had the same beginning, are equally ancient and have been made by nature in one mode. Strip all of us naked, you will see that we are alike; dress us in their clothes and them in ours, and without a doubt we shall appear noble and they ignoble, for only poverty and riches make us unequal. It pains me much when I hear that out of conscience many of you repent the deeds that have been done and that you wish to abstain from new deeds ... But if you will take note of the mode of proceeding of men, you will see that all those who come to great riches and great power have obtained them either by fraud or by force; and afterwards, to hide the ugliness of acquisition, they make it decent by applying the false title of earnings to things they usurped by deceit or by violence. And those who, out of either little prudence or too much foolishness, shun these modes always suffocate in servitude or poverty. For faithful servants are always servants and good men are always poor; nor do they ever rise out of servitude unless they are unfaithful and bold, nor out of poverty unless they are rapacious and fraudulent.[61]

In his analysis of the creative role that violence plays in Machiavelli's political theory, Yves Winter has rightly stressed the rhetorical sophistication of this speech and the degree to which it crisply and economically enumerates numerous themes central to Machiavelli's political vision: "the preference for conflict over harmony; the advice to the workers to seize the occasion; the insight that when many transgress, they will not be penalized and that small misdeeds are punished while great crimes are rewarded; the rejection of a Christian model of conscience as arbiter of political action; the claim that power and wealth often have their origins in violence and fraud, shrouded in tales of merit and entitlement; and the counsel that boldness is prudence, and that a failure to act decisively and, if necessary, violently may lead to greater violence and misery down the road."[65]

Without disputing the originality of Machiavelli's provocative deployment of these themes, we should nevertheless recognize that many of these terms and assumptions were articulated by Guicciardini prior to Machiavelli. Guicciardini urges the people to recognize that they are equal to the *uomini da bene* in patriotism and competence, that accommodation of their exalted position is tantamount to servitude, that the *ottimati*'s pre-eminent status and riches reflect criminality rather than virtue, and that continued submission will only invite greater abuse that will eventually require recourse to violence. Machiavelli's violent populism was far more likely sustained and sincere, whereas Guicciardini's articulation of these themes was likely his method of testing the weaknesses of his aristocratic preferences and anticipating counter-arguments. Nevertheless, motives aside, by the time Machiavelli began composing his major works, Guicciardini had already beaten a conceptual path that exposed the self-regarding vanities of the Florentine aristocracy as vehicles of injustice.

Unlike Machiavelli, whose relationship to humanism and the republican tradition is the subject of considerable controversy, Guicciardini is identified by all the landmark scholarly contributions to Renaissance political culture as straightforwardly reiterating the values of Florentine civic humanism. Although they acknowledge Machiavelli's and Guicciardini's contrasting popular and aristocratic perspectives, the deans of the Cambridge school, John Pocock and Quentin Skinner, nevertheless portray them both as inheritors of the classical and humanist advocation of the mixed regime. For much the same reasons as did Leonardo Bruni, Poggio Bracciolini, and Pier Paolo Vergerio before them, Machiavelli and Guicciardini valued the Polybian tradition because it encouraged citizens to pursue the common good, conceived of politics in terms of individual responsibilities rather than rights, and balanced the power of the one, the few, and the many in ways that maximized civic unity and concord over conflict. Critics of that view dissent only regarding Machiavelli. John McCormick, most notably, underscoring Machiavelli's innovative advocacy of popular empowerment, stresses that if we wish to interpret early sixteenth-century Florentine political thought as an affirmation of civic humanism and its embrace of Aristotle and Cicero, we must instead label it a "Guicciardinian moment."[66] Italian scholarship largely concurs. Gennaro Sasso, perhaps Guicciardini's closest reader, although acknowledging his frequent reversals of opinions, ultimately concludes that he identified disunity as the gravest political danger and therefore, consistent with Florentine tradition, built his political thought around the ancient concept of *concordia*.[67]

Although many of Guicciardini's utterances indisputably uphold a vision of politics fully consistent with the political ideals of Renaissance humanists, we should also recognize the clarity and force of his writings that complicate or outright contradict his apparent compatibility with Florentine tradition and putative contrast with Machiavelli. Guicciardini was no intellectually gifted parvenu from Arezzo or Colle Val d'Elsa for whom prosperity and upward mobility depended in part on idealizing the metropolitan elite or averting one's gaze from contradictions between its ideals and its practice. As a distinguished and informed member of that very elite and a shrewd intellect always dismissive of easy, uncomplicated truths, Guicciardini clearly recognized, much as did Machiavelli – in Najemy's words, the "disillusioned debunker of civic humanist ideals" – the messier social and political function of civic humanism that Florentine specialists have exposed.[68]

As Najemy has persuasively argued, civic humanism functioned as an ideology to justify, in the most literal sense of that word, "participation without power."[69] As hierarchical patronage politics dominated by elite families gradually superseded the vertically structured guild republicanism of the Middle Ages, the Florentine *ottimati* engineered the consent of the broad ranks of the *popolo* to elite domination by vastly expanding the latter's access to minor positions while restricting major offices to their inner circle: "They [the popolo] thus accepted occasional election to prestigious offices as the reward – or consolation prize – for relinquishing any real share of power" (or as Guicciardini expressed it, only a select few members of the people who achieve "the level of an Aristotle or Solon" can hope for election).[70] Humanism sanded the rough edges of that unequal exchange by idealizing leadership in terms of individuals of exceptional personal virtue and by condemning all forms of conflict and protest as the worst political evil, immediate proof of the absence of virtue. As Najemy put it, civic humanist promoted "at its core … an ethic of dutiful passivity."[71] Najemy's survey of supporting texts privileged fifteenth-century writers, but Guicciardini provides a perfect illustration in the first half of *On the Method of Electing* in his anecdote of the humble, patriotic Spartan who, upon learning that he had not been elected to the Council of Three Hundred, returned home happy to have learned that the city enjoyed three hundred citizens more competent than he. Turned away from a direct role in the politics of his city, he demonstrated his virtue as someone who "suppresses his own ambition, who steadfastly exhibits deference towards the reggimento (or, simply, those who govern), whose willingness to cooperate borders on unquestioning obedience."[72]

We see from *On the Method of Electing*, however, that even at the outset of his career as a politician and writer, Guicciardini understood the distinction between Florentine politics as rationalized by humanist virtue politics (rule by a virtuous few voluntarily placed in power by an appreciative many) and how it functioned in practice – a kleptocratic regime that promoted an inner circle of the worst citizens whose domination of the people, owing to the people's moderation and innate reluctance to embrace extreme measures, was largely unavoidable. Unlike Guicciardini, Machiavelli devised institutional mechanisms to protect the people against the worst abuses of elite rule, whereas Guicciardini simply acknowledged the problem. Machiavelli offered those popular institutional mechanisms most thoroughly in his *Discourses on Livy*, the text with which Guicciardini disagreed most substantially. *On the Method of Electing* nevertheless reveals that, even if he did not share Machiavelli's methods for constraining elite misconduct in political life, he anticipated and therefore must have recognized the legitimacy of Machiavelli's diagnosis of the problem. Between such disparate elements the politics of concord and unity was impossible.

If Guicciardini's subsequent constitutional writings in his *Discorso di Logrogno* and *Dialogue on the Government of Florence* aspired to establish a regime built on the common good, when he composed the final version of his *Ricordi* in 1530, Guicciardini had returned to his view in *On the Method of Electing* that elite politics by definition could not provide for the people's desires: "Generally, it is the few, not the many, who determine the affairs of the world. And since the aims of the few are almost always different from those of the many, they give birth to effects different from those desired by the many."[73]

This chapter has demonstrated that, from the first moment that Guicciardini put pen to paper in reflection of Florentine politics, he thought about politics in terms of an irresolvable tension between the interests of the many and those of the few. Further, he elaborated a detailed view of aristocratic culture as characterized chiefly by criminality, violence, and contempt for the people. Machiavelli had not yet written *The Prince*, his first major treatise that described politics in similar terms, so he cannot have been an influence on Guicciardini's analysis of electoral politics. Whether Guicciardini genuinely saw aristocratic culture as inherently problematic or merely had a precocious capacity for inhabiting the world view of the populist critic remains an open question. In the next chapter, however, we will turn to his *Ricordi*, a series of private and personal reflections on politics and strategies for self-promotion that, because they were private and intended only for himself and his heirs, display none of his otherwise characteristic and deliberately ambiguous reasoning from both sides. The *Ricordi* contain numerous convictions that echoed Machiavelli's most provocative counsels in *The Prince*, many of which Guicciardini justifies with the same view of nobles and people that is evident in *On the Method of Electing.*

Chapter Three

Radical *Virtù* in *The Prince* and the *Ricordi*

As we saw in the previous chapter, even if Guicciardini at times shared Machiavelli's populist conception of nobles and people, he was unwilling to engage, even as a thought experiment, in Machiavellian democracy – in how to devise extra-electoral mechanisms to offset the corrupting effects of the disproportionate wealth and status wielded by elites. Since Guicciardini's only overtly formal acknowledgment of Machiavelli's political thought was his refutation of *The Discourses on Livy*, scholarship tends to portray their relationship in terms of contrasting republican theories: one a senatorial, elitist, and largely traditional variation on humanist consensus politics and the other a radical critique of that tradition in favour of innovative mechanisms to constrain the corruption caused by wealthy elites. In comparisons of these two thinkers, Machiavelli's *Prince* is nowhere to be found.[1]

This chapter takes a different approach. It focuses less on the question of Machiavelli's influence and more on the striking degree to which, irrespective of who influenced whom and when, Guicciardini's *Ricordi* advanced similar arguments as Machiavelli's *Prince*, made similarly provocative challenges to the ethical assumptions of prevailing political thought, and defended those provocations with similar justifications. In particular, I examine the similarity of Guicciardini's views in the *Ricordi* on the major ethical issues that Machiavelli famously raised in *The Prince*: the false virtue of generosity, the value of cruelty well used, the tactical superiority of fear over affection, the value of calculated deceit, the degree to which traditional virtues functioned as vices in many contexts, and the church's role in the peninsula's political servitude. I conclude that Guicciardini tended to identify Machiavelli's ideas explicitly only on points of disagreement in Machiavelli's republican theory (the value of a citizen militia and the salutary nature of class conflict, in particular), but that the substance of his *Ricordi* amounted to precisely the same radical reinterpretation of *virtù* that is evident in Machiavelli's *Prince*.

To be clear at the outset: the analysis offered here is not an argument that Machiavelli's *Prince* formally influenced the development of Guicciardini's various political counsels in the *Ricordi*. Perhaps it did, given the degree to which Guicciardini frequently arrived at similar conclusions as Machiavelli did and often used similar rhetorical strategies. The fact remains, however, that Guicciardini nowhere alludes to having read *The Prince* and he justifies virtually all of his political lessons in terms of his own specific experiences as a courtier and ruler without any reference to external influences. If they shared a substantial consensus on a wide range of ethical questions, that was most likely the result of each thinker's own independent reasoning from experience. This chapter argues, rather, that portrayals of the two as advocates of rival republican political theories miss a much more profound common intellectual agenda. Guicciardini fully shared Machiavelli's revolutionary reappraisal of ethics in political life, a point of considerably more intellectual significance – given the impact that their assault on virtue politics had on subsequent political thought – than their class-specific contrasting republican theories.

In chapter 15 of *The Prince* Machiavelli provided his first explicit rationale for the radical recasting of virtue and vice that characterized not only the subsequent chapters of that book but all his subsequent utterances on ethics. In the opening paragraph he prepared the reader for the degree to which his "little book on princedoms" departed from both mediaeval and humanist tradition, the former grounded in Christian virtues and the latter in pagan. He acknowledged that distance with a notional apology and justified it as a necessity imposed by his commitment to pragmatic utility: "And because I know that many have written about this, I fear that, when I too write about it, I shall be thought conceited, since in discussing this material I depart very far from the methods of others. But since my purpose is to write something useful to him who comprehends it, I have decided that I must concern myself with the truth of the matter as facts show it rather than with any fanciful notion."[2]

In perhaps one of the most controversial utterances in early modern political thought, Machiavelli announced that his political thought would provide counsel based on analysis of how people actually conducted themselves rather than how ethical norms stipulated that they ought to act. He rejected the virtue politics of his humanist contemporaries and the Platonic, Aristotelian, and Ciceronian teaching that had inspired them, as examples of the latter approach: flawed at the outset because it was based on excessively abstract and idealistic conceptions of politics. This flaw rendered them not only useless from Machiavelli's methodological point of view but positively dangerous for all those who strove to conduct themselves in accordance with classical and Christian ethical norms. "[M]any have fancied for themselves republics and principalities that have never been seen or known to exist in reality. For there is such a difference between how men live and how they ought to live that he who abandons what is done for what ought to be done learns his destruction rather than his preservation, because any man who under all conditions insists on making it his business to be good will surely be destroyed among so many who are not good."[3]

Guicciardini clearly agreed. Most striking about Guicciardini is the degree to which he casually dismissed the relevance of ethics for those in political life. The *Ricordi* simply took for granted what Machiavelli had to frame, with rhetorical apology, as a necessity imposed upon him by a regrettable reality. In one of his briefest *ricordi* Guicciardini declared a starker and more unbridgeable divide than had Machiavelli between political power and ethical conduct. Power cannot ever be exercised in accordance with traditional virtues because its origins are always by definition criminal. What begins as an act of transgression and usurpation cannot subsequently be transformed into legitimate rule: "Political power cannot be wielded according to the dictates of good conscience. If you consider its origin, you will always find it in violence – except in the case of republics within their territories, but not beyond."[4] More provocatively still and equally casually, Guicciardini indicted Christianity as an institution of power – its spiritual mission was simply another form of violent usurpation: "Not even the emperor is exempt from this rule [power stemming from violence]; nor are the priests, whose violence is double, since they assault us with both temporal and spiritual arms."[5] What Machiavelli had to prepare his reader for – the rejection of moral considerations – Guicciardini expressed bluntly and without apology (perhaps because Machiavelli wrote *The Prince* with an immediate Florentine audience in mind, such as Francesco Vettori and, he hoped, Giuliano and Lorenzo de' Medici, whereas Guicciardini composed his *Ricordi* for his own private reflection).

A subsequent *ricordo* on the political utility of courtly skills concluded with only a slight variation on Machiavelli's lament regarding the gap between "how one lives and how one ought to live" and "what is done" for "what ought to be done." Reflecting on his youthful austere ambition (his fellow students nicknamed him Alcibiades because of that trait), Guicciardini regretted his dismissal of what he deemed frivolous pursuits such as dancing, singing, dressing well, and riding, among other aristocratic pastimes. Lacking experience in political life, he dismissed such activities as "more decorative than substantial in a man." Later, he came to recognize that such "ornaments," irrespective of their superficiality, heightened the reputation of those who excelled at them, thereby opening additional routes to princely favour and hence opportunities for wealth and power. He conceded the limiting idealism of his youthful outlook, acknowledging that "the world and prices are no longer made as they should be, but as they are."[6]

The Dangers of Generosity

In the first of his polemics against the virtue politics that defined Renaissance political culture, Machiavelli considers the conventional wisdom that a prince should always display generosity. By the end of the chapter he concedes the tactical benefits and inherent virtuosity of generosity, understood and practised prudently, but only after dramatically and fundamentally redefining its meaning in realist terms. As Hankins has so thoroughly demonstrated, Renaissance political thought privileged means over ends – by definition, no vicious action could result in a virtuous outcome.[7] Machiavelli challenged the humanist celebration of generosity, by privileging ends over means, demonstrating the damaging outcomes caused by virtuous methods. First, for generosity to be recognized and praised, it must be regularly seen, requiring the prince to engage in frequent lavish displays of spending that will cause him equally frequently to acquire wealth via escalating taxation of subjects, thereby incurring the people's disfavour: "If a prince wishes to maintain his reputation for generosity among men, it is necessary for him not to neglect any possible means of sumptuous display; in so doing, such a prince will always use up his resources in such displays, and will eventually be obliged, if he wishes to maintain his reputation for generosity, to burden then people with excessive taxes and to do all those things one does to procure money. This will make him hateful to his subjects and, if he becomes impoverished, he will be held in low regard by everyone."[8] The only way for a prince to avoid the contempt-inducing impoverishment that inevitably results from pursuing a reputation for generosity is to correct course by zealously guarding whatever wealth remains, thereby incurring the vicious reputation of miserliness and the very opprobrium that a generous reputation was meant to protect against. "There is nothing that uses itself up faster than generosity; for as you employ it, you lose the means of employing it and you become either poor or despised or else, to escape poverty, you become rapacious and hated."[9] Should his immediate readership question his analysis at a theoretical level, he concludes with three examples of powerful parsimonious monarchs – the warrior pope Julius II, the French king Louis XII, and the Spanish king Ferdinand I – whose mutual quarrels were devastating the Italian peninsula.

Machiavelli instead advises princes to embrace a reputation for miserliness at the outset, for several reasons that all use the language of the many and the few and reiterate the book's overarching argument that a wise prince always allies with the former against the latter. While people may criticize a miserly prince for failing to live up to an ideal, the criticism generated falls far short of hatred. By contrast, pursuing a reputation for generosity ultimately results in the wrath of one's subjects – one of the prince's most dire existential threats, in Machiavelli's view – in part because of the consequent rapaciousness necessitated but also because it reveals the prince's misguided loyalties. Traditional displays of generosity benefit a few people while the costs are paid for by many people: "As a consequence of this generosity of his, having injured the many and rewarded the few, he will feel the effects of any discontent."[10] Better still, Machiavelli reasons, over time the people will gradually recognize the artificiality of the generosity championed by humanist culture and begin to appreciate that a stingy prince bestows real gifts upon his subjects.

Renaissance virtue politics, preoccupied as it was with ruling elites, conceived of generosity in terms of conspicuous wealth and giving, a virtue that could only be bestowed upon some. Machiavelli continued to champion generosity but reconceived it from giving to *not* taking, a higher virtue because it could be bestowed on everyone. In spite of Machiavelli's dim view of humanity and his subsequent argument that people rarely distinguish between appearance and reality ("Men in general judge more by their eyes than their hands: everyone can see, but few can feel. Everyone sees what you seem to be, few touch upon what you are." [11]), he asserts here a variation on one of his most recurring themes: regarding their own material self-interest, the people are rational and shrewd judges, abundantly capable of distinguishing between actual virtues and the normative virtues championed by humanist culture. "With time [the miserly prince] will come to be considered more generous, once it is evident that, as a result of his parsimony, his income is sufficient, he can defend himself from anyone who wages war against him, and he can undertake enterprises without overburdening his people. In this way he appears as generous to all those from whom he takes nothing, who are countless, and as miserly to all those to whom he gives nothing, who are few."[12]

Guicciardini arrived at precisely the same conclusion in his *Ricordi* regarding the false virtue of generosity as did Machiavelli, though he did so from an aristocratic rather than a popular perspective. Much like Machiavelli and in direct contrast to his humanist predecessors, Guicciardini justified his position by privileging ends over means: however much the practice of generosity might reflect an individual of moral character, only by looking at ends and outcomes can one arrive at a true measure of its political value (Guicciardini would employ the same method in his analysis of regime types in his *Dialogue on the Government of Florence*). Like Machiavelli, he recognizes that, for the many, not taking has greater tangible value than giving has: "prodigality in a prince is more detestable and more pernicious than parsimony. For a prince cannot be prodigal without taking something from many of his subjects, and thus they are worse off than if he were parsimonious and gave them nothing."[13] A subsequent *ricordo* refines that observation along more precisely Machiavellian lines by stressing the inherent social injustice of princely generosity. By necessity, it requires taking from the many to reward the few: "the prodigal prince must resort to extortion and rapacity, whereas the other takes from no one. Many more are the men who suffer from the exactions of a prodigal prince than those who benefit from his generosity."[14]

If Guicciardini agreed on the virtuous consequences of parsimony, however, he did not share Machiavelli's confidence that the many possessed adequate rationality to value true rather than notional virtues. Guicciardini expressed his sentiment ironically, as an actual truth nevertheless at odds with political reality. Machiavelli was certain that the people would, over time, come to appreciate the true generosity of a parsimonious prince as more valuable than the periodic and unequally distributed gifts of a generous prince. Guicciardini was equally certain that the people would not, even if they should. In *ricordo* 72 he asserts: "Without doubt, a prodigal prince is more popular than a tight-fisted one. And yet it should be the contrary."[15] In *ricordo* 172 he reiterates that the people are "worse off [under a generous prince] than if he were parsimonious and gave them nothing ... And yet it seems the public prefers a prodigal prince to a stingy one."[16] For Guicciardini, the people persist in valuing a false virtue because the many are more powerfully moved by their appetites than by reason. Even if the odds of receiving benefits from a generous prince are plainly more remote than suffering his exactions, hope for gain, however unlikely, motivates more powerfully the human psyche than it does the fear of loss, however probable. "Although the prodigality of the prince favours few men compared to the necessarily large number from which it takes, it is nevertheless true, as I have said at other times, that men hope more than they fear. They like to think they will be one of the few who will be favoured rather than one of the many from whom something will be taken."[17]

Although he stops short of declaring it outright, Guicciardini challenges the virtue politics assumption of his humanist predecessors that virtuous conduct reflects wisdom. Unlike Machiavelli, who believes the people capable of distinguishing between real and false virtues, Guicciardini concludes the opposite: the many will never recognize that they fund the so-called generosity of a prodigal prince. As a result, for Guicciardini, the truly wise prince must rise above the conduct counselled by humanist virtue politics and disregard the popular approval that it promises as a consequence. "The sort of generosity that pleases the public is very seldom found in truly wise men. A man who appears generous, therefore, is not as praiseworthy as a judicious man."[18]

In a *ricordo* on effective household management Guicciardini introduces another motive based on personal experience for prudent rulers to shun generosity – the people's diminished capacity for respect and gratitude. In principle, the master of a household should regularly reward his servants. How better to earn their loyalty? In practice, however, servants do not reward generosity with elevated allegiance. On the contrary, they adjust immediately and take previous acts of generosity for granted, such that they abandon the master's service at the first lapse in largesse: "If men were respectful or grateful enough, it would be the duty of a master to benefit his servants on every occasion, as much as he could. But experience shows – and I have seen this to be the case with my own servants – that as soon as they get their fill, or as soon as the master is unable to treat them as generously as he has in the past, they leave him flat. Thus, to best serve his own interests, a master must be tight-fisted, more readily inclined to be stingy rather than liberal."[19] This *ricordo* reflects the long-standing parallel in Western political thought between the domestic household and the kingdom: what is good for the *pater familias* is good for the king.

Not always! In keeping with Guicciardini's larger political philosophy, a prudent violation of the rule is always a periodic necessity. Since Guicciardini views hope as stronger than fear, the prudent patrician head of household inculcates loyalty by stimulating hope, in this case a rare but recurring act of extreme largesse bestowed upon a single individual: "He must retain their allegiance with hopes rather than deeds. Now, for that to be successful, he must occasionally be very generous to just one of them; and that is enough. For the nature of men is such that hope, as a rule, is stronger than fear. They are more excited and pleased by the sight of one man well rewarded than they are frightened by seeing many men treated poorly."[20] Guicciardini expresses here a variation on Machiavelli's notion of cruelty well used. Generosity, like cruelty, is vicious only if routinely and habitually displayed, without discretion, and directed at many. Used tactically (meaning displayed rarely), directed at an individual, and chosen with discretion, the virtuous ends – in this case colonizing the minds of the many – trump the vicious means.

The Value of Cruelty Well Used

Of all the notoriety Machiavelli earned from his political thought, perhaps no topic was as provocative as his defence of cruelty. While he displayed an implicit fascination with spectacular violence and its political potential in all his major works of political thought and history, he addressed it most explicitly in chapters 8 and 17 of *The Prince*.[21] Chapter 8 considers the case of princes who rise to power via criminal methods, using Agathocles the Sicilian and Liverotto da Fermo, respectively, as ancient and modern examples of princes who enjoyed stable and secure rule in spite of having risen to power via sudden acts of terrible violence.[22] To explain their seemingly surprising success, Machiavelli focuses on the specific tactics of their violence. In contrast to the Renaissance humanists, a community that spoke with one voice in condemning all forms of princely cruelty, Machiavelli introduces a distinction between "cruelties badly used and well used," one of the most striking phrases in his lexicon. In his economy of violence, acts of cruelty could often be politically salutary provided they were motivated by absolute necessity, carried out swiftly and all at once, rather than piecemeal and persistently, and conferred benefits to a prince's subjects as much as to the prince himself: "Those [acts of cruelty] can be called well used (if it is permissible to speak well of evil) that are done at a stroke, out of the necessity to secure oneself, and then are not persisted in but are turned to as much utility for the subjects as one can."[23]

Chapter 17 introduces a corresponding distinction that similarly distinguished Machiavelli from the humanist movement. If cruelty is vicious only when deployed for the wrong reasons, it follows that its counterpart – mercy, a virtue championed by humanists unconditionally – is also only a virtue when displayed in the right way and at the right time. Machiavelli again uses ancient and modern examples – Scipio Africanus's tolerance of his soldiers' licence and the Florentine republic's tolerance of factional discord in Pistoia – to demonstrate the unnecessary violence and disorder resulting from an excess of mercy. Guicciardini evidently concurred – mercy was neither inherently virtuous nor vicious but rather depended on the context and purpose of its deployment. To show mercy irrespective of context or outcome was tantamount to insanity. Drawing on ancient examples, Guicciardini concludes: "Neither Alexander the Great, nor Caesar, or anyone else famous for his clemency, ever exercised it when he knew it would endanger the fruits of his victory. That, indeed, would have been folly. They showed mercy only when it did not diminish their security and when it added to their fame."[24] The subsequent *ricordo* on revenge provides an explanatory example. If wronged, one should always pursue revenge, even in the absence of hate, for the simple reason that reacting with mercy merely encourages people to continue to harm you. Just as one should not always show mercy, one should not always shrink from vengeance: "Revenge does not always stem from hate or from an evil nature. Sometimes it is necessary so that people will learn not to offend you. It is perfectly all right to avenge yourself even though you feel no deep rancour against the person who is the object of your revenge."[25]

Machiavelli's discussion of cruelty in chapter 17 of the *Prince* effectively applied the lessons of chapter 8 more widely, now arguing that necessity obliged all new princes, not merely those who rose to power via criminal methods, to engage in periodic acts of cruelty, and therefore that rulers in general, contrary to the advice of their humanist educators, should never shrink from a reputation for cruelty. As a result of the periodic necessity for cruelty, Machiavelli then concluded that a wise prince, given a choice between being loved and feared, should always privilege a fearsome reputation: "And men have less hesitation to offend one who makes himself loved than one who makes himself feared; for love is held by a chain of obligation, which, because men are wicked, is broken at every opportunity for their own utility, but fear is held by a dread of punishment that never forsakes you ... I conclude then ... that since men love at their convenience and fear at the convenience of the prince, a wise prince should found himself on what is his, not on what is someone else's."[26]

Here, too, we see that Guicciardini arrived at largely similar conclusions and for similar reasons, though his reasoning was based entirely on his own experience as a ruler. Echoing the dismal view of human nature that underpinned so many of *The Prince*'s provocative lessons, Guicciardini opens a *ricordo* on cruelty with the axiom that "[t]he wickedness of men is such that you cannot govern well without severity."[27] Just as Machiavelli observed that appearances often counted for more than reality, Guicciardini's only caution regarding the use of cruelty involved not acquiring a reputation for it. His explanation of how to carry out requisite acts of cruelty without becoming known for it, and therefore hated, echoes two of Machiavelli's three conditions for cruelty well used – that it be strictly necessary and carried out with benefit to the people: "You must be clever about it [cruelty]. You must do everything possible to have people believe that you dislike cruelty and that you use it only out of necessity and for the public welfare."[28]

For both writers, advocacy of periodic, tactical cruelty resulted from a prior implicit agreement on the necessity of a fearsome reputation. On this topic, too, their reasoning and qualifications substantially overlapped. Before proclaiming the thesis that all successful rulers must instil a measure of fear in their subjects, Machiavelli first acknowledges that in a perfect world, one should strive for both love and fear. He then goes on to explain, however, why pursuing the affection of one's subjects is both improbable and dangerous, given the corruption of our world and the inherent selfishness of humanity: "For one can generally say this about men: they are ungrateful, fickle, simulators and deceivers, avoiders of danger, and greedy for gain."[29] Although less specific, Guicciardini concurs: "If men were wise and good, those in authority should certainly be gentle rather than severe with them. But since the majority of men are either not very good or not very wise, one must rely more on severity than on kindness. Whoever thinks otherwise is mistaken. Surely, anyone who can skilfully mix and blend the one with the other would produce sweetest possible accord and harmony. But heaven endows few with such talents; perhaps no one."[30] Machiavelli also concedes that, in principle, a ruler should aspire to be both loved and feared, but given the improbability of such an exceptional scenario, when he is forced to choose, fear is the superior choice.

Whereas *The Prince* at least acknowledged that urging rulers to cultivate a fearsome reputation required sustained explanatory rationale, given its distance from the norms of Renaissance political theory, Guicciardini's subsequent *ricordi* casually take for granted the value of fear. For example, reflecting on his own judicial experience, he declares: "In my administrations I never liked cruelty or excessive punishments. Nor are they necessary. Except for certain cases that must serve as example, you can sufficiently maintain fear [mantenere el terrore] if you punish crimes with three quarters of the penalty, provided that you make it a rule to punish all crimes."[31] In his final revisions to the *Ricordi* he reiterates more explicitly the value of fear and violence: "It is hardly surprising that a ruler who frequently resorts to cruelty and severity is feared. For subjects will surely fear someone who can hurt or ruin them and who does not hesitate to do so. But I praise those rulers who, with little severity and few punishments, know how to acquire and preserve a reputation for terror" (and given the earlier *ricordo,* he must have had himself in mind as that very praiseworthy prince).[32] Just as Machiavelli urged the wise prince to learn how not to be good, Guicciardini urges prudent rulers, however moderate by nature, to cultivate a reputation for vicious cruelty.

The Church's Role in Italy's Flawed Religious Culture

In addition to acute awareness of the moral failings of the clergy and a precocious relativity about the exclusive truth of Christianity, Guicciardini shared Machiavelli's view that the institutional church contributed to

Italy's political weakness and that its spiritual ideals had effeminized the present. Machiavelli articulated these two points in a variety of texts and in a variety of ways but expressed them most directly in *discorsos* 1.12 and 2.2. In *discorso*1.12, on the importance of strict observation of religious rituals, Machiavelli contrasts Roman religious discipline and respect for ceremonial sanctity with his contemporaries' general disregard for Christian ideals, an inevitable result of the excessive corruption of the Roman court. If through its poor example the church contributed substantially to the decline of Italian religion, it contributed even more to the decline of the peninsula's political power that had once conquered the known world. While the church was never powerful enough to subdue all of Italy and unite the peninsula so that it might collectively amass enough force to equal the martial power of centralized monarchies like France and Spain, the church always retained enough power to obstruct any attempt by Italian princes to do the same. Contrary to many of his contemporaries who perceived proximity to the seat of Christendom as advantageous to the Italian city states, Machiavelli concludes, the church threatened Italian autonomy at an existential level: "Italy has been under many princes and lords, who have brought about the great disunion and the great weakness that have made her the prey not merely of powerful barbarians but of whoever assails her. For this we Italians are indebted to the Church and not to any other."[33]

Guicciardini shared a similar conviction about the church's role in peninsular political life, adding a local observation that if the church obstructed peninsular powers, it did so doubly for Florence owing to its proximity. In his *Considerations on Machiavelli's "Discourses on Livy"* (a text that always privileged dissent over agreement, as we will see in chapter 5), Guicciardini endorses the thesis of *discorso* 1.12 (with an admittedly different conclusion): "And I also think it is true that the greatness of the Church, that is, the authority lent her by religion, has been the cause of Italy never having fallen under a monarchy. For on the one hand, it has enjoyed such credit that it has been able to assume leadership and call up as many foreign princes as it liked against those who sought to oppress Italy. On the other hand, stripped of her own arms the Church was not strong enough to establish a temporal dominion, or only one willingly allowed her by others."[34] Given the content of the *Considerations*, the question of the church's role in peninsular politics was effectively put to him by Machiavelli, but his *Ricordi* reveals his own interest in the question (unsurprising, of course, given his role in the papal administration). There he twice reflects that on the church's role in impeding Florence's power in Tuscany. Whereas the Venetians benefited from neighbours accustomed to servitude and disinclined to rebellion, the Florentines' immediate neighbours in Tuscany prized and stubbornly clung to their ancient liberty, and just beyond them lay the border with Rome, where the church enjoyed ancient roots "and very much impeded the course of our dominion."[35]

Further and worse still, both Machiavelli and Guicciardini underscored that the obstacles to unification thrown up by the church were insurmountable owing to its unique spiritual identity. As Guicciardini put it in his contrast of Florence and Venice, Florence had as its neighbour the church, both "strong and immortal. Though it sometimes seems to stagger, in the end it reaffirms its rights more strongly than ever." The Venetians, by contrast, had secular princes for neighbours, "whose lives and memories are not everlasting."[36] Were the pontiffs in Rome merely secular princes, they could be conquered and their state incorporated. As Machiavelli elaborated in *The Prince*, however, ecclesiastical states are maintained and endure even in the absence of ability or good fortune. "They are supported by customs grown old in church history, which are now so powerful and of such a sort that they keep their prince in his position, however he acts and lives. The pope alone has states and does not defend them, subjects and does not keep them in order; yet his states, through being undefended, never are snatched away."[37] Although Machiavelli's language borders on wonder in this passage, his tone reflects a combination of contempt at the level of indulgence his culture permits the popes and frustration at the unique peninsular weakness that that indulgence causes.

Years later, when Guicciardini was composing his *History of Italy*, he expressed the same combination of contempt and frustration in his treatment of the sack of Rome in 1527. The sack was doubly tragic for Guicciardini because it was a catastrophic event at the peninsular level and for him personally. Until that moment he had been enjoying a powerful – perhaps the most powerful – position in the Medici pope Clement VII's regime: in 1524 Clement had appointed him president of the Romagna and elevated him further still in 1526 as lieutenant general of papal forces. Following the sack, which Guicciardini saw as a personal failure as well as a failure of broader papal policy, he retreated to his villa to commence a period of writing, much as Machiavelli had done in the aftermath of the Boscoli-Capponi conspiracy in 1512. Reflecting on the surprisingly swift restoration of the pope's freedom and territories, Guicciardini reiterated Machiavelli's caustic lament. "Certainly a most noteworthy example, something perhaps which has never happened since the Church became great: that a Pope, fallen from such power and reverence, is held in captivity, loses Rome, and his entire domain falls into the power of others; and that the same Pope, within the space of a few months, is restored to liberty, that which was taken from him is restored, and in a very short time, he is once more returned to his former greatness. So authoritative is the papacy among Christian princes, and the respect which all of them have for it."[38] The detailed account of the sack in his *History of Italy* stressed, just as Machiavelli had in the aforementioned passage, the degree to which the fundamentally unearned and illegitimate reverence that the church enjoyed permitted it to survive without ever having to confront its moral failings.

In addition to a similar view of the church's geopolitical contribution to Italian weakness, they both viewed the church – using largely similar language – as rendering individuals psychologically weak, effeminate, and abject. In *discorso* 2.2 Machiavelli contrasted the ferocious love of freedom in the ancient world with the enfeebled present. The cause of that contrast was the difference between ancient religion that prized a particularly virile notion of glory, and modern Christianity that prized humility and contempt for worldly glory: "Our religion has glorified humble and contemplative more than active men. It has then placed the highest good in humility, abjectness, and contempt of things human; the other placed it in greatness of spirit, strength of body, and all other things capable of making men very strong ... This mode of life thus seems to have rendered the world weak."[39] Guicciardini expressed virtually the same sentiment in his private reflection that "too much religion spoils the world, because it makes the mind effeminate, involves men in thousands of errors, and diverts them from many generous and virile enterprises."[40]

Machiavelli and Guicciardini both must have also have recognized the danger in statements that condemned Christianity as inferior to pagan religion, because they qualified those statements to suggest that they were quarrelling not with the religion itself but with erroneous interpretations. Guicciardini concluded his *ricordo* by stressing a distinction between Christianity's fundamental truth and superfluous, misguided misinterpretations: "I do not hereby wish to derogate from the Christian faith and divine worship, but rather to confirm and augment them by distinguishing what is excessive from what is sufficient, and by stimulating men's minds to consider carefully what should be taken into account and what may safely be ignored."[41] Machiavelli's disclaimer more pointedly condemned the church's teaching as deliberately obscuring the truth with "educations and false interpretations" rather than containing inadvertent superfluities: "And although the world appears to be made effeminate and heaven disarmed, it arises without doubt more from the cowardice of the men who have interpreted our religion according to idleness and not according to virtue."[42] In backing away from the full implications of their critique of Christian teaching, they were both effectively following Guicciardini's advice in an adjacent *ricordo* that one should "never argue against religion or against things that seem to depend on God. These matters are too strongly rooted in the minds of fools."[43]

Agency and Fate

Machiavelli and Guicciardini both framed their political thought in general as attempts to protect against the destabilizing, even anarchic, power of fortune. Machiavelli privileged a unique conception of *virtù* as the best safeguard against unforeseen contingencies, whereas Guicciardini championed a more circumspect understanding of prudence. In this respect, both thinkers were following directly in the steps of their humanist predecessors. They all conceived of fortune as an inherently capricious and destructive force, rather than as a Christian, providential plan that individuals could and should struggle against rather than passively accept, and they all agreed that the best weapon in that struggle was a proper code of conduct. Given their contrasting stress on means versus ends, however, the comparison between Machiavelli and Guicciardini on fortune and the political thought that preceded them ends. The virtue politics of the humanist movement insisted that virtuous conduct – hence means – was always the best safeguard against fortune. Machiavelli and Guicciardini, always focused on outcomes rather than methods, both embraced a relative and context-specific definition of virtue and vice, in which any given disposition could be either vicious or virtuous depending ultimately on its outcome. Unsurprisingly, they both articulated a more guarded, limited, and complicated sense of how best to counter fortune, shifting the analysis of method from the moral categories of the humanists – liberality, clemency, moderation, honesty – to the morally neutral categories of action, caution, impetuousness, patience, force, and skill.

Their reasoning, expressed in *The Prince* and the *Ricordi*, again demonstrates a similar pattern. Although both meditated at length on the most effective methods for individuals to protect against malignant fortune, they also concluded, far more than their predecessors did, that the fundamental inscrutability of the future implied diminished prospects for autonomy over contingency. Contrary to the central conviction of humanist virtue politics, they both stressed that effective outcomes required a propitious and unpredictable compatibility between individual strategy and larger context. No single code of conduct, whether traditionally virtuous or traditionally vicious, could ever achieve success as a rule; effective conduct, by definition, needed to vary in style and tactics consistent with variations in the larger cultural and political arena, or fortune itself. One could experience greater or lesser success by aligning one's plans, to whatever possible extent, with fortune, but one could never transcend fortune altogether. Nevertheless, in spite of that limited view of individual potential, they concluded that action was superior to caution and expressed that conclusion in similar language and metaphors.

Machiavelli's views on this topic are well known, expressed most famously in chapter 25 of *The Prince* that likens fortune to a flooded river, most destructive to those who fail to prepare dikes and embankments during periods of calm. He opens that chapter by acknowledging the degree to which recent calamities in Italy, following so swiftly upon the relative calm and prosperity of the peninsula's *pax laurenziana*, seem to affirm the view that humanity is irretrievably powerless against fortune ("This belief has been the more firmly held in our times by reason of the great variations in affairs that we have seen in the past and now see every day beyond all human prediction. Thinking on these variations, I myself now and then incline in some respects to their belief."[44]) He then goes on to elaborate, however, that to preserve free will, fortune dominates only half of our actions, leaving the other half to us, followed by analysis of how best to maximize the limited autonomy we are given. Machiavelli reasons that one must adapt one's methods to the context of the times: "I believe that a prince succeeds who adapts his way of proceeding to the nature of the times, and conversely one does not succeed whose procedure is out of harmony with the times."[45] Success depends on reading the tea leaves accurately and timing one's endeavours appropriately. In spite of his counsel against consistently deploying a single strategy (and somewhat contrary to his own advice), he nevertheless concludes the chapter by arguing that one should favour impetuosity over caution.[46]

On all Machiavelli's main points, Guicciardini concurred, first in recognition of the magnitude of fortune's power, second in his view that one must align one's strategy with the times, and third that in general one should favour action over caution. All of Guicciardini's utterances on effective action were set against the certain conviction of future inscrutability: "How wisely the philosopher spoke when he said: 'Of future contingencies there can be no predetermined truth.' Go where you will: the farther you go, the more you will find this saying to be absolutely true."[47] Guicciardini allowed no exceptions to this rule, even for wise men: "If you were to have a wise man judge what effects a particular event will have and then wrote down his judgment, you would find when you looked at it later that few of his predictions had come true: just as few as if, on New Year's Day, you looked at an astrologer's predictions for the previous year. The affairs of this world are simply too uncertain."[48]

Much like Machiavelli, however, he was centrally preoccupied with how to maximize one's success in the affairs of palace and market. He certainly shared Machiavelli's view that there was no correct method capable of success irrespective of context and timing. One must always assess the larger context and align one's plans judiciously: "If you attempt certain things at the right time, they are easy to accomplish – in fact, they almost get done by themselves. If you undertake them before the time is right, not only will they fail, but they will often become impossible to accomplish even when the time would have been right. Therefore, do not rush things madly, do not precipitate them; wait for them to mature, wait for the right season."[49] Much as Machiavelli attributed success to those who adapted their strategy to the times, Guicciardini recognized that sound tactics and strategy could not be assessed outside of a shifting context.

He also shared Machiavelli's somewhat contradictory view that, despite having recognized the inscrutability of the future and the necessity of aligning one's plans with a propitious context, one should nevertheless generally privilege action over caution. Machiavelli rationalized that advice via his infamous simile that fortune is a woman and therefore favours young, bold, and violent men willing to subdue her. Guicciardini's argument instead relied on probabilities – potential dangers abound, to be sure, but not all occur and some are manageable. When calculating risks, therefore, the cautious actor who factors in all dangers operates with an exaggerated view of an undertaking's probability of failure. Guicciardini attributes political wisdom to the brave man willing to accept risk.

> It is an old saying that all wise men are timid, because they know all the dangers and therefore have cause to be afraid. I think this saying is wrong … A brave man … ought sooner to be called wise than a timid man. Assuming that both see matters clearly, the difference between them lies in that the timid man takes into account all the dangers he recognizes, and supposes the worst; whereas the brave man, though he too recognizes them all, considers that some can be avoided by human industry and that some will disappear by chance. He will not let himself be abashed by them all, but will embark on his course with the knowledge and hope that not everything that can happen need happen.[50]

For the same reason ("the future is so deceptive and subject to so many accidents, that very often even the wisest of men is fooled when he tries to predict it"), Guicciardini also concludes that "to give up a present good for fear for a future evil is, most of the time, madness – unless the evil is very certain, very near, or very great compared to the good."[51] Action in the present takes precedence over caution regarding future contingency.

Their discussions of agency and fate also share a similar inherent contradiction, expressed almost identically. In spite of Machiavelli's argument in chapter 25 that successful princes adapt their strategies and style to remain compatible with changes in context, he also concedes the impossibility of that scenario: our natures are fixed, unvarying, and beyond our control. Given the immutability of individual temperament, the best we can do is proceed with our plans and hope that circumstances are propitious. As he explains, a person might attain success via cautious forbearance one day, yet come to ruin the next: "On this depends variation in success: if, for one whose policy is caution and patience, times and affairs circle about in such a way that his policy is good, he continues to succeed; if times and affairs change, he falls, because he does not change his way of proceeding."[52] Immediately following this statement, however, Machiavelli concedes that none of us is actually capable of changing our methods. "Nor is any man living so prudent that he knows how to accommodate himself to this condition, both because he cannot deviate from that to which nature disposes him, and also because, always having prospered walking in the same road, he cannot be induced to leave it. Therefore the cautious man, when it is time to adopt impetuosity, does not know how. Hence he falls."[53] Having discounted the possibility of individual change in universal terms, he concludes the chapter by considering the specific case study of Julius II. Mercurial, ambitious, and restless, Julius carried out all his affairs with a bold rashness that, because it was unexpected, resulted in consistently favourable outcomes. His success, as Machiavelli sees it, resulted primarily from the good fortune of circumstances being propitious to impetuous action and the relative brevity of his life (although he lived to seventy!). Had he lived longer, circumstances would have shifted in ways that required caution, inevitably causing his downfall.

Guicciardini agreed on all points. In one *ricordo* he expresses the same universal recognition that the seemingly abundant virtue of many successful people results in fact from the good fortune of their personalities aligning with the times. "Some men attribute everything to prudence and virtue and try to ignore fortune. But even they cannot deny that it is a great stroke of luck to be around at a time when your virtues and the things you do best are highly valued … the same act will be pleasing at one time, displeasing at another."[54] Where Machiavelli illustrates this truth by considering Julius II, Guicciardini illustrates it by considering the Roman general Fabius Maximus, famously cautious and hence

Julius's conceptual counterpart. "Take the example of Fabius Maximus, whose great reputation resulted from his being by nature hesitant. He found himself in a war in which impetuosity was ruinous, whereas procrastination was useful. At another time, the opposite could have been true. His times needed his qualities, and that was his fortune."[55] Like Machiavelli, Guicciardini also concludes, in the *ricordo*, with the concession that adapting one's tactics to the time is difficult at least and most likely impossible: "To be sure, if a man could change his nature to suit the conditions of the times, he would be much less dominated by Fortune. But that is most difficult, and perhaps even impossible."[56] Although both thinkers generally counselled action over caution, their internal contradictions on the topic suggest that their counsel was more a token of a wish than a reality.

The Value of Deception

For Machiavelli, whose contemporary fame was based more on his status as a celebrated playwright than that as a political philosopher, the parallels between politics and theatre are substantial and well explored.[57] Virtually all of his writings explore the degree to which appearances frequently count for more than reality. He addresses that thesis most explicitly, however, in chapter 18 of *The Prince*, "How Princes Should Keep Their Promises." In that chapter he famously declares that a wise prince should always strive to appear merciful, faithful, humane, and religious. To the maximum extent possible, a prince should also practise those virtues but also be ready, when necessary, to act contrary to those virtues: "He holds to what is right when he can but knows how to do wrong when he must." Owing to the inevitable contrast between substance and appearance, it follows that those with a precocious talent for theatre prosper most: "The one who knows best how to play the fox comes out best, but he must understand well how to disguise the animal's nature and must be a great simulator and dissimulator."[58] Nor is exceptional acting required. Since most people perceive little and their vision is constrained by their immediate needs, "he who deceives will always find someone who will let himself be deceived."[59] As an example demonstrating the truth of that general conviction, Machiavelli offers the case of Alexander VI, a chronically faithless and deceptive papal monarch who nevertheless always benefited from his dishonesty, owing to the chronic blindness caused by self-serving human nature.

Guicciardini advanced similar arguments in similar language. Much like Machiavelli, he professed to esteem honesty and disdain deception while also – ostensibly – recognizing that circumstances occasionally required one to abandon the former in favour of the latter: "A truthful, open nature is universally liked and is, indeed, a noble thing; but it can be harmful. Deception, on the other hand, is useful and sometimes even necessary, given the wickedness of man; but it is odious and ugly."[60] His subsequent analysis of that regrettable reality, however, encouraged honesty not for its own sake but because possessing a reputation for honesty enabled greater success and advantage from one's lies. "In the ordinary course of events practise the former [truthful, open nature] so that you will gain a reputation for being a sincere person. And nevertheless, on certain important and rare occasions, use deception. If you do this, your deceptions will be more useful and more successful because, having a reputation for sincerity, you will be more easily believed."[61] He subsequently attempts again to portray his counsel as a reluctant concession to an unfortunate reality ("I cannot praise those who always live by deception and wiles; but I can excuse those who use them occasionally"), but his final revision of that *ricordo* reveals the degree to which he valued deceit. The final revision was mostly verbatim repetition but added additional explication on the value of deceit: "Deception is very useful, whereas your frankness tends to profit others rather than you."[62]

Like Machiavelli, Guicciardini concludes with a historical example – Ferdinand of Aragon – that perfectly mirrors Machiavelli's argument and language of chapter 18. Of the Spanish pope Machiavelli writes: "Alexander VI never did anything else and dreamed of anything else than deceiving men, yet he always found a subject to work on. Never was there a man more effective in swearing and who with stronger oaths confirmed a promise, but yet honoured it less."[63] Of the Spanish king Guicciardini writes: "Even though a man be a known dissimulator and deceiver, his deceptions will nevertheless, on occasion, find believers. It seems strange, but it is very true. I remember that His Catholic Majesty, more than any other man, had such a reputation; and yet there was never any lack of people who believed him more than they should."[64] As to why both monarchs found such an abundant supply of gullible victims, Machiavelli and Guicciardini offer identical responses. For Machiavelli, "[m]en are so simple-minded and so controlled by their immediate needs that he who deceives will always find someone who will let himself be deceived."[65] For Guicciardini, "this stems necessarily either from the simplicity or from the greed of men. The latter believe too easily what they wish were true; the former simply do not know what is happening."[66]

While these passages make a formal case for the advantages of effective deception, many of Guicciardini's other *ricordi* generally normalize deception, dispensing advice on how best to conceal one's true intentions or on the assumption that one is always being deceived by others.

For example, he counsels, if one wishes to disguise one's intentions, the best method is to vocally articulate clear and compelling arguments for the opposite plan: "If you want to disguise or conceal one of your intentions, always take pains to show you have its opposite in mind, using the strongest and most convincing reasons you can find."[67] Another *ricordo* stressed the importance of conducting one's affairs with strict secrecy without appearing secretive. Guicciardini must have considered the need for secrecy self-evident, but he did elaborate on why, even if everyone recognized its importance, it was prudent to appear trusting: "You have everything to gain from managing your affairs secretly. And you will gain even more if you can do it without appearing secretive to your friends. For many men feel slighted and become indignant when they see that you refuse to confide in them."[68] Just as Machiavelli's counsel to princes to learn how not to be good was predicated on the assumption of the vicious conduct of others, so was Guicciardini's estimation of the utility of deceit predicated on the assumption of humanity's generally deceitful nature: "A master knows less about his servants than does anyone else; and the same is true of a ruler and his subjects. For they do not show themselves to him the same way they do to others. With him, they try to disguise themselves, and in fact try to seem completely different from what they really are."[69] Guicciardini's implicit lesson is clear: in a world of deceitful actors one must learn to dissemble as a condition of survival (or, as Machiavelli put it, "any man who under all conditions insists on making it his business to be good will surely be destroyed among so many who are not good"[70]).

A number of Guicciardini's *ricordi* regularly deploy theatrical metaphors and the relationship between rulers and ruled as analogous to actors and audiences. When judging those around you, one *ricordo* instructs, one should not assign praise or blame based on others' status and rank, because those are externally ordered irrespective of individual merit, but rather how effective they are in their station, just as "in a comedy or a tragedy we do not have higher respect for the actor who plays the part of the master or the king than for the one who plays the servant. Instead, we pay attention only to the quality of the performance."[71] Both Guicciardini and Machiavelli recognized that perception frequently counted for as much or more than reality: "If you are … seeking power, you must always hide your failures and exaggerate your successes. It is a form of swindling and very much against my nature. But, since your fate more often depends upon the opinion of others rather than on facts, it is a good idea to create the impression that things are going well."[72] Guicciardini championed the value of secrecy in part because of basic pragmatism – one's plans are more difficult to obstruct by enemies to the extent that they are unknown – but also because of the psychological effect on allies at court: "Ignorance of [a ruler's plans] keeps men … eager to observe his every move. His slightest act will cause a thousand comments, which in turn bring him great reputation."[73] By concealing narrative purpose, secrecy enables rulers to capture the permanent gaze of their subjects: "If your subjects and those around you know nothing of your affairs, they will always be in suspense, almost in wonderment, and will pay heed to your every step."[74] Machiavelli used identical language in *The Prince* to describe the beneficial consequences of Ferdinand of Aragon's military campaigns: "He performed and planned great actions, which kept the minds of his subjects always in suspense and wonder, watching for the outcome."[75] An effective performance transforms fiction into reality.

Ingratitude

The two shared a bedrock pessimistic view of humanity, expressed in strikingly similar ways, as self-serving, ungrateful, dishonest, and inclined towards evil which underpinned almost all of the specifics of the common political vision expressed in the *Ricordi* and *The Prince.* As a consequence of that conviction, both thinkers legitimized their rejection of virtue politics as a defensive posture, an externally imposed pre-emptive survival tactic. One must treat people instrumentally for the simple and inescapable reason that people will always treat others that way.[76] Machiavelli expressed variations on this view throughout his political and literary writings but addressed it first and most explicitly in chapters 18 and 19 of *The Prince.* "For one can generally say this about men: they are ungrateful, fickle, simulators and deceivers, avoiders of danger, and greedy for gain."[77] Given humanity's immutable baseness, Machiavelli discounts as unreliable all relationships based on virtues such as affection and loyalty: "Love is held together by a chain of obligation that, since men are a wretched lot, is broken on every occasion for their own self-interest."[78] The subsequent chapter on honouring one's promises makes explicit the instrumental, defensive logic that guided all of Machiavelli's radical recasting of traditional ethics. "If men were all good, this precept [value of faithlessness] would not be good. But since men are a wicked lot and will not keep their promises to you, you likewise need not keep yours to them."[79]

Guicciardini's *Ricordi* frequently reiterate the same axiom about human nature and the same instrumental logic regarding the consequent dangers of virtuous conduct. For example, even if society theoretically valued those with reputations as trusting and forthright, Guicciardini reasoned, such traits in practice were liabilities, given human nature: "To get a reputation for being suspicious and distrustful is certainly not desirable. Nevertheless, men are so false, so insidious, so deceitful and cunning in their wiles, so avid in their own interest, and so oblivious to other's interests, that you cannot go wrong if you believe little and trust less."[80] In one's conduct with others, one should always presume their potentially hostile intentions and act accordingly, hence his strict counsel never to divulge a secret unless compelled by necessity: "You become a slave to those who know your secrets – aside from all of the other evils that knowledge of them can bring about. Even when necessity forces you to tell them, you should do so as late as possible. For when men have lots of time, they will think a thousand and one evil thoughts."[81] Another *ricordo* cautions more broadly against exposing any form of vulnerability to others because "any security founded on the will and discretion of others is worthless, seeing how little goodness and faith is to be found in men."[82] Survival dictates that one must always adopt a defensive, guarded posture because "generally men's actions are more determined by their self-interest or by their evil character rather than by considerations of reason, your merits, or of their obligations to you."[83]

Given their common view of human nature as being depraved, both thinkers shared the conviction that people had an inverse capacity for gratitude and offence. No matter how much extraordinary generosity or favour one might show someone, that person will invariably tend to take it for granted, assume that it reflected justifiable merit, or even forget it altogether, whereas should one offend the same person, the memory of that offence will burn forever, creating an equally perpetual thirst for revenge. Machiavelli meditates on the implications of this observation in chapter 17 of *The Prince*: "While you work for their benefit they are completely yours, offering you their blood, their property, their lives, and their sons, as I said above, when the need to do so is far away. But when it draws nearer to you, they turn away." He concludes, concisely and provocatively, that "men forget the death of their father more quickly than the loss of their patrimony."[84] Having declared in universal terms people's superior capacity for remembering an offence than being grateful for a favour, Machiavelli furnishes an historical example in the case of Cesare Borgia and Giuliano della Rovere. While a cardinal, Giuliano had been a bitter rival and foe of the Borgia family and was eventually exiled by Alexander VI for a decade. Years later, however, Cesare struck a deal with Giuliano to enable him to win the papacy (as Julius II) by ensuring favourable votes from the delegation of Spanish cardinals. Cesare evidently believed that the benefits of the present alliance would outweigh the injuries that his father, Rodrigo, had inflicted on Giuliano years ago. Upon gaining the papacy, however, Julius wielded his new power to undermine Cesare's state in north central Italy. "Anyone who believes that new benefits make men of high station forget old injuries deceives himself. The Duke [Cesare], then, erred in this election, and it was the cause of his ultimate ruin."[85] For Machiavelli, the universal lesson was clear: never hope or expect that new benefits will cause someone to forget old injuries.

Guicciardini's conception of prudence counselled the same advice, elaborated in several contexts. One *ricordo* declares that all reliable alliances must be based on mutual advantage rather than gratitude for benefits granted: "You can better rely on someone who needs you or who happens to have a common objective than on someone you have benefited. For men generally are not grateful. If you do not want to be deceived, make your calculations according to this rule."[86] He consequently warns against benefiting anyone with a favour that at the same time injures someone else. The beneficiary will soon forget the benefit, but the injured person will never forget the offence, resulting in a temporary ally and a permanent foe. "Be careful not to do anyone the sort of favour that cannot be done without at the same time displeasing others. For injured men do not forget offences; in fact, they exaggerate them. Whereas the favoured party will either forget or will deem the favour smaller than it was. Therefore, other things being equal, you lose a great deal more than you gain."[87] Guicciardini expressed the dangers of dealing with those one has injured in more extreme terms than Machiavelli does. Whereas Machiavelli warns that benefits will never extinguish memory of injury and the desire for revenge, Guicciardini adds that injured people's thirst for revenge is so great they will pursue it when contrary to their self-interest. "If you have offended a man, do not trust or confide in him, even in a business deal which, if successful, would bring him profit and honour. There are some men for whom the memory of an offence can be so strong that it drives them to avenge themselves, even against their own self-interest – either because they value that satisfaction higher, or because passion so blinds them that they can no longer discern their own honour and profit. Keep this *ricordo* in mind, for many err on this score."[88]

In his recent *Virtue Politics* James Hankins writes that "no prominent writer of the Italian Renaissance showed less interest than Machiavelli in promoting the moral authority of ancient authors."[89] Machiavelli's political thought, however much draped in the superficial garb of reverence for antiquity – the intellectual coin of the realm in Renaissance Florence – mined ancient histories for useful political lessons, but only after a process of interrogation, based on his experiences, that frequently culminated in conclusions at stark moral odds with the ancient sources themselves. Machiavelli's methodology followed logically from the nature of his larger intellectual project of "demoralizing" virtue, in Hankins's apt phrase.[90] Ancient political thought consisted of strictly moral counsel that Machiavelli had concluded was a dangerous source of weakness in the political arena. As a consequence, Machiavelli used classical authors as subversive ornamentation rather than intellectual substance, designed to capture the attention of his readers while imparting to them his own radically different conception of *virtù* as the pursuit of agency, power, and individual autonomy at all costs.

On the question of political ethics, it is hoped that this chapter has shown that Guicciardini was Machiavelli's alter ego. His *Ricordi* performed the same function as Machiavelli's *Prince* – both were distillations of experience into prescriptions for effective conduct in the present. Like Machiavelli, Guicciardini had no interest in the moral teachings of ancient authors. Aside from a passing reference to Livy, Guicciardini expresses praise only for Tacitus, whom he admired for his clinical dissections of life under a tyrannical culture. In a text devoted exclusively to pragmatic political advice Guicciardini not once invokes Plato, Aristotle, Cicero, or any of the ancient authorities so cherished by his and Machiavelli's contemporaries. More than once, he declares outright that the most valuable political attribute – discretion – cannot be learned from books, a statement that, expressed however casually, places him squarely with Machiavelli in terms of conceptual distance from Renaissance intellectual orthodoxy and its penchant for ancient precedent.[91] Although speaking of legal culture rather than political philosophy, Guicciardini nevertheless expressed the same sensibility as did Machiavelli that the invocation of authority mattered less than the application of reason:

> The science of law has come to such a pass that if one side of a case presents a cogent argument and the other presents the authority of a scholar who has written on the subject, more attention will be paid to the authority. And so practising lawyers are forced to read everyone who has written, with the result that the time which should be devoted to reasoning is consumed in reading books. And such reading is so fatiguing to the mind and body that it is more like the work of a porter than that of an educated man.[92]

The morally subversive content of Guicciardini's *Ricordi* clearly explains why he shared Machiavelli's higher estimation of reason over authority. How could he invoke the stature and gravitas of ancient authorities when the substance of his counsel violated every one of their major ethical norms? Like Machiavelli's, his experience in the storm-tossed politics of the Italian wars had taught him that political and material prosperity – survival, even – depended on the tactical and periodic deployment of cruelty, deception, lack of faith, and the a priori presumption of such conduct in others.

This chapter has demonstrated the degree to which Guicciardini's *Ricordi* and Machiavelli's *Prince* portrayed politics in identical, radical terms and with a similar radical detachment from the prevailing consensus of humanist virtue politics. Further, it underscores the degree to which Guicciardini justified his positions with similar views about noble and popular culture as explored in the previous chapter. The *Ricordi* is a particularly revealing source for understanding Guicciardini's core convictions because, unlike in many of his other writings, he never deploys his lawyerly instinct to argue both sides of a question. In this text, written for self and family and intended for private consumption, he had no need for the strategic ambiguities of *in utramque partem* reasoning or the dialogic genre. Every word reflects Guicciardini's proudly accumulated and hard-won political wisdom, much of which either echoed, anticipated, or reflected Machiavelli's populism. In the following chapter we will examine the way in which Guicciardini amplified his early critique of aristocratic political culture, in his *Dialogue on the Government of Florence,* his most ambitious analysis of Florentine politics. That amplification reflects in part the fact that Guicciardini's *Dialogue* was also the first text he wrote in which Machiavelli began to exert a discernable influence on Guicciardini's vocabulary and reasoning.

Chapter Four

Deconstructing Regimes of the Few in Guicciardini's *Dialogue on the Government of Florence*

This chapter demonstrates that Guicciardini's *Dialogue on the Government of Florence*, his most extensive analysis of Florentine political culture that he wrote during his years of friendship with Machiavelli, displays a striking awareness of the legitimacy of Machiavelli's populist outlook.[1] It considers in particular Guicciardini's contrasting comments about the Albizzi oligarchy that ruled Florence from 1393 to 1434 and aristocratic oligarchy in general in three texts: *The History of Florence*, begun in 1508; the *Discorso di Logrogno*, written in 1512; and the *Dialogue on the Government of Florence*, written sometime between 1521 and 1524.[2] In the two early texts Guicciardini praised the politics of the few, in general abstract terms and in historical terms with specific reference to the Albizzi regime. In the *Dialogue*, however, Guicciardini quarrels at length with his earlier self, revisiting those early statements only to subject them to sustained scrutiny, revision, and at times outright rejection. He chooses Bernardo del Nero, a working-class "new man" who had successfully climbed Florence's political and social ladder, as the voice of wisdom and experience and as the final arbiter of the convictions voiced by the other interlocutors, all of whom were his social superiors. Via Del Nero, Guicciardini condemns the Albizzi oligarchy as a corrupt faction that caused considerable violence and discord and that excluded the people from an appropriate role in politics. Nor does he limit his argument to the specifics of the Albizzean context – he argues at a theoretical level that such sins are an inevitable result whenever government is in the hands of the few.

The *Dialogue*'s critique of oligarchic rule in general and the Albizzi regime in particular suggests intimate familiarity and sympathy with a number of Machiavellian arguments.[3] Guicciardini argues against the adoption of the Albizzi regime as a model for the present or future, condemning it as an exclusionary, unstable, and tyrannical faction. In doing so, Guicciardini literally deploys Machiavellian criticism and language – the very same critique that Machiavelli makes in contemporaneous texts, the *Florentine Histories* and the *Discourse on Florentine Affairs after the Death of Lorenzo.* Further, the *Dialogue*'s condemnation of the Albizzi functions as a historical example of a larger and more theoretically abstract condemnation of the politics of the few in general that concurs with Machiavelli's provocative condemnation of elite politics in *The Prince* and *The Discourses.*

In spite of those criticisms, however, when Guicciardini outlines in the *Dialogue* his ideal vision for the Florentine government, it does not substantially change from his earlier constitutional writings: a lifetime standard bearer, a great council, and a senate made up of the city's most wise and influential citizens that controlled all the key issues of war, diplomacy, legislation, and finances. From a rhetorical point of view, if nothing else, we must ask why Guicciardini includes such sustained criticism of aristocratic rule in a text that ultimately argues, as his earlier works have done, for an aristocratic senatorial order in Florence. Why demonstrate such acute awareness of the dangers of elite rule in a text that positions the Florentine elite as the driving force of his ideal regime? And why place the most sustained and elaborate articulation of his senatorial ideal in the mouth of a Medici protégé of humble origins?[4]

The *Dialogue* was – among other things, to be sure – an attempt to persuade Machiavelli that Guicciardini's senatorial preferences were the best method to safeguard Florentine republican liberty and therefore were also compatible with the primary goal of popular regimes. To do so, however, required an altogether different rhetorical strategy that substantively engaged Machiavelli's critique of noble culture. In the 1520s and in a context in which many people – Machiavelli included, whose language Guicciardini repeats almost verbatim – were counselling the Medici on the reform of the Florentine government, Guicciardini went to some considerable length to incorporate Machiavelli's perspective to indicate that he saw the problematic implications of elite political culture, agreed with its condemnation, and had therefore conceptualized his political order in ways that prevented elite potential for discord.

As we saw in chapter 1, we have already seen Guicciardini's penchant for *in utramque partem* analysis, in which he advances a position, only to critique it from an opposing viewpoint. A formidable intellect rather than an aristocratic shill, Guicciardini from his first writings subjected the self-regarding pieties of the *ottimati* class to searching scrutiny and anticipated populist counter-arguments. The *Dialogue* stands out, however, for the sheer magnitude, thoroughness, and polemical verve of Guicciardini's "other voice." I argue that in the *Dialogue* we see that Guicciardini began to employ Machiavelli – his populism, his political vocabulary, and his interpretation of Florentine history – as his intellectual foil, an equally formidable (or perhaps greater) intellect against which Guicciardini would have to measure the viability of his aristocratic preferences. Guicciardini's dramatic reversal of opinion regarding the virtues of the Albizzi oligarchy reveals the degree to which Machiavelli expanded and sharpened Guicciardini's style of adversarial reasoning.

By way of an introductory point of departure, the first section of this chapter situates its arguments in comparison and contrast with Gennaro Sasso's fundamental study of the relationship between Machiavelli and Guicciardini, still the most substantial interpretation of their relationship. The second section turns to Guicciardini's praise of the Albizzi regime in *The History of Florence* and his praise of aristocratic oligarchy in general in *The History of Florence* and *Discorso di Logrogno.* The third section analyses his subsequent radical critique of the Albizzi and demonstrates that it was not an isolated case but was rather part of a larger and more theoretical condemnation of oligarchic regimes. The fourth section addresses longstanding debates about Guicciardini's choice of Bernardo del Nero as the *Dialogue*'s chief interlocutor, via an analysis of Machiavelli's and Guicciardini's many connections to the Del Nero family. The conclusion shifts the focus to Machiavelli and considers the implications of Guicciardini's surprising acknowledgment of elite misrule for current debates about how to interpret Machiavelli's similarly unexpected reversal of position on noble and popular culture in his later historical and political writings.

Gennaro Sasso's Guicciardini

In positing Machiavelli as an implicit interlocutor in Guicciardini's *Dialogue,* this chapter takes up themes and questions explored in a lengthy article by Gennaro Sasso that remains the most substantial treatment of the relationship between the two thinkers. In Sasso's interpretation the question of Machiavelli's relationship with Guicciardini, his impact on Guicciardini's political and historical vision, and his implicit presence in the *Dialogue* are all fundamentally unrelated to Guicciardini's equivocations and reversals of opinion about the merits and historical accomplishments of the Florentine aristocracy. On the first topic – the Machiavellian connection – Sasso interprets the *Dialogue* in terms of discontinuity, a decisive refutation of Machiavelli's arguments that departed from Guicciardini's earlier texts that had displayed a certain openness to Machiavellian ideas. On the third topic – the *Dialogue*'s biting criticism of aristocratic rule in book 1 – Sasso interprets the *Dialogue* in terms of continuity, a consistent feature of Guicciardini's thinking created by the unbridgeable gap between his theoretical preference for an aristocratic ideal and his historical awareness of the flaws of the Florentine aristocracy.

For Sasso, there is nothing particularly surprising or difficult to explain about Guicciardini's criticism of the Albizzi regime in the *Dialogue*. He interprets it as the result of an irresolvable tension caused by Guicciardini's idealistic vision of and instinctive preference for elitist regimes, combined with his granular knowledge of the actual shortcomings of the Florentine aristocrats, their tendency towards internal divisiveness, and consequent weakness in the face of popular and princely challenges to their supremacy, a tension that Sasso sees in all his writings.[5] Bernardo del Nero's disquisition on the flaws of the aristocratic rule thus merely states more baldly the implicit arguments in the larger narrative of *The History of Florence*, Guicciardini's earliest writing. His *History*, in spite of its opening paean to the wisdom of Maso degli Albizzi and Niccolò Uzzano, goes on to trace in detail Cosimo and Lorenzo's subsequent deft manipulation of aristocratic decadence and corruption to their own advantage in the fifteenth century, and aristocratic impotence to the mismanagement of the Soderini government in the sixteenth. Guicciardini the historian recognized that Florence had had elite-dominated regimes in the past that were not too dissimilar from his ideal, yet none had proved durable, largely for reasons of aristocratic vanity, mutual jealousy, and bad judgment. As much as he may have wished to, he could not entirely repress that historical awareness when elaborating theoretical arguments in favour of his senatorial ideal, hence Sasso's conclusion that "the scission between [Guicciardini's] historical and political judgment ... was the constant characteristic, and constant limit, of his realistic thought."[6]

On the topic of Guicciardini's engagement with Machiavellian themes, Sasso sees a broad arc that demonstrates early familiarity with Machiavellian ideas and occasional common ground and ultimately culminates in a sustained, polemical rejection of *The Discourses on Livy*. Guicciardini's first work of political theory, the *Discorso di Logrogno*, praised the Great Council, an institution that Machiavelli would later defend at length, and a citizen militia, a project championed and led by Machiavelli only a few years earlier. Guicciardini's treatment of Cesare Borgia and Piero Soderini's regime in his *History of Florence* includes details suggesting access, respectively, to Machiavelli's dispatches from Borgia's camp in Urbino, Imola, and Rome in 1502–3 and Machiavelli's *First Decennale*; and Sasso posits Machiavelli's militia writings as Guicciardini's source for his related discussion in chapter 26.[7]

By the 1520s, however, Guicciardini had definitively rejected his earlier flirtation with Machiavellian themes and arguments. Via Del Nero's proposals in book 2 of the *Dialogue on the Government of Florence*, Guicciardini acknowledges his earlier appreciation of a citizen militia, only to abandon it: whereas Florentine political culture initially possessed enough discipline and effective institutions for a militia to work, its current context of aristocratic vanity and corruption precludes capable leadership; once armed, Florentine peasants will direct their weapons against the Florentine elite rather than its external aggressors.[8] Book 2 concludes with an elaborate rejection by Del Nero of all the aspects of Roman political culture – in contrast to Venetian practice – that Machiavelli had championed in *The Discourses*: their recurring class conflict, the salutary consequences of establishing the Tribunes of the People, and their military system. Guicciardini's Del Nero, like other actual parvenus embraced by the elite such as Leonardo Bruni and Poggio Bracciolini, adopts the central axioms at the heart of Florentine elite politics: disunity is the greatest, most existential danger for any republic, and therefore consensus and concord are the highest and most indisputably urgent political ideals. For Sasso, book 2 of the *Dialogue* marks Guicciardini's definitive break with Machiavelli's political thought: "In adopting this ancient concept [Concordia] and in making it the ideal centre of his vision, Guicciardini knowingly imprinted on the *Dialogue* its character of continuous, uninterrupted, anti-Machiavellian polemic."[9]

The following analysis does not dispute Sasso's reading of book 2 but offers a different interpretation of and explanation for Guicciardini's criticisms of aristocratic rule in book 1, rooted in answers to some questions that Sasso for the most part does not raise. First and foremost, Sasso's reading of the *Dialogue* downplays the novelty and extremity of its assessment of the flaws of elite hegemony. It is certainly true that its overall combination of book 1's criticism and book 2's advocacy of a Venetian-style aristocratic senatorial order is part of the larger pattern of Guicciardini's equivocations that Sasso identifies, particularly in Guicciardini's early texts. In the latter, however, Guicciardini loudly trumpeted his aristocratic allegiances while expressing his inner doubts indirectly and without any overt declaration. The *Dialogue* reveals an altogether new perspective: book 1 explicitly announces the shortcomings of aristocratic rule as a razor-sharp thesis that Del Nero defends at length. What in earlier texts was an inner conflict that manifested itself in apparent inconsistencies and contradictions becomes in the *Dialogue* a major category of analysis that Guicciardini explores in detail and with unambiguous self-awareness.

Further, if we accept Sasso's argument that the *Dialogue*'s fusion of criticism and advocacy of elite rule reflects the permanent tension between Guicciardini's ideal preference for aristocratic rule and his substantial historical knowledge of the Florentine aristocracy's numerous political vices, we are then unable to explain why Guicciardini did not limit himself to historical condemnation of the Albizzi regime but rather went on to mount an extended criticism of elite rule in general non-historical terms. In Del Nero's analysis, the Albizzi regime is not an idiosyncratic corrupted example of a potentially ideal regime type; it is a standard reflection of that regime type's inherent and inevitable flaws. Guicciardini displays here not only an unprecedented acknowledgment of his own doubts about the putative wisdom of the Florentine aristocracy but also a new willingness to consider critical perspectives of elite rule in general. Although Guicciardini never abandons his desire for an aristocratic regime in Florence, as the outcome of the *Dialogue* makes clear, he now defends that desire via a recognition of the validity of more populist perspectives, implied from the outset by Guicciardini's choice of Del Nero as the dialogue's voice of authority.

Whereas Sasso reads book 2 as Guicciardini's external dialogue with Machiavelli and book 1 as internal dialogue with himself, the analysis offered here posits Machiavelli as a major interlocutor for book 1 and the catalyst for its new perspectives. In addition to the wide array of Machiavellian vocabulary and ideas in book 1 of the *Dialogue*, there are compelling contextual reasons for doing so. The dense and intimate correspondence between the two began in 1520 and continued until Machiavelli's death in 1527; thus Guicciardini wrote the *Dialogue* (1521–4) during the period when Machiavelli was literally a major interlocutor in his life. In 1521, the year Guicciardini began writing the *Dialogue*, Machiavelli had just finished his own constitutional recommendation for the Medici that began with an historical consideration of the relative strengths and weaknesses of the Albizzi and fifteenth-century Medici regimes, the same subject with which Guicciardini began his constitutional treatise. Sasso's analysis of their relationship draws on Machiavelli's correspondence to document their early moments of contact and shared community prior to the collapse of the republic in 1512, but he largely ignores the sustained correspondence between the two later in their lives. However much the two may have differed in terms of ideal preferences, the correspondence indicates a profound mutual respect for each other's understanding of Florentine history, articulated as they each were assessing the historical strengths and weaknesses of the Albizzean and Medici regimes.

I turn now to sustained explication of these contextual and textual connections linking Machiavelli to book 1 of Guicciardini's *Dialogue.* If we accept the argument presented here, that Machiavelli was both catalyst and audience for much of book 1's critique of aristocratic rule, we see that the *Dialogue*'s rejection of *The Discourses* in book 2 was only one aspect of that text's engagement with Machiavelli. Via Bernardo del Nero in book 1, Guicciardini made a number of arguments about Florentine history and politics similar to those recently made by Machiavelli in his

1521 constitutional treatise on the Florentine government and that he was in the process of elaborating in the *Florentine Histories*, completed a year after Guicciardini's *Dialogue*. If Guicciardini's ultimate priority has not changed – a Venetian-style senatorial order in Florence – his rationale and defence of that priority has. Among its virtues, he has added a new element: it is uniquely effective at limiting the potential for discord of governments in the "hands of the few."

The Albizzi Regime in Guicciardini's Early Writings

Guicciardini's first sustained commentary on the relative merits of the politics of the few and the many was his *History of Florence*, written between 1508 and 1509 and thus in the context of one of Florence's more open and inclusive regimes.[10] The periodization he deployed in *The History of Florence* and its overarching narrative was a form of implicit political theory (unlike Machiavelli, he did not declare his themes and arguments at the outset) intended to demonstrate the virtues of aristocratic hegemony via the detailed exposition of the shortcomings of its alternatives.

Guicciardini opens *The History* with a thorough denunciation of plebeian politics as manifested in the Ciompi revolt and its bloody aftermath. Like all Florentine *ottimati*, Guicciardini viewed the Ciompi revolt as proof that working-class politics amounted to little more than chaos, violence, and systematic theft. Unlike Machiavelli, who provided a relatively sympathetic account of the revolt as a product of structural economic injustices in the guild hierarchy, Guicciardini portrays the origins of the revolt as the corrupt workaround by the Eight of War, the committee entrusted with conducting Florence's war with the papacy, to remove the reasonable constraints on its power that had been advocated by the city's best citizens.[11] To counter the influence and stature of those best citizens, the Eight cynically catered to the lower classes and weaponized them by encouraging them to revolt, hoping to guide the proletarian horde according to their own design. The Eight had hoped merely to use the spectre of class rebellion to beat back the leading citizens, but, having made their fateful Faustian bargain, they found themselves equally at the mercy of the *sottoposti* woolworkers who had taken control of the government, ruling according to their own whims rather than the Eight's agenda. In spite of the reasonable intervention of Michele di Lando, himself a woolworker, to restrain the worst excesses of the Ciompi, the ensuing regime was a toxic combination of plebeian rabble led by elite demagogues and was plagued by constant riots and frequent, arbitrary executions. The plebeians' support for their extremist demagogic leaders, however, was fickle and fleeting (Guicciardini would later universalize this as the primary characteristic of all truly popular regimes). The regime collapsed, ushering in more chaos but also fresh opportunity for wiser heads to impose a stable form on the disorganized matter of Florentine politics.

Guicciardini then relates the city's delivery from plebeian evil by a small group of aristocrats led by Maso degli Albizzi. They establish a narrow oligarchy that Guicciardini idealizes as the city's only moment of political perfection, a precise historical example of his later general thesis that regimes dominated by a wealthy, prudential few confer the greatest benefits to all. Guicciardini lauds Maso and the oligarchs because they ruled over a united city, expanded Florence's territory, and defended the city against foreign aggression. Guicciardini's praise of the Albizzi oligarchy is unambiguous. He writes: "Finally, in 1393, a [parlamento] brought order to the state. The Gonfalonier of Justice was Maso degli Albizzi ... and the government was in the hands of the wise and well-to-do, who provided great unity and security until 1420 ... Men were so worn out by the recent turbulence that they were glad to keep the peace under this orderly régime. In this period, our city did indeed show how strong it could be when it was united."[12] He then outlines the city's chief military and diplomatic successes: for twelve years Florence sustained a costly war against the Duke of Milan; it acquired Pisa, Cortona, and Castrocaro; and it fought the king of Naples. He concludes: "Florence was successful both at home and abroad: at home, because it remained free, united, and governed by well-to-do, good, and capable men; abroad, because it defended itself against powerful enemies and greatly expanded its dominion. Florentine successes were so great that this government is deservedly said to be the wisest, the most glorious, and the happiest that our city had had for a long time."[13]

In spite of its manifest virtues, however, the Albizzi regime succumbed roughly thirty years later to the rising power of Cosimo de' Medici. Having demonstrated in a brisk few pages the worst and best possible regimes for Florence, the remainder of Guicciardini's grim *History* chronicles the ways in which oligarchy's alternatives – rule by one and by the many – each excluded the city's wisest and best citizens, to the general detriment of all.

The first half of his *History* chronicles the corruption of political life under the Medici. His portrait of Medici rule is consistent with all his subsequent treatments of the family in his *Ricordi*, *Dialogue*, and *History of Italy*: although individually, Cosimo and Lorenzo were exceptional, charismatic, and in many ways glorious individuals who contributed substantially to Florence's greater glory, they were nevertheless tyrants. As all tyrants do, they instinctively mistrusted excellence and ambition in others and hence generally excluded or banished outright the city's wisest citizens. As a consequence, they tended to rely on only their own counsel or on the counsel of new men, who were by definition lacking in experience and whose dependence on the Medici for their socially unwarranted status guaranteed their loyalty. On multiple occasions Guicciardini shows Cosimo de' Medici's paranoid streak. Upon assuming power in 1434, Cosimo banished many enemies, "all of noble and rich families. Then he began to exalt many vile men of low station to replace them."[14] His grandson Lorenzo did the same, promoting "men from whom he had nothing to fear, men who were then devoid of connections and standing, such as Bernardo Buongirolami and Antonio di Puccio."[15] Even on the occasions when Lorenzo did surround himself with "noble and wise" citizens, he still "in many cases ... followed only his own counsel and opinion, against the will of the others; and he took extreme care that no one in the city grew powerful enough for him to fear."[16] His son Piero was even worse in this regard. Upon his assumption of power, he too followed his own ill-considered counsel, culminating in tragedy for the family (the collapse of Medici power and his own expulsion from Florence) and tragedy for Italy (the French descent into Italy and the beginning of Italian servitude to foreign powers).[17]

In spite of their many considerable accomplishments, amply documented and respected by Guicciardini, he underscores an overall narrative of decline, corruption, and eventual extinction. Deprived of the wisdom of the city's best citizens, their regime was ultimately doomed to fail. He inserts an early, prophetic coda to Medici rule, following his discussion of the Pazzi conspiracy, that hints at the tragedies to come: "That is the way civil discord and strife end: the one side is exterminated, the head of the other becomes lord of the city. His supporters and adherents, once companions, become almost subjects; the people and the multitude become slaves; power is passed on by inheritance, and very often it passes from a wise man to a madman who then plunges the city into the abyss."[18]

The second half *The History* chronicles all the ways in which the renewed republic that was established after the expulsion of the Medici also alienated – albeit for different reasons – the city's elite families. His analysis of the Soderinian republic repeatedly praises the wisdom and prudence of the city's elite families and identifies their legitimate mistrust of Soderini as the regime's greatest weakness. His survey of the regime's defects opens with technical problems related to continuity in office-holding: the excessively rapid rotation of office in the Signoria and the colleges that discouraged any sense of personal responsibility in officials; the absence of a corresponding magistracy entrusted with long-term oversight of policy; and laws that insisted on long intervals between consecutive appointments to the government that applied not just to individuals but also to their families. Such a context was hardly conducive to elite control of policy, a problem compounded by the evident mutual suspicion between the middle ranks and the aristocracy. For Guicciardini, this state of affairs will inevitably lead to the regime's demise: "The result is that most of the time, these offices can only be filled by weak and inexperienced men of little ability. If such men will not listen to the wise and expert citizens, but prefer instead to act according to their own minds and their own authority – as was the case then because they feared the leading citizens wanted to overthrow the government – it is impossible for the city not to go to perdition."[19]

Guicciardini goes on to stress the degree to which the elite were hostile to the regime and the problems that their alienation created. Those making decisions were frequently uninformed, decisions were invariably reached too late, and administrative inefficiency resulted in wasteful and ineffective expenditure, with the collective result that foreign powers viewed the regime with scorn as untrustworthy and unreliable. Worse still, its defences, in terms of both soldiers and fortresses, were hopelessly inadequate. Now wishing for the regime's downfall owing to the structural mismanagement of affairs, the Florentine elite escalated the effects of their exclusion by actively refusing to serve, a position that Guicciardini defends as a necessary consequence of the middle ranks' illegitimate suspicion of them: "These awful conditions made the wise and honoured citizens malcontent and desperate, and estranged them completely from the government. Nor could they try to remedy the situation, for every time they did they were loudly accused by everyone of wanting to overthrow the government. Most of them were behind in their taxes. None would take on commissions and legations unless forced, for our disorder was so great that everything was sure to come out badly. These citizens did not want to reap the censure and criticism of the people for something that was not their fault."[20]

Although his account certainly seems to imply an unpatriotic unwillingness on the part of the best citizens to offer up their expertise for the greater good, irrespective of the offer's ungrateful reception, Guicciardini resists that conclusion. He unequivocally defends the *ottimati*'s desire to establish an oligarchic regime centred around a standard bearer for life. The catalyst for and intensity of their desire he fundamentally attributes to the excesses of the popular regime that ultimately gave the aristocrats no alternative:

> The wise citizens, who were accustomed to having authority, were so displeased by this state of affairs that they were nearly disgusted with this form

> of government. They saw the city being ruined and declining at the rate of a hundred miles per hour. They saw themselves being divested of reputation and power; and that hurt them not only because of self-interest, but also because the city is sure to suffer when men of quality do not have, I will not say tyrannical power, but at least the rank they justly deserve. To all this was added the fact that every time some tumult arose the public suspected them, and there was danger that their houses would be attacked. Indeed, every day that passed seemed to them to be fraught with great risk. For all these reasons they ardently desired a change – at least a reform – of the government so that the city could be run well.[21]

Having defended the legitimacy, rationality, and beneficial implications of their desire for change, Guicciardini proceeds to identify both the self-serving motives of those opposed to aristocratic reforms and the damaging consequences of their widespread opposition. Guicciardini explains that the "bulk of the city was made up of men of small houses, men who knew that under a more oligarchic government, people like them would have little to say. Then there were some men who did in fact come from good houses, but who belonged to clans that included men of higher quality and authority than they; and such men also realized that in an oligarchy they would be left behind."[22] Combined, these two groups made up a decisive majority who successfully opposed substantive reforms because they benefited from the regime's tendency to discriminate "very little among men and among houses. They realized the government had some defects, but they nevertheless guarded it jealously. Indeed, they were so afraid it would be taken away from them that they immediately opposed any talk of change or reform."[23]

In his subsequent text, the *Discorso di Logrogno*, Guicciardini set himself the task of devising an optimal regime for Florence that would be capable of succeeding where the Medici and Soderini regimes had failed.[24] Assessing the flaws of the Soderini regime in 1512, immediately prior to its collapse, he advances a theoretical variation on the role of the elite largely if not entirely consistent with his sentiments in *The History of Florence* about the enlightened rule of the Albizzi oligarchy and the popular republic's misrule caused by their shabby treatment of the aristocrats. Using an aristocratic vocabulary that disdained commerce and praised glory, Guicciardini criticizes both the excessive and presumptuous interference in affairs of state by those who are ill suited to the task and the inadequate opportunities for those who are well suited: "Able and worthy men do not have regular opportunities to demonstrate their qualities, nor are there rewards for those who perform meritorious deeds for our republic; there is an overweening ambition in everyone to seize public offices, and an arrogant desire to interfere in all public matters of any importance; the spirits of men are effeminate and enervated, and dedicated to a way of life that is soft and ... sumptuous; and there is little love of true glory and honour, but much love of possessions and money."[25] Owing to these problems, he argues that the Soderini regime would soon devolve into either popular anarchy or tyranny, a prescient conclusion given the restoration of the Medici later that year.

A positive vision of the politics and psychology of the few underpins his subsequent discussion in the *Discorso* of how the regime should configure its constitution to correct its flaws. Guicciardini acknowledges that his uncompromising criteria for the lifetime gonfalonier's eligibility will attract relatively few candidates – only those who "act outstandingly" and perform "meritorious deeds." Tellingly, however, he sees this as evidence of his plan's rationality and consequently an argument in its favour: "And even if this is a prospect likely to inspire only a few men, this stimulus is not therefore worthless, because in every well-ordered republic it is obvious that it is always a few able and virtuous citizens who exercise control: glorious deeds and great achievements have always been initiated and performed by a few men, because to be in charge of great enterprises and to be heads of government in free cities, great and varied talents and virtues are required, and these are to be found in very few men."[26] He champions lifetime tenure primarily because the correspondingly high status conferred will stimulate "this honourable ambition in men of great spirit and give them the opportunity to perform glorious deeds."[27]

To explain the method of electing the gonfalonier Guicciardini turns to discussion of a senate, his major institutional innovation and another opportunity to proclaim the probity and virtue of the prudential few. He acknowledges that in theory, according to his earlier approval of the Great Council's chief responsibility of electing officials, the Great Council should select the gonfalonier. Guicciardini makes an exception, however, owing to the importance of the position and the Council's lack of "detailed knowledge and fine judgment." Electing the gonfalonier should be one of many important tasks reserved for a senate "in which all the wise and prudent men will sit."[28] Guicciardini devises his senate in such a way that "all the most important work of governing will really be carried out by very few men, which is what always happens in republics, in both ancient and modern times."[29]

The senate becomes the chief institutional mechanism by which these few men effectively control a wide range of the most important aspects of politics: "it must be the guiding body of our city and the controller of everything important."[30] Guicciardini grants the senate power to choose the republic's ambassadors and commissaries and to ratify the Council of Ten's mercenary contracts. The senate also appoints the city's judges, assumes responsibility for the passage of fiscal laws, and of course elects the gonfalonier. At the broadest level, the senate "should decide about affairs of state and play a prominent part in legislation." After elaborating on the specifics, Guicciardini sums up the advantages of his senatorial order in terms of its ability to harness the benevolent and considerable talents of the few. For Guicciardini, that combination of benevolence and talent is crucial – without their virtuous inclinations, concentrating power so intensely around so few would threaten the republic's liberty: "And happy are the republics that are full of such noble ambitions, because they always cause those things to flourish that lead men to these high public offices, namely, outstanding abilities and fine deeds, as well as a burning desire to want to rise to this exalted office and in those who already hold office. Their great power and standing are not incompatible with a free society, nor do they threaten it."[31]

The *Dialogue*'s Critique of Aristocratic Regimes

Roughly a decade later, between 1521 and 1524, Guicciardini revisited the relative merits and flaws of the Albizzi regime and considered the ideal Florentine regime in his *Dialogue on the Government of Florence*, his most substantial work of Florentine constitutional analysis. Significantly, he composed this text during the early years of his friendship with Machiavelli in which Machiavelli was also writing a constitutional proposal framed in terms of the potential lessons offered by previous regimes in the city's history. Their correspondence certainly suggests that the two men were often in the habit of discussing Florentine history.[32] Guicciardini had already loaned Machiavelli his *History of Florence* during the composition of the latter's *Art of War* in 1519.[33] In their first exchange of letters Guicciardini elaborates his theory of the value of history and the importance of prudence, in the context of enthusiastic acknowledgment of Machiavelli's commission to write the *Histories*:

> You see that, with only the faces of the men and the extrinsic colours changed, all the very same things return; and we do not see any incident that has not been seen in other times. But changing the names and forms of things means that only the prudent recognize them; therefore history is good and useful because it sets before you and makes you recognize and see again what you had never known or seen. There follows from this a brotherly syllogism: that he who gave you the task of writing annals is greatly to be commended; and you are to be exhorted to carry out the charge given to you with diligence.[34]

In 1524 Machiavelli wrote to Guicciardini about the composition of the *Florentine Histories* and to lament Guicciardini's absence as a source of advice. "Here in the country I have been applying myself, and continue to do so, to writing the history, and I would pay ten soldi – but no more – to have you by my side so that I might show you where I am, because, since I am about to come to certain details, I would need to learn from you whether or not I am being too offensive in my exaggerating or understating the facts."[35] In 1525 he again wrote to Guicciardini about the *Histories*, this time mentioning that he had received "that" raise, which suggests their prior discussion of Machiavelli's salary, and announcing his princely targets: "I received that raise to a hundred ducats, for the *History*. I am just now beginning to write again, and I vent my feelings by accusing the princes who have all done everything they can to bring us to this situation." Tellingly, Machiavelli signed off a letter to Guicciardini by indicating the primacy of history in his self-conception: "storico, comico, e tragico."[36]

In a context of regular intellectual exchange with Machiavelli, Guicciardini returns to a key question left unanswered by his younger self in *The History of Florence*: why did the Albizzi oligarchy – the greatest regime in the city's history and one that benefited from unity, strength, and security – collapse after a relatively modest reign of twenty-seven years? In light of Guicciardini's evident admiration for the Albizzi regime in that early text, we might have expected him to linger on the circumstances of its relatively swift demise. However, his treatment of the factional rivalry between Rinaldo degli Albizzi and Niccolò da Uzzano, on the one hand, and Giovanni di Bicci and Cosimo de' Medici, on the other, is surprisingly cursory. After recounting the exile of Cosimo in 1433 and the brief seeming victory of his heroes, he writes: "With Cosimo gone, Rinaldo degli Albizzi, Niccolò Barbadori ... and others like them remained in power. But they did not know how to stay there."[37] At the crucial moment in his account of the critical reversal of fortune, he uses a passive verb: "The following September ... a [parlamento] was convened." This of course was the meeting that recalled Cosimo from exile and granted him the extraordinary emergency powers that he used to crush his enemies and consolidate his victory.

Guicciardini's *Dialogue* answers that question with a sustained, detailed, and polemical re-evaluation of the Albizzi's regime's few virtues and many flaws. We are first presented in the *Dialogue* with the following description of the Albizzi oligarchy:

> In the days of Messer Maso degli Albizzi, Gino my great-grandfather, Niccolò da Uzzano and those others, the government was in the hands of the

> leading citizens of most worth, but it was not so narrow that the city wasn't free. The regime remained united for many years and governed in Florence and outside with the highest repute. For they avoided revolutions and not only defended themselves from the very powerful enemies who attempted to oppress us at that time, but they also acquired Pisa and many other places and considerably increased the dominion and reputation of the city. For this reason, in the opinion of everyone who has talked or written about these matters, Florence has never had a regime that governed her better or was more honoured than this one.[38]

This assessment repeats almost verbatim the summary we previously considered in *The History of Florence*: the city was ruled by the best citizens, they ruled with unity and stability, defended Florence from powerful aggressors, and expanded its territory, hence Guicciardini's invocation of an alleged widespread common consensus that it was the best regime the city had ever enjoyed (as Sasso observed, in invoking that historical consensus, Guicciardini was footnoting himself).[39] So far, so similar.

This encomiastic tribute to aristocratic prudential wisdom, however, is not uttered by Bernardo del Nero, the *Dialogue*'s anchor, but by Piero Capponi, who praises that regime as part of his larger defence of the expulsion of the Medici and the popular regime that followed in its wake. In ousting the Medici, Piero Capponi and his allies had intended to re-establish a narrow aristocratically dominated republic, described in terms virtually identical to the language that Guicciardini uses in the *Discorso di Logrogno*: "Our intention was to remove the city from the power of one man and restore liberty, as has been done. It is true that we wanted to avoid giving the government absolutely to the people, but rather to place it in the hands of the leading and worthiest citizens, to make it a government of men of worth rather than a totally popular regime."[40] A few pages later, Capponi goes on to say that in attempting to create "a government of men of worth," they modelled their efforts explicitly on the Albizzean oligarchy: "Therefore we shouldn't despair that what existed then might not return another time, especially since we were all set – and had already begun – to get as close as possible to that form of government [the regime of Maso degli Albizzi, Gino Capponi, and Niccolò da Uzzano]."[41]

The validity of their plan is then challenged by Del Nero, who elaborates at length on its various shortcomings. Given that Guicciardini's *Dialogue* does not equitably divide its points of view among the four interlocutors – Bernardo del Nero, Piero Capponi, Piero Guicciardini, and Pagolantonio Soderini – but is designed instead as a vehicle for the elaboration of Del Nero's opinions, it is particularly significant that Del

Nero is a vocal critic of the aristocratic regime that governed Florence from 1393 to 1434.

Through Del Nero, Guicciardini critically and thoroughly deconstructs the myth of the oligarchic regime's unity and stability. "Don't let yourselves be deceived by the example of the regime at the time of messer Maso and the others ... I've often heard from our oldest citizens that an extraordinary combination of two conditions was responsible for keeping this regime more united than those which preceded it usually were."[42] Note the use of the term *extraordinary* – so frequently used by Machiavelli – in precisely the same sense of beyond or outside of existing legitimate institutional arrangements. Once triumphant, the oligarchs would have immediately descended into destabilizing internal factional quarrels were it not for the particularities of context. Their apparent unity was in part the result of their state of collective shock and indignation caused by the recent Ciompi revolt and the plebeian regime dominated by Giorgio Scali. More importantly, the city was at war with Milan and Naples for much of that period: "The second was that our city had never waged longer or more dangerous wars than at this time, nor against more powerful enemies ... [They] weighed so heavily on us and were so dangerous that these men were all the more forced to lay their rivalries on one side and devote themselves to saving their city."[43]

Having dispensed with the regime's false reputation for unity, Del Nero goes on to condemn the regime's narrow elitism and the consequent turbulence that led to the rise of the Medici:

> If you read and digest your chronicles carefully, you will see that it was not a free type of regime because everything was in the hands of a few citizens and the people had, in effect, no part in it at all. Nor was it even peaceful, since there were often insurrections and disturbances. Scarcely had it secured itself in power when new divisions developed, giving rise to the parties which caused the events of 1433 and 1434. So this is why I say that, if you think carefully about all this, you will see that the regime was not such, nor so long-lasting, to be pleased about it, even if you'd managed to produce one similar to it."[44]

In book 2, Del Nero reiterates these condemnations in bolder language still: "either ... a few people have held power in the city, as happened from the fall of Messer Giorgio Scali until 1434 ... Then the few oppressed the other citizens and held them in servitude with a thousand insults and rudenesses; and they were so factious among themselves that they exiled, decapitated and destroyed each other, and did far more damage to this poor city of ours than our enemies ever did."[45] Guicciardini offers us a quintessentially Machiavellian portrait of the few ruling in the manner of the few: they concentrate power disproportionately in their own hands, they exclude the people and treat them abusively, and thereby generate the discontent, discords, and instability that enables Cosimo de' Medici to defeat them and subvert the republic altogether. In short, Del Nero believes that the regime deserved to fail and was responsible for Medici tyranny.

In this passage Guicciardini may have been invoking Machiavelli directly. As he wrote those words – "if you read and digest your chronicles carefully" – his friend and interlocutor was at work writing one of the chief chronicle sources that explored in detail the defects of the Albizzi regime and the reasons for its inevitable collapse, a chronicle that the two men evidently discussed on several occasions.[46] Guicciardini certainly could not have been referring to his own history that held up the Albizzi regime as an example worthy of emulation. But Machiavelli's introduction of the Albizzi regime stressed precisely these aspects – the misleading appearance of stability, insurrections and disturbances, the hostility of the people, and the degree to which their misrule made possible the Medici rise to power. His *Histories* explains that, although under Maso and Niccolò da Uzzano the city "lived quietly from 1414 to 1421 ... the parties born out of the discord between the Albizzi and the Ricci ... were never eliminated." Recognizing that, the oligarchs, still fearful of their noble rivals who enjoyed popular support – the Alberti, Ricci, and Medici – harshly persecuted them with "frequent [parlamenti] and continual persecutions." Machiavelli concludes: "Thus every day these men with their sinister modes were renewing the hatred of the generality of the people; and by not watching out for harmful things because they did not fear them or by nourishing them through their envy of one another, they made the Medici family regain authority."[47]

Guicciardini's interpretation and vocabulary echo not only Machiavelli's *Florentine Histories* but also his constitutional blueprint, the *Discourse on Florentine Affairs after the Death of Lorenzo*, written while Guicciardini began the *Dialogue*. There Machiavelli began his survey of defective Florentine regimes by refuting the myth of the Albizzean regime's stability and unity. "Beginning with the alteration made at that date by Messer Maso degli Albizzi, we see that then the lawmakers intended to give her the form of a republic governed by aristocrats, but their form had so many defects that it did not last longer than forty years; and it would have been less permanent if the Visconti wars had not ensued, which kept it united."[48] Machiavelli explains the "insurrections and disturbances" that Del Nero condemned as the result of the excessive power wielded by the Signoria: "The Signoria ... had too much power, being able to dispose without appeal of the life and property of citizens, and being able to call the populace to a [parlamento]. Hence it came to be not the defender of the state but a means for causing its ruin."[49] Reiterating Del Nero's objection that the "people had no part in it at all," Machiavelli concludes: "To these failings of that constitution [established by Maso] was added another, which amounted to as much as all the rest: the people did not have their share. These conditions, altogether, caused countless injustices, and if, as I have said, external wars had not kept that government solid, it would have fallen sooner than it did" – precisely the conclusion reached by Bernardo del Nero and in virtually identical words.[50]

Throughout the *Dialogue*, Guicciardini critiqued not only the Albizzi regime specifically but also moments in Florentine history when power had been concentrated in the hands of a few. Here too there is reason to believe that Guicciardini's new ambivalent view of elite politics was the product of his intellectual encounter with Machiavelli. If we look at the one text that we definitively know that Guicciardini wrote with Machiavelli in mind – his 1530 *Considerations on the "Discourses" of Machiavelli* – we see a similarly frank acknowledgment of the dangers of *ottimati* rule. Although Guicciardini ultimately makes arguments in that text (as we will see in the next chapter) in favour of aristocratic hegemony as being beneficial to republican orders in general, he does so in dramatically more qualified terms. Instead of defining the *ottimati* in terms of their natural inclination towards prudence, wisdom, and glory, he now writes about them as a group with as much potential for harm as for good. Whereas in his first writings the *ottimati* were the solution to the shortcomings of the popular republic, he now concedes that their potential to make vital contributions to republican government depends on whether they are incorporated in ways that contain the problematic aspects of their political culture:

> In government by the optimates there is this advantage ... as they are the best qualified men in the city they rule it with more intelligence and prudence than a multitude might. And being publicly honoured they have less reason to intrigue, which they might easily do if discontented. The trouble is that as their authority is great they favour those measures useful to themselves and oppressive to the rest of the population, and as there are no bounds to men's ambition to increase their estate, they come into conflict with others like themselves, and commit acts of sedition. From this ensues the city's ruin, either through tyranny or by some other means.[51]

In the *Dialogue* Guicciardini offers a more detailed explanation of that brief but significant concession in the *Considerations* that, whatever its merits, the political culture of the *ottimati* also poses a threat to republican order. For example, Del Nero explains to Capponi that Florentine history demonstrates the inherent fragility and instability of aristocratic oligarchy in general and argues, on the basis of that observation, that the Florentines naturally incline towards one-man rule or popular rule. Any regime that falls between those two opposite ends of the political spectrum – what Del Nero calls "every middle course" – inevitably and swiftly degenerates into anarchic violence. Worse still, especially considering the elitist motives of Del Nero's interlocutors, governments of the few actually prove to be more suspicious of and lethal to the city's outstanding citizens:

> This is what experience has taught me in the past, for every time power has been held by a few citizens, the city has always been full of discord, with revolutions and plebiscites every day. There have been extremely few great citizens in these types of regimes who have not been decapitated or exiled; when after a brief time power has finally slipped from the grasp of the few, it is either restricted to one man alone or it returns to the people at large. Examples of this are so frequent and so well known that I don't want to waste time reciting them.[52]

Del Nero's explanation of why the Florentine context naturally militates against oligarchy essentially rules out the possibility of stable, unified rule by a prudential elite. He locates the problem in a combination of the general collective psychology of the Florentines and the city's longstanding obsession with the ideal of liberty. As a point of departure, stable rule would require that the governing few remain unified. However, internal divisiveness plagued all ruling elites in the city's history because their natural and intense love of liberty prevents Florentines from ever acknowledging the legitimacy of anyone else's superiority:

> We are by temperament full of strong passions and restlessness, and it is this which is the cause of discord and disunity among the ruling elite. Through their strong desire to dominate each other, they pull this person here and that one there, so that due to their own shortcomings they lose even more power. The fact that others dislike anyone being superior to themselves ensures that whenever this happens, these men are destroyed – for, as everyone in Florence who does not belong to the inner circle resents the dominance of others, it is impossible to remain great without a foundation and a supporting shoulder. And if the rulers are not in agreement, who is there who can provide this shoulder and this foundation?[53]

Those "strong passions and restlessness" are not restricted to the elite but are rather universal and irrepressible products of Florentine culture, such that rivalry and discord must inevitably result not only between those in power but also between those in power and everyone else. In short, the Florentine context limits the rule of the few to a turbulent and fitful existence at best.

Guicciardini concludes book 1 of the *Dialogue* by having Del Nero counsel moderation to his *ottimati* interlocutors and warn them that the actions of the city's leading citizens have an impact on the city's political life, for good and for ill, proportional to their prominence and status. The city's leading citizens in the past failed to recognize that special responsibility, and Del Nero holds them accountable for creating the circumstances that ushered in the city's worst regimes, both popular and tyrannical:

> Discords arise when the leading citizens in a republic – who in the end are the most potent cause of the prosperity and adversity of cities – resolve to achieve certain objectives and, failing to do so, try to upset everything to attain them, thinking more about their own ambition and desires than about the quiet of the city. It is then that these discords and divisions arise, and then that they plot sedition, which often ruins them and always causes suffering to the city. These troubles caused by civil discord give rise either to a new tyranny or to the return of the old tyrant, or they encourage depravity and licence among the people and the plebs which tumultuously shake the city. These provided the basis for the Duke of Athens' lordship, for Cosimo's return and power, and for the Ciompi storm."[54]

In the second book of the *Dialogue*, in which Del Nero outlines his theoretical and prescriptive recommendations for the Florentine constitution, we see a similar critical interrogation of the language and convictions that Guicciardini championed in his *Discorso di Logrogno* and a reaffirmation of Del Nero's doubts about the rule of the few expressed in book 1.

Pagolantonio Soderini elaborates on and amplifies Capponi's earlier idealistic arguments about the virtuous political culture of the *ottimati* and its beneficial contexts for republics ancient and modern. Early in book 1, Capponi explained that even though the sudden and unexpected intervention of Savonarola had forced the *ottimati* to establish a more popular regime than they had intended, he remained optimistic that the city would come around to their vision. In the context of renewed republican freedom the Florentines would begin to esteem the leading citizens such that they would be able to establish "good customs" and "refine things" and, little by little, restore the government to their initial aristocratic vision: "burdens, as our proverb has it, settle down while travelling."[55] In

Soderini's more elaborate defence of Capponi's optimism he reiterates every point, in almost identical language, that Guicciardini made earlier about the aristocratic appetite for glory, its beneficial consequences, and the recurring historic truth that all important accomplishments in any republican context are the product of the prudential few:

> The men of outstanding talent, who savour more than the others the taste of true honour and glory, will have greater freedom and opportunity [in the post-Medici context of 1494] to demonstrate their worth and put it to use. I set store by this, not to satisfy or foment their ambition, but for the benefit of the city. For if one examines carefully the course of all history, ancient and modern, one finds it is always the virtue of a few people that counts, for only a few are capable of such elevated deeds, and they are the ones gifted by nature with more intelligence and judgment than the others. Such men … all devote themselves to attaining true glory and true honour, which consists entirely in doing generous and praiseworthy deeds to benefit and exalt their native city … A careful reading of Greek and Roman history, as well as our own chronicles, will show that in every ordered political society the weight of the city rests upon the shoulders of such men, who in every age are few; great and glorious undertakings have never been initiated and carried out by anyone else.[56]

Just as Capponi's praise of the Albizzi oligarchy in book 1 repeated almost verbatim Guicciardini's language from *The History of Florence*, Soderini's praise of the few directly invoked Guicciardini's *Discorso di Logrogno*.

Mirroring the narrative structure of book 1, Soderini's lofty account of the politics of the few is followed by Bernardo del Nero's critical refutation. Del Nero begins by recapitulating the traditional philosophical hierarchy of ideal regimes but then subjects them to pragmatic contextual scrutiny, resulting in an inversion of the hierarchy. The philosophers praise the government of one as the best regime when the one is good, but Del Nero observes that rarely happens in present times. Most of the princes of Italy rose to power as a result of chaos, force, or factions, none of which tend to favour those one might wish to see in power. Further, in the Florentine case a benevolent rule of one is even more improbable. Owing to the Florentines' "natural appetite for liberty" and love of equality, a prince would have to rule through force rather than love and would therefore be "inevitably accompanied by many evils in substantial matters."[57]

Del Nero condemns the rule of the few more forcefully than he does the rule of the one, both in general terms and specifically for Florence. His objections here reiterate his warnings to Soderini and Capponi that their intended regime, even if Savonarola had not intervened, would necessarily have degenerated and collapsed. Del Nero explains that the rule of the few rarely turns out well in general, but in Florence it must inevitably degenerate. For the reason he returns to the Florentines' intense culture of equality: "There is little to choose between one family and another, nor are they so outstanding as to be able to differentiate between them without using force. Equality is natural to us and it is totally alien to us to see so many chiefs – apart from the fact that rivalries and discords would arise between them for endless reasons, so it would be impossible to prevent them rapidly, and in disorder, collapsing into either a tyranny or popular licentiousness." Del Nero therefore concludes that "government of the *ottimati* is the worst our city could have, worse even than government by one man, for it would share all the evils that spring from being violent, plus all those born of civil conflicts and faction."[58]

To return to the qualification offered at the outset, when Guicciardini, via Benardo del Nero, eventually offers a constitutional recommendation for Florence, he outlines an aristocratically dominated senatorial order that does not substantially differ from that outlined in the *Discorso di Logrogno*: a lifetime standard bearer of justice for continuity, a great council for elections and approval of laws, and a senate responsible for the main burden of proposing new laws and conducting diplomacy and war.

If the main conclusions remain largely consistent, however, the same cannot be said for the *Dialogue's* style of argument, political vocabulary, and interpretation of Florentine history. Guicciardini no longer builds his arguments on the assumption that the politics of the few naturally inclines towards prudence, sacrifice, glory, and the common good. In *The History of Florence* and the *Discorso di Logrogno* Guicciardini for the most part praised the Albizzi oligarchy and aristocratic oligarchies in general. Both texts championed aristocratic republicanism in Florence, the former via detailed exposition of the shortcomings of its princely and popular alternatives and the latter via overt advocacy. In the *Dialogue*, however, Guicciardini invokes those earlier convictions, only to have Bernardo del Nero refute them, at length and in detail. In the latter text he clearly wishes to demonstrate that he recognizes that the Florentine elite, far from being the answer to the problems of Florence, have been historically complicit in its political failures. In short, Guicciardini now adopts an apologetic tone and builds his larger argument in ways that appear sympathetic to and meant to engage a reader with a popular outlook and popular priorities.

We see evidence of this in Guicciardini's efforts to underscore the degree to which his preferred regime is compatible with popular priorities. Bernardo del Nero commences his lengthy exposition on the ideal Florentine constitution in book 2 with praise for popular regimes and the degree to which he has devised his proposal to preserve Florentine liberty, the first priority of all popular regimes. He begins with general remarks on the nature of popular government: "This leaves us with popular government to consider. Since it's our own and natural to us, one hopes that it can be established to function well, especially since – despite all the tyrannies and narrow governments this city has had in the past – the ancient basis of our liberties has never been eroded; on the contrary it has been preserved as though the city had always been free: this is the citizen's equality, which is the ground absolutely most suited to receive liberty."[59] Although Del Nero eventually ends up reiterating Guicciardini's traditional preference for a senatorial order, he defends it as a pragmatic concession, an acceptable compromise that will ultimately prove to be more capable of preserving the city's liberty, the defining feature of the popular regime: "[D]espite the city's fondness for liberty, it is not enough to have introduced a free regime, for it too can conceal many mistakes and disorders. It must be established in such a way that we can taste the fruits of liberty, otherwise it will be good and pleasing only in name, and in effect very often resemble a tyranny."[60]

We see further evidence of Guicciardini writing to persuade a populist reader in Del Nero's assessment of the Venetian republic. Del Nero frequently praises the Venetian government – "as fine as any free republic has ever had" – and consequently adopts many Venetian practices in his constitution.[61] On the one hand, praise of Venice should not surprise us given Guicciardini's preferences and the degree to which many of Guicciardini's aristocratic contemporaries had long been advocating the adoption of the Venetian model as the best way to preserve their status and power in Florence.[62] On the other hand, Del Nero's discussion includes a distinctive feature that is not evident in other invocations of Venice: he disputes the traditional distinction between Venice as a "government of nobles" and Florence as a "popular government." His advocacy of Venetian practices begins with the argument that "our popular government belongs to the same type as Venice's." Del Nero explains that the Venetian system's formal class vocabulary obscures the practical similarities between the Venetian and the Florentine systems. Whereas the Venetian system formally excludes the plebeians from the government, the Florentines do so in practice: "And if the plebs don't participate, they don't in ours either, since infinite numbers of workers, newcomers to the city and others, do not belong to our Council. And although it is more difficult in Venice for the ineligible to be qualified for office than with us, this is not because the type of government is different, but because within the same type they have different institutions."[63] The same parallel exists for the Venetian nobles and the Florentine *ottimati*. Del Nero explains that the Venetian requirement of noble status for holding office functions less as a way to restrict the office-holding class to a small group of nobles than as a de facto language for indicating the ruling group in general. Although noble status does not theoretically exist in Florence, the *ottimati* nevertheless generally occupy positions of power and function as a group much like their Venetian counterparts: "So if we were to call our citizens gentlemen and reserved this title for those who were qualified for office, you would find that the government of Venice is as 'popular' as ours and that ours is no less a government of optimates as theirs."[64] Bernardo concedes only one significant distinction between the two systems: the ruling group designated as Venetian "nobles" is actually larger and more inclusive than the community of Florentine *ottimati*.

Why Bernardo del Nero?

This chapter now turns to a question that all interpretations of the *Dialogue* must confront: Why does Guicciardini, an apologist for the wisdom of the prudential few, assign the voice of authority in the *Dialogue* to a parvenu like Del Nero? By the standards of the Florentine aristocracy, the Del Nero family members were virtually foreigners. They were originally from Genoa and settled in Florence in the late fourteenth century, making them relatively "new" Florentines by the standards of Florence's aristocratic clans. They became and remained minor guildsmen throughout the fifteenth century.[65] Prior to his promotion as a "powerful member of Lorenzo's inner circle," as Najemy put it, Bernardo del Nero was a used-clothes merchant – hardly an obvious candidate to choose for the *Dialogue*'s role of senior dispenser of political wisdom to members of the Capponi, Soderini, and Guicciardini families.[66] In the first pages of the *Dialogue* Guicciardini alerts us to this very aspect of Del Nero's character when Bernardo announces: "I have enjoyed a very long friendship with the Medici and I am infinitely indebted to that family. Not being of noble birth nor surrounded by relations, like you three, I have received favours from them and have been elevated and made equal to all those who would normally have preceded me in being awarded political offices and honours in the city."[67]

Del Nero's presence, in and of itself, stands out as another novel aspect of the *Dialogue* and leaves us with some puzzling questions. Why does Guicciardini, from one of the city's oldest and most illustrious houses, choose a relative outsider of low social station as the text's primary dispenser of wisdom? Why, in a text that culminates in a sustained reiteration of Guicciardini's already established preference for a republican government anchored around an aristocratic senate, does he have Del Nero engage in a devastating critique of the aristocratic chauvinism of the Albizzi regime in particular and regimes of the few in general?

These are central questions for everyone who has worked on the *Dialogue.* Alison Brown suggests that Guicciardini built the text around deliberately inscrutable ambiguities as a survival strategy for a political context in which it was not clear whether Florence's future would be Medicean or republican. In her reading, the choice of Del Nero, who was executed for conspiring against the republic on behalf of the Medici, reflects Guicciardini's tacit acknowledgment that he too had benefited from Medici power and feared republican persecution.[68] Of course, many other aristocrats had similarly benefited from the Medici, and members of the aristocratic Ridolfi and Tornabuoni houses were also executed along with Del Nero, so there is no reason that he needed to choose from among the conspirators a member of the most striking class contrast with himself. John Najemy, acknowledging the oddity of making Del Nero a vehicle for Guicciardini's views, speculates that Guicciardini was dramatizing the contradictions of the elite's relationship to the Medici: on the one hand, supporting the family for protection against the ambitions of the people, but on the other, traditionally preferring a mixed constitution led by them.[69] While this explanation reconciles book 1's praise of the Medici with book 2's aristocratic republic, it does not address the choice of a plebeian to stand in for a proud and famously status-conscious member of one of the city's greatest houses.

Gennaro Sasso indirectly hints at a Machiavellian connection to the character of Bernardo del Nero. In Sasso's analysis, Del Nero exposes his aristocratic interlocutors' understanding of the Albizzi regime as more aristocratic self-serving nostalgia than reality by demonstrating its incompatibility with the concrete historical realities of the regime.[70] Put in terms familiar to any reader of Machiavelli's *Prince,* Del Nero goes directly "to the truth of the matter [*verità effetuale*] as facts show it rather than with any fanciful notion."[71] In terms of method, Del Nero follows in the footsteps of *The Prince.*

Context from the 1520s adds further Machiavellian connections. Machiavelli's correspondence during the 1520s – also the years of close contact with Guicciardini – reveals a close relationship between Machiavelli and the Del Nero family, which was also part of the circle of contacts Machiavelli shared with Guicciardini and Francesco Vettori. Machiavelli was related to Francesco del Nero – his "honoured brother-in-law," in Machiavelli's words – through his wife, Marietta Corsini, sister to Francesco del Nero's wife.[72] Francesco del Nero was also an official of the

Florentine Studio that offered Machiavelli, at the behest of Clement VII, the formal commission to write the *Florentine Histories*.[73] Machiavelli was close to Francesco del Nero: he wrote to him often and sent him gifts, and letters to Machiavelli from Filippo de' Nerli and Francesco Vettori mention Francesco del Nero as a mutual friend. Francesco del Nero's letters to Machiavelli suggest that Francesco fraternized regularly with Guicciardini and Vettori.[74] Machiavelli was evidently also close to Francesco del Nero's brother, Agostino, whose letter to Machiavelli addressed him as "honoured foster father."[75] In addition to a shared circle of mutual friendships, Guicciardini, and to a lesser extent Machiavelli, must have been in nearly constant professional contact with Francesco and Agostino del Nero after Clement VII had joined the Holy League of Cognac. The Del Nero brothers played major roles in Clement VII's treasury, raising Florentine funds for the war effort that were ultimately transferred to Guicciardini, head of the papal armies.[76]

Given the close personal and political connections between Machiavelli, Guicciardini, and Francesco del Nero, Guicciardini's choice of Bernardo del Nero as the *Dialogue*'s central protagonist suggests that he had this community in mind as the *Dialogue*'s readers. We can answer many questions – in ways compatible with the arguments by Brown and Najemy – about Guicciardini's choice of Del Nero if we conclude that he was speaking directly to Machiavelli. His protagonist was politically experienced, an insider of the Medici regime, and therefore well positioned to speak with authority, but he was also an artisan whose world view and rise to power were fundamentally at odds with aristocratic politics. Unsurprisingly, then, throughout book 1 Del Nero repeatedly and at length deconstructs the pieties of Florentine aristocratic wisdom, grafting specific Machiavellian critiques of the Albizzi oligarchy onto his populist interrogation of Florentine aristocratic pieties. Machiavelli's texts from this period share similar arguments and even similar wording to Del Nero's utterances. Guicciardini's choice of Del Nero must be an early signal of the text's novel populist elements and a specific invocation of the circle that Guicciardini shared with Machiavelli.

Guicciardini's Impact on Machiavelli's *Florentine Histories*

By way of conclusion we return to the friendship between Machiavelli and Guicciardini and what we might conclude about its impact on the historical and political writings of these two towering figures of the late Renaissance. Analysing the correspondence between Machiavelli and Guicciardini and the one-sided degree to which almost all of the substantive political commentary comes from Machiavelli, Robert Black speculates that Guicciardini always disagreed and was disinclined to engage in any detail. For this reason, Black concludes that "their correspondence – lively and significant as it was – did not rise to the overarching unity and profound dialogue characteristics of the earlier Machiavelli-Vettori correspondence."[77] If we limit the discussion strictly to correspondence, Black's conclusion is indisputable – for whatever reason, Guicciardini did not concede substantive points or counter-argue at length in his letters to Machiavelli. This chapter, however, has demonstrated compelling textual evidence that Guicciardini took Machiavelli's politics seriously, invoked his language explicitly, and tried to demonstrate considerable recognition of and sympathy with Machiavelli's scepticism about elite politics and its historic role in Florence's troubled history of factional discord. What appear to be Bernardo del Nero's inconsistencies in his discussion of the politics of the few should be read as a dialogue with Machiavelli intended to persuade him that Guicciardini's senatorial order would be different from the corrupt oligarchies of the past. Through their friendship, intellectual sparring, and mutual respect, Machiavelli evidently tempered the intensity of Guicciardini's aristocratic convictions and persuaded him that the people merited a significant role in Florentine politics.

If we accept that his friendship with Machiavelli pushed Guicciardini in new directions and compelled him to alter his language and rhetorical strategies, we should consider the possibility that Guicciardini's friendship may have had a similar effect on Machiavelli. As John Najemy shows in his analysis of Machiavelli's correspondence with Francesco Vettori and of the composition of *The Prince*, Machiavelli's language and arguments were driven in notable ways by his friendship with Vettori and their contrasting convictions about political life. Machiavelli clearly had a robust capacity for intense intellectually engaged friendship throughout his life. In a 1527 letter to Vettori shortly before his death, Machiavelli proclaimed his friendship with Guicciardini in the strongest possible terms: "I love Messer Francesco Guicciardini, I love my native city."[78] Can we identify the presence of Guicciardini in Machiavelli's writings from the 1520s, the period of their friendship?

I argue not only that we can and should but also that doing so helps resolve an interpretive dilemma regarding Machiavelli's late writings. Recent studies by Robert Black, James Hankins, me, and others have stressed the way in which Machiavelli's later writings – the *Florentine Histories*, most significantly – display a social and political conservatism at odds with *The Prince* and *The Discourses on Livy*.[79] These scholars point to many conventional aspects of Machiavelli's *Histories* that contrast with his earlier position of radical distance from received wisdom; for example, Machiavelli praises unity and condemns tumults, he shows repeated and evident concern for the common good, and he faults the Duke of Athens for wishing to be feared rather than loved. The clearest evidence that these scholars adduce, however, in support of Machiavelli's late conservative turn is his surprising and repeated utterances about the fickle and unreasonable nature of the Florentine people, the martial generosity of the nobles, and the nobles' willingness to compromise. Nowhere does Machiavelli more plainly contradict his earlier favourable contrast of the people's rationality and constancy with the nobles' destabilizing sense of entitlement. Explaining this transformation, Robert Black points to the simple fact of Machiavelli's improved circumstances: now that he was close to the ruling group, a recipient of Medici patronage, and a successful playwright, Machiavelli was able to accept the status quo against which he had railed so provocatively in *The Prince* and *The Discourses,* texts written after his political humiliation and during a period of political ostracization. Small wonder that Machiavelli in a Medici commission was now expressing establishment views entirely typical of the Florentine *ottimati.*

John McCormick, however, has recently raised some powerful objections to the view that Machiavelli abandoned his populist agenda. He has shown a recurring contradiction throughout the *Histories* in which Machiavelli's own narrative contradicts his formal proclamations about the nature of nobles and people in general. When Machiavelli describes nobles and people directly, his adjectives – *generous, immoderate, reasonable, injurious, unjust* – add up to a wholesale rejection of the categories of social analysis in *The Prince* and *The Discourses.* However, when Machiavelli shows the nobles and people in action, their deeds do not often demonstrate the validity of those adjectives but rather bear out the conduct and attitudes that Machiavelli had attributed to them in his early works. As McCormick puts it, "it is worth asking whether Machiavelli's adjectives match his verbs when he discusses the political actions of the Florentine nobles and people."[80] For example, Machiavelli announces in sweeping terms that the Florentine people are unwilling to share office, but in many chapters he shows us the people earnestly engaging in a power-sharing arrangement with the nobles. Elsewhere he laments that the Florentine people's triumph over the nobility resulted in the city's loss of "arms and generosity," yet he had earlier shown notable examples of noble cowardice and martial incompetence. On the basis of these and other examples, McCormick concludes that Machiavelli's *Histories,* read astutely and alert to its manifest contradictions, demonstrate broad continuity with *The Prince* and the *Discourses.* If Machiavelli was indeed in these years "the voice of the Florentine establishment," as Black would have it, it is difficult to understand why he surreptitiously embedded an alternate narrative in his *Histories* that bore out the accuracy of his earlier populist arguments.[81]

McCormick's demonstration that the *Histories* displays an incompatibility between verbs and adjectives invites an esoteric reading that raises a significant question: Why would Machiavelli camouflage opinions that he had earlier delivered in provocatively plain terms? McCormick's explanation stresses the politically charged context of the early 1520s in which Medici rule and their aristocratic lieutenants were deeply and bitterly resented by many Florentines – as much as three quarters of the city, according to the chronicler Bartolomeo Cerretani.[82] Machiavelli's rapprochement with the Medici and their patronage of him both as the city's formal historian and as a constitutional theorist unfolded in this potentially explosive context of open mistrust and suspicion between the Medici and the Florentine people. In such a context, McCormick infers, Machiavelli could not advocate for the people and against the nobles with the transparency that was evident when he was writing as a rejected outsider to Florentine politics. Given the urgency and determination with which he attempted to recover his lost political standing, the stakes were simply too high for his earlier provocative style. Neither did he wish to renounce his core convictions that new princes and well-ordered republics should look to the people as natural allies, hence his covert writing in the *Histories*.

However politically loaded the context, it is hard to accept that Machiavelli would shy away from delivering politically unpalatable opinions to the Medici, given how extensively he did just that on other more potentially explosive topics. At a similarly critical moment in 1512, before his fall from grace but after the Medici's triumphant return to Florence, his *Memorandum* warned the Medici that the very aristocrats who had engineered their return had their own interests at heart and should not be trusted – a risky move that backfired tragically. In the Medici-commissioned *Histories*, Machiavelli did not shy away from impugning the methods and motives of the founder of the family's power in Florence, Cosimo *il vecchio* de' Medici. After elaborating in detail in the introduction to book 7 on the dangers of citizens acquiring influence through private methods and partisans, Machiavelli went on in the following chapter to declare that Cosimo de' Medici rose to power by precisely those private ways and with extensive partisans.[83] His treatment of the fifteenth-century Medici – not only Cosimo but also Piero and Lorenzo – frequently and openly condemned their rule as paranoid, violent, and unstable, as emphasized by several scholars.[84] Reflecting on the *Histories*' numerous provocative passages, Carlo Dionisotti concludes that it was a "miracle" that Machiavelli was not punished.[85] Guicciardini's *Dialogue* may have recommended exterminating the entire Medici family, but it was a private text. Machiavelli made his controversial comments while looking a Medici pope directly in the eye.

As we saw, Machiavelli's related constitutional proposal to the Medici, composed in the same tense context, was no less risky. He plainly announced to the Medici that maintaining their rule in any regime other than a republic anchored by the Great Council would be highly perilous owing to the people's widespread dislike of their presence. Of all the people solicited by the Medici for proposals on anchoring their power, he was alone in advocating a republican system. The risks that Machiavelli took in his critical analysis of Clement VII's illustrious ancestors, his political advice to Leo X to plan on the family's obsolescence, and his frank declarations of the Florentine people's bitter enmity towards them were far greater than those of historicizing a positive view of the people and a critical view of the nobles in thirteenth- and fourteenth-century Florentine history.

For these reasons it seems improbable that Machiavelli began to utter insincere comments about nobles and people typical of the Florentine aristocracy because he feared the consequences of a more transparent approach. On the one hand, fear rarely seems to have played a role in Machiavelli's life and writings. On the other, friendship clearly played a powerful role. Given Machiavelli's declaration in the last year of his life that "I love Messer Francesco Guicciardini," his friendship with Guicciardini must have been among his most important. Their correspondence indicates that they discussed the composition of the *Histories* and that Machiavelli looked to Guicciardini for strategic and historical advice. We know that Machiavelli read Guicciardini's *History of Florence*.[86] Although they differed in the class orientation of their ideal regime, they were both republicans and Florentine patriots. Given the near open hostility between the two and the considerable political gulf that separated them during the Soderini years, the fact of their friendship alone demonstrates a mutual intellectual respect that transcended their equally mutual class prejudice.

This chapter has shown the impact of their discussions of Florentine politics and history on Guicciardini's *Dialogue*, his first substantial text written in the context of friendship with Machiavelli. That text certainly invites an esoteric reading because it ultimately argues for an aristocratic republic, but its advocate and theorist, Bernardo del Nero, paradoxically elaborates at length on the theoretical and historical shortcomings of the politics of the few. Guicciardini must have been writing with Machiavelli in mind as his reader, anticipating Machiavelli's objections, communicating respect for them, and therefore implicitly arguing that his ideal senatorial order was the product of a shared awareness of the potential flaws of aristocratic hegemony. If we envision Guicciardini as Machiavelli's primary reader for his *Histories*, we are able to see why Machiavelli's verbs and adjectives do not always match up in his discussion of the few and the many. Machiavelli still retained his earlier populism but wanted to offer an interpretation of Florentine history that acknowledged the historical legitimacy of Guicciardini's aristocratic interpretation of Florentine history and that offered moments of agreement. The apparent contradictions in these two major texts must reflect an ongoing dialogue between Machiavelli and Guicciardini in which they privileged common ground rather than distance.

In the next chapter we turn to the only text that Guicciardini wrote formally and explicitly addressing Machiavelli's political thought, his *Considerations on the "Discourses of Machiavelli."* Much like the *Ricordi*, the *Considerations* do not feature Guicciardini's habitually cryptic instinct to argue both sides of a question but rather consist of direct statements intended to refute the validity of Machiavelli's populist republicanism. Even there, however, in his strident refutation of major arguments in Machiavelli's *Discourses*, we will see that Guicciardini continued to display deep affinities with Machiavelli's critique of noble culture and approval of popular politics.

Chapter Five

Cognitive Dissonance in Guicciardini's *Considerations on the "Discourses of Machiavelli"*

This chapter considers Guicciardini's *Considerations on the "Discourses of Machiavelli,"* the text most routinely invoked to demonstrate Guicciardini's rejection of Machiavellian political thought. At first reading, such invocations make perfect textual sense. Of the thirty-nine *discorsi* that Guicciardini discusses, he agrees with Machiavelli fewer than five times and always grudgingly. Without a doubt, Guicciardini's overall intent is systematic rejection of Machiavelli's account of Roman history and the abstract principles that he derives from it. While we have abundantly encountered in previous chapters Guicciardini's love of nuance, contextual equivocation, and exploration of both sides of any question, the *Considerations* stands out in Guicciardini's oeuvre for its uncharacteristically unequivocal declarations: "It is advanced too absolutely," "I do not understand," "I do not therefore see," "On the contrary," "I do not agree with him," "I would lean rather to the opposite view," and "The *Discourse* is very far from the truth," to quote only a small selection of his oppositional statements.

Additional readings, however, reveal that Guicciardini retained his characteristic ambivalence about his own aristocratic preferences and continued to share several of Machiavelli's core convictions, even while ostensibly disagreeing. The *Considerations* intends to draw sharp lines of division between Guicciardini's esteem for aristocratic prudence and Machiavelli's contrasting populism, which Guicciardini argues is rooted in a flawed reading of Roman history and a blinkered perception of populist politics in general. To refute Machiavelli, Guicciardini engages in a sustained dissenting reading of Roman history. He also combines his considerable experience as a ruler and the supporting authority of tradition to portray Machiavelli's populism as both an isolated case and confused. But Guicciardini's reasoning in each of those three categories of analysis – seemingly inadvertently – betrays the same doubts about the merits of aristocratic rule and the same reluctant acknowledgment of popular rationality and moderation that we witnessed more overtly in his earlier texts. Whereas most scholars point to the *Considerations* as definitive proof of Guicciardini's anti-Machiavellian sentiments, the fact that Guicciardini continued to exhibit those same doubts even while attempting a systematic refutation suggests instead that the *Considerations* is the best evidence that Guicciardini's characteristic equivocation about his preferences was not a rhetorical strategy but rather a genuine, sustained acknowledgment of common ground with Machiavelli's political thought (even while he denied it).

By way of contextual point of departure, this chapter opens with a review of the unique context – Guicciardini's recent elevation by the Medici to the status of an Italian prince, followed by his first taste of professional catastrophe and persecution by a populist regime – that likely inspired his motivation to condemn Machiavelli's republicanism as confused and misguided. The second section assesses Guicciardini's main quarrels with Machiavelli's reading of Roman history and the ways in which Guicciardini's optimal mixed regime differed substantially in its conception of the nature of nobles and people. The third section revisits Guicciardini's arguments about Rome to show that his reasoning, despite his dissenting intentions, continued to align in substantial ways with major Machiavellian arguments, in some cases even amplifying them. The fourth and final section summarizes Guicciardini's invocation of authority and tradition as proof of Machiavelli's flawed thinking, but shows that, in small but significant and revealing ways, Machiavelli's influence had altered Guicciardini's position.

From Medici Prince to Persecuted Victim

Guicciardini's systematic rejection of Machiavelli's republicanism in his *Considerations* and his atypical reluctance formally to critique his own preferences must stem from two major contextual factors. The first is the degree to which Guicciardini's career was tethered to the Medici family, whose control of the papacy under Leo X from 1513 to 1521 and under Clement VII from 1523 to 1534 elevated its power beyond the confines of its traditional primus inter pares role in Florentine politics. Before Guicciardini's first appointment in 1516 as a papal governor, his political career had followed the traditional *cursus honorum* of the Florentine republican elite – more distinguished than many, perhaps, but still squarely within Florentine civic, republican traditions. His ability and willingness in his early texts to reflect upon how the self-regarding pieties of aristocratic culture might appear violently transgressive from a popular perspective corresponded to political offices that defined him first and foremost in terms of traditional republican government (even if it was unofficially dominated by the Medici): in 1508 he, along with his father, participated in his first *pratica*, a meeting of esteemed citizens summoned to provide informal counsel to the Signoria; in 1512 he was appointed the city's ambassador to Spain; in August of 1514 he was elected to the Otto di guardia; and in September of the same year he was elected to the Signoria.[1] As John Najemy has persuasively argued, however exclusionary and narrow aristocratic regimes may have been, since the Ordinances of Justice of 1215 the elite had defined themselves as humble citizen servants of the republic, *patres conscripti*, and celebrated the shared values of citizenship, even if in name more than in substance.

After 1516, however, the Medici began to reward Guicciardini with offices that defined him more as a prince than as a citizen. In 1516 Pope Leo appointed him governor of Modena, and in 1517, governor of Reggio; in 1521 he assumed command of papal forces against the French as commissary general; in 1524 Pope Clement appointed him president of the Romagna and two years later entrusted him to combat Charles V as lieutenant general of the papal armies. Between his military authority and presidency, Guicciardini was effectively the reigning monarch of the northern papal states. Given his ambition (evident from his school years in which his classmates nicknamed him Alcibiades) and pride, it is difficult to imagine that such postings did not introduce a new self-conception that was incompatible with the citizen's world view. Nor need we infer that new world view. Guicciardini amply confirmed the transition from citizen to prince in a self-portrait from his presidency of the Romagna:

> If you had seen messer Francesco in the Romagna ... with his house full of tapestries, silver, servants thronged from the entire province where – since everything was completely referred to him – no one, from the pope down, recognized anyone as his superior; surrounded by a guard of more than a hundred landsknechts, with halberdiers and other cavalry in attendance ... never riding out with less than one hundred or one hundred and fifty horse; immersed in governing bodies, titles, "Most illustrious lords," you would not have recognized him as your fellow citizen ... but considering the importance of his affairs, his boundless authority, the very great domain and government under him, his court and his pomp, he would have seemed on a par with any duke rather than lesser princes.[2]

The uncharacteristically dogmatic, elite chauvinism of the *Considerations* surely must reflect, at least in part, his new persona as a prince ruling over subjects, rather than as a citizen sharing power with equals. As Machiavelli acknowledged in the preface to *The Prince*, to view the nature of princes one must have the perspective of the people; whereas to know the people, one must have the perspective of a prince. By the time Guicciardini was composing the *Considerations*, his perspective had shifted unequivocally from citizen to prince. He no longer viewed the people as a community with whom he might rub elbows in the marketplace and city hall, possessing at the very least the potential for rationality and prudence, but rather as an inherently destabilizing force. Instead of drawing on his Florentine experiences, which underpin the nuanced portraits of class conflict in chapters 3 and 5, his *Considerations* condemns the people based entirely on his experiences as a prince, as we will soon see in detail.

The second major contextual factor accounting for Guicciardini's rejection of Machiavelli's *Discourses* was Guicciardini's colossal and unprecedented reversal of fortune in 1527 caused by the sack of Rome, which led to his persecution by a radical popular regime in Florence. Clement VII's incarceration by Charles V in Castel Sant'Angelo imploded Medici power in Rome, triggering in turn an anti-Medici revolt in Florence that put an end to the staggeringly impressive political good fortune that Guicciardini had hitherto exclusively enjoyed. Effectively stripped of all the offices and titles acquired in service of the Medici, he suddenly lost his princely identity and was compelled to return to Florence as a citizen viewed unsurprisingly by the new republican regime as possessing questionable loyalties. As he correctly anticipated in his *Accusatoria* and *Defensoria*, texts written at his rural villa in 1527, Guicciardini foresaw that he would likely face persecution for having so successfully and faithfully served the Medici, and specifically for his loyalty to Clement VII during the first, early signs of anti-Medici agitation in Florence.[3] Although leading elite families led the revolt of 1527, much as they had in 1494, popular forces inspired by Savonarola's memory soon overtook control of the regime, and their intransigence towards negotiation with Clement led to a protracted siege that only heightened the extremism of the city's internal politics. As John Najemy summarized it, "At each stage of the conflict, *ottimati* voices grew weaker and more suspect to a radicalized popolo that refused compromise with Clement, revived the memory of Savonarola and his vision of the holy republic, and put a huge portion of the city's population under arms in a resurrected militia," along with reopening the Great Council and in 1528, for the second time, proclaiming Christ the king of Florence.[4] Although Guicciardini benefited from a respectful relationship with the gonfalonier Niccolò Capponi, the regime nevertheless singled him out, along with other prominent former Mediceans, for punitive taxation and fines. After Clement had persuaded Charles V to restore the Medici to power, the city's populist regime increasingly viewed Guicciardini as a potential enemy of the state. Fearing possible imprisonment, he fled the city in 1529 to join Clement in Rome, beginning the *Considerations* as he travelled south. By 1530 the republican regime had declared him an exile and seized his property.[5]

Although the populist government was inspired first and foremost by Savonarolism, the two institutional centrepieces of the regime – the restoration of the Great Council and the establishment of a citizen militia – were also vocally and recently championed by Machiavelli. Guicciardini clearly saw its punitive radicalism as an inevitable consequence of the class conflict that Machiavelli had praised in the *Discourses* and as a raw refutation of Machiavelli's high estimation of the people's capacity for prudence and moderation. We see this in the frequency with which Guicciardini's quarrel with Machiavelli in the *Considerations* invoked his own recent persecution by the third republic and faulted its excesses with clear parallels to his own experience. For example, in his reflections on *discorso* 1.10, in which Machiavelli specially condemns the founders of tyrannies (clearly a fraught topic for Guicciardini in 1530 as he worked with Clement and the imperial army to restore the Medici to Florence), he autobiographically observes that some so-called free regimes behave so licentiously that they compel good citizens to incline in tyrannical directions:

> The example may be given of our own city where after the change of government of 1526, some distinguished citizens were prosecuted and penalized, and, finally, on the arrival of the Prince of Orange, were forced either to disobey the orders of the Eight to stay in Florence under pain of rebellion, or to remain with the risk of being assassinated, or at the very least the certainty of being arrested. These were forced either to desire the change of a government, which, under colour of liberty was tyrannous and destructive of the liberty of the nation, or to allow themselves in silence, and unjustly, to be deprived of their country and their possessions."[6]

In his response to *discorso* 1.16 and the prevalence of sons of Brutus in newly established republics, Guicciardini again faulted the excesses of the popular regime for driving otherwise freedom-loving citizens towards the Medici: "The harsh, indiscriminate persecution in 1526 of those who had been their friends, made many desire their return who otherwise would have hated them just as much as anyone else did."[7]

Guicciardini began the *Considerations* in the wake of his first experience of grave misfortune and persecution by forces that he clearly associated with Machiavelli's populist preferences. The severity of his treatment of the regime's leaders that same year, after the combined papal and imperial forces had toppled the republic and re-established Medici authority, further suggests that for the entire duration of the composition of *Considerations* Guicciardini was militantly and vengefully stewing over what he perceived as his outrageous and unjust treatment by an ideologically vindictive *popolo*. Guicciardini arrived as a conqueror in Florence, "the pope's enforcer," in Najemy's words, and wrote back to Clement that "we have made a good beginning, having detained all those rogues and begun to examine Carduccio, and thus we shall continue, for indeed, if one wishes to put this state on a proper footing, mild measures are useless."[8] Several leading members of the republic were executed: some, like Francesco Carducci, were tortured and decapitated, while others were more discreetly eliminated, such as Rafaello Girolami, who died under mysterious circumstances in his jail cell, and Benedetto da Foiano, who Clement starved to death in Rome. In the imposition of banishments and exiles, Guicciardini was "merciless beyond all others," in Roberto Ridolfi's words, earning him the nickname "Ser Cerretieri," the despised Duke of Athens's still more despised hatchet man. The historian Benedetto Varchi, a supporter of the republic and a victim of Guicciardini's proscriptions, recorded that in his summary justice Guicciardini revealed himself as "the cruellest and most enraged of all," a position that Guicciardini justified as necessary because "we [*ottimati*] have as our enemy an entire people."[9]

Contrasting Views of Rome

In terms of political theory, Guicciardini's most substantial quarrel with Machiavelli's *Discourses* concerns their prioritization, respectively, of unity and social conflict. Machiavelli broke with tradition in asserting, both in *The Prince* and the *Discourses*, that conflict was an inevitable aspect of political life. All states, whether princely or republican, were made up of two groups, the nobles and the people, whose natures – the former's instinct to oppress and the latter's desire for freedom from oppression – ensured a permanent state of conflict. Rather than deploring humanity's irrepressible capacity for conflict, Machiavelli breaks further with tradition in the *Discourses* when he declares: "In every republic there are two opposed factions, that of the people and that of the rich, and ... all the laws made in favour of liberty result from their discord."[10]

Guicciardini shared Machiavelli's instinct to interpret politics in binary terms of nobles and people but disputed the inevitability of their conflict and vigorously rejected the notion that conflict could ever have beneficial consequences. Guicciardini – along with virtually all ancient and Renaissance political thought – instead championed unity as the highest ideal in political life. Rome's recurring social conflict was therefore a sure indicator for Guicciardini of a flawed constitution and an argument against adopting their methods and values in the present.

Much of Guicciardini's quarrel unfolds in his rebuttal to *discorso* 1.4 in which Machiavelli had argued that the struggles between the people and the Roman senate were the cause of the republic's power. Guicciardini shifts the focus by considering the historical circumstances that caused Rome's internal dissensions, a question that Machiavelli's axiomatic assumption about the universality of conflict largely avoids. The conflict between senators and plebeians was not the product of universal tendencies but rather the result of avoidable errors in political judgment, first in the formal division of classes into plebeian and patrician and second in the allocation of office-holding rights exclusively to the latter: "The cause of the disunity of Rome between patricians and plebs was that the classes of the city were divided, that is, on the one hand all the patricians, on the other all the plebs ... if there had not been from the beginning this distinction between patricians and plebs ... those divisions would not have arisen."[11]

Although Guicciardini does not state it explicitly, he suggests that in its early history the Roman republic was not a mixed constitution, his ultimate ideal, because it did not include the people. It eventually did and therefore ultimately achieved the balance that Guicciardini saw as the chief attribute of the mixed regime, but because of its initial political imbalance the route necessarily involved frequent tumults and "seditious movements" that would have destroyed the republic were it not for Rome's exceptional martial virtue. He concludes his counter-argument with the observation that "rarely, if ever, has a republic attained from the beginning a perfect order," a sly, indirect critique of Machiavelli's purpose in book 1 of the *Discourses*, given its overall praise of republican Rome's first founders, first laws, and first religion.[12]

Guicciardini thus implicitly agrees with Machiavelli that Rome arrived at the ideal mixed constitution as a result of dissension. His larger quarrel is with Machiavelli's extrapolation from the Roman example that dissension is a necessary – indeed salutary – method to attain and sustain a mixed constitution. The two both championed the superiority of the mixed regime but they used the term in radically different ways. For Machiavelli, the mixed constitution balanced a permanent state of conflict between nobles and people via class-specific institutions for each group, hence his conclusion that "those enmities rising between the people and Senate must be borne, being taken as an evil necessary to the attainment of Roman greatness."[13] For Guicciardini, the mixed constitution resolved the problem of conflict by harmoniously incorporating the one, the few, and the many. Since the entire purpose of the mixed regime is the sublimation of conflict, Guicciardini reasons, any regime plagued by chronic conflict cannot provide an exemplary method, hence his dismissal of Rome as a model: "I do not therefore see that the Romans could not have organized the state so that plots and disorders need not arise between the senate and the plebs. I rather judge it to have been quite easy ..."[14] His version of the mixed regime diminishes, rather than formalizes, political distinctions between social groups, a point he elaborates in his reply to Machiavelli's argument that the people make better guardians of liberty: "I would like the protection of liberty against any seeking to oppress the republic, to belong to all, always avoiding as far as possible the distinction between nobles and plebeians."[15]

In his reply to *discorso* 1.2, Guicciardini outlines his vision of how to construct a harmonious mixed regime from the outset, thereby avoiding the dangerous methods made necessary by Rome's initial artificial divisions. Reiterating arguments he had earlier made in his *Discorso di Logrogno* and *Dialogue on the Government of Florence*, Guicciardini anchors his ideal regime in an aristocratic senatorial order whose composition, crucially, must be meritocratically porous. He dismisses regimes with circumscribed aristocracies (another critique of Venice) as inherently prone to corruption: "If they are optimates by birth and not by election, from prudent and good men at first, affairs soon fall into the hands of imprudent and wicked ones."[16] Guicciardini always possessed the traditionally aristocratic conviction that ambitious and talented people are by definition few and the inner circle upon whom all regimes vitally depend. However, as a proud citizen of a republican city state with a relatively high degree of social mobility and no legally defined noble class, he recognized that such people could be found among all social ranks. He advocates for an optimate elite who "must not be drawn always from the same lines and families, but from the whole body of the city, from all who according to the law are qualified to take part in the magistrature." From this group he appoints a senate whose members are "very numerous so as to be more easily accepted by the others who will be able to hope that they or their house may succeed when vacancies occur. And also with a large number there is hope that all those who deserve to may enter."[17] As optimate status is open to all and the optimate senate has many seats, and therefore many opportunities for people to serve, Guicciardini expects his system to distribute rewards sufficiently broadly to achieve unity, a point he defends with a Spartan historical precedent: "The Spartans had optimates of this kind, drawn not from a special class of men but from the whole body of the city; the Romans had them, but differently, for with them the patricians were from the first the optimates and the rest formed the plebs, which was the origin of all their seditious movements."[18]

Their contrasting conceptions of the ideal mixed regime resulted in large part from their equally contrasting conceptions of nobles and people. Machiavelli built much of his political thought on axiomatic assumptions about the two groups' permanent, universal dispositions, which placed them in a state of oppositional conflict. In contrast to Guicciardini and all his contemporaries, he defined them in terms of instinctive collective psychological tendencies that, for the most part, implicated the elite as a political problem to which the people were the solution.[19] Machiavelli viewed noble culture as inherently problematic: as a group the nobles oppressed the people, behaved violently, and did not recognize authority above their own, while as individuals each thought himself a prince in his own right and therefore always fought other nobles for pre-eminence and in princely contexts against his own rulers. The people by contrast wished merely to live unmolested and secure in the enjoyment of their possessions. In chapter 9 of *The Prince*, Machiavelli argues on the basis of these observations that shrewd princes should ally with the people against their nobility: "a ruler cannot creditably and without injury to others satisfy the rich, but certainly he can satisfy the people, because the people's object is more creditable than that of the rich ... not to be oppressed."[20] The same observations underpin the numerous chapters in book 1 of the *Discourses* that attribute a critical role to the people in preserving Rome's freedom and power, such as the tribunes' protection of Rome's liberty, the people's superior capacity for judgment, Rome's popular tribunals, and of course the people's formidable military skills. Whether in a republican or a princely context, it followed that all regimes benefited from capitalizing on that conflict by using the people to contain the potential for discord caused by elite ambition.

Expressing the far more conventional establishment view, Guicciardini conceives of nobles and people in terms of a contrasting capacity for prudence and reason that requires the assigning of active decision-making power to the former and passive ratification power to the latter. The nobles are the fulcrum of Guicciardini's ideal state because of their capacity for prudence, constancy, intelligence, and boldness. He elaborates his view in his responses to three of Machiavelli's *discorsi*. In his reply to *discorso* 2.2 on the mixed constitution, Guicciardini considers the advantages of governments of the few over the one and the many: "In government by the optimates there is this advantage, that being many they can less easily set up a tyranny than one man could. As they are the best qualified men in the city they rule it with more intelligence and prudence than a multitude might."[21] He reiterates this view of governments of the few in his reply to *discorso* 1.5: "But if it were necessary to give a city a government either of nobles or of plebs, I believe it would be better to choose the nobles, for ... they have greater prudence and good qualities."[22] And finally, in his reply to *discorso* 1.40's consideration of the decemvirate and the respective contributions that nobles and people offer to aspiring tyrants, Guicciardini declares that tyrants "who have with them the nobility, enjoy support more vigorous, efficacious, and bold, for the nobility does not change its mind as often or as easily for trifling reasons as do the people." Owing to these positive qualities, Guicciardini assigns them exclusive jurisdiction over virtually all aspects of weighty political deliberation: "Their function must be to discuss and decide those matters where human prudence is most needed, that is, wars, peace, negotiations with princes, and all matters essential for the preservation and expansion of the state."[23]

Guicciardini's *Considerations* frequently vilifies the people as inconstant, irrational, and informed only by superficial appearances, hence his constitution's exclusion of them from participation in important deliberations, a consistent feature of all his writing. For example, in his reply to *discorso* 1.2, Guicciardini declares that "the people, on account of their ignorance, are not capable of deciding matters of great importance ... [they are] easily deceived and misled by ambitious men and traitors."[24] He offers another variation in his counter to *discorso* 1.7: the people "are not able to understand or examine well, and are easily moved by rumour and false calumny."[25] In his response to *discorso* 1.47, even while agreeing with Machiavelli that the people responsibly and capably distribute honours and offices, Guicciardini still avers that the populace "does not examine or distinguish with subtlety, so that it is often wrong ... It believes false rumours, it acts from frivolous motives, and in fact its ignorance is much more dangerous than the decisions of a few may be."[26] Guicciardini asserted such reservations about popular judgment throughout his writings.

Within these reservations, however, Guicciardini introduces a new and yet more pointed challenge to Machiavelli's view of noble culture. Without anywhere declaring a thesis, the *Considerations* implicitly portrays the people as vindictive aggressors who instigate the noble conduct that Machiavelli deplores and mistakenly attributes to internal rather than external causes. In his response to *discorso* 1.29, in which Machiavelli argues that princes are more prone than the people to ingratitude, Guicciardini attributes to the people – in addition to lack of perspicacity – an inherently destructive resentment and envy of excellence, the chief etymological characteristic of aristocracy: "As for envy it arises much more easily in men of the people for whom every kind of eminence of birth, riches, valour, or reputation, is usually unwelcome. There is nothing they dislike as much as seeing other citizens higher than themselves and they always want to pull them down."[27] He puts the same accusation in different terms in his analysis of the ideal mixed regime in his response to *discorso* 1.2: "[The people] are fond of persecuting well qualified citizens for they need novelty and disturbances."[28]

In his reply to *discorso* 1.7, in which Machiavelli argues for the necessity of popular tribunals through which to bring charges against citizens conspiring against the republic, Guicciardini outlines one method by which he fears the people will "pull down" those eminent in birth, riches, and reputation. Although he agrees in principle with the necessity of those tribunals, he alters their composition to ensure they do not become vehicles through which the people might persecute their betters, causing them to retaliate in ways injurious to the city: "One must also be careful that these should be so arranged that innocent people may not be easily vexed or punished. For besides injustice it is also harmful to the city, for where this danger threatens the nobility and upper classes, and they live with this perpetual fear, they naturally become discontented, and the discontent of the powerful becomes dangerous in many ways to the republic."[29]

In his rebuttal to Machiavelli's criticism of fortresses as a weak source of security in *discorso* 1.24, Guicciardini dismisses the very possibility of Machiavelli's superior source – the people's good will. Guicciardini again portrays the people as malicious aggressors who compel violent treatment by their rulers:

> If [the people] loved their prince when they were well treated, I agree that fortresses would be useless for any prince who ruled well ... But considering how often peoples even when well treated behave unreasonably, how much they like change, how powerful the memory of a former prince may be once they are under a new power, how great their appetite for freedom if they have been used to it, and how often for this or other reasons a prince or tyrant is obliged to rule his citizens or subjects with some offence to them ... [and] must base themselves to some extent on force, and holding their people in some fear. Otherwise they would too often be in the grip of malice.[30]

What Machiavelli viewed as the nobles' inherent desire to dominate, Guicciardini reinterprets as justified self-defence in the face of popular aggression.

Guicciardini's Doubts Persist

Even in this text, however, composed in an adversarial mode and targeted directly at Machiavelli's identification of wealthy elites as permanently abusive political actors, we still see Guicciardini's instinct to recognize that the historical record often complicates or outright contradicts his own aristocratic preferences. Most significantly, as John McCormick has explained in detail, Guicciardini's rejection of Machiavelli's insistence on the inevitability of social conflict implicitly concedes the basic validity of Machiavelli's perspective.[31] Machiavelli predicated that insistence with a general axiom: that all states at all times consist of nobles and people, who are motivated by contrasting instincts. The nobles inherently wish to oppress others, while the people desire only freedom from such oppression. From this general observation Machiavelli deduced that conflict between those two social groups was a structural, permanent feature of political life, rather than a local and momentary breakdown from an otherwise pacific status quo of harmonious unity.

Although Guicciardini denies the inevitability of conflict, the analysis of Roman history that he offers in support of that denial largely confirms Machiavelli's view of the problematic nature of the noble class and the moderate nature of the people. Guicciardini counters Machiavelli's theory of inevitable conflict by arguing that Rome's dissensions were the result of an ill-considered political choice and that, for Rome specifically and political life in general, conflict was avoidable. The ideal principles of representation and inclusion that he offers as the optimal constitutional method of achieving unity are consistent with his earlier visions in the *Discorso di Logrogno* and *Dialogue on the Government of Florence*. But his reflections on Rome's early mistakes that created unnecessary dissension reveal another instance of Guicciardini implicitly arguing with himself, subjecting his aristocratic preferences to critical scrutiny, and implicitly recognizing that elite conduct in practice rarely lives up to this theoretical ideal.[32]

Guicciardini reveals most clearly his implicit and unacknowledged agreement with Machiavelli's view of Roman history in his discussion of Rome's first political divisions. Disputing Machiavelli's axiom regarding the inevitability of conflict, Guicciardini counters that Rome could have avoided its notable tradition of internal conflict if only it had settled on an equitable distribution of office from the outset:

> My conclusion is that the cause of the disunity of Rome between patricians and plebs was that the classes of the city were divided, that is, on the one hand all the patricians, on the other all the plebs, and that all the officers of

> the state were patricians, the plebs being totally excluded and without any hope of ever attaining office. If there had not been from the beginning this distinction between patricians and plebs, or if at least they had given half the honours to the plebs as was done later [but only when compelled by force!], those divisions would not have arisen."[33]

For Guicciardini, the thrust of his sentence concerns the unnecessary and damaging consequences of dividing a city into separate classes with distinct rights and responsibilities; he thereby connects his identification of Roman missteps with his elaboration of an ideal regime in his commentary on *discorso* 1.2, in which all citizens are equally eligible for office so long as they have the estimation of their peers. Without intending to, Guicciardini here provides a singularly apt illustration of what Machiavelli universally attributed to elites: the early Roman elite's first instinct was to establish a domineering, thoroughly exclusionary regime in which they monopolized the government, thereby compelling the plebeians to seek class-specific protection in the form of the tribunes of the people.

Guicciardini also implicitly concurs with Machiavelli on the cause of that exclusionary instinct – class contempt for social inferiors – and faults the elite, rather than the plebeians, for diminishing Rome's power. Rome would have enjoyed even greater power than it did if only the Roman patricians had been capable of a measure of respect for the people: "It would have been a far greater contribution to [Rome's] power if the patricians had given way earlier to the will of the people, rather than thinking as they did at first, that they had no need of the plebs."[34] As McCormick has observed, Guicciardini never asks the key question of why the patricians behaved in such an extreme fashion in the first place. Machiavelli, of course, had a ready answer: those with conspicuous wealth, status, and power always wish to monopolize politics and exclude the people.

Guicciardini's account of the triangular relationship of the early Roman kings, the patrician-dominated senate, and the people also confirms Machiavelli's condemnation of the inherently abusive nature of elite culture, even while ostensibly quarrelling with Machiavelli. Guicciardini explains that under the kings the artificial division of the city into patricians and plebeians caused a relatively minor disruption because of the restraining power of the monarchs. Since the preponderance of power lay in royal hands, the senate had relatively little ability to oppress the plebeians. The monarchs, in contrast to the patricians, recognized the understandable frustration of the plebeian class and, to mitigate it, would on occasion confer patrician status on certain plebeians so that the people might have some representation in the ruling group: "Under the kings, however, it [legal distinction between social groups] was not harmful, for as power rested in the kings the senate could not itself oppress the plebs. And whatever the senate failed to see to regarding the interests of the plebs, the kings sometimes remedied ... they also used sometimes to elect plebeians into the ranks of the patricians, which enabled the plebeians to tolerate that class to which they might hope to attain."[35]

While ostensibly disputing Machiavelli's account of Roman history, Guicciardini nevertheless perfectly reiterates Machiavelli's account of the origins of the tribunes of the people. As Machiavelli recounts in *discorso* 1.3, under the Tarquins it appeared that the nobles "had put away that pride of theirs and become democratic in spirit and could be tolerated by anyone however humble." Their apparent humility, however, was not the result of an innate transformation but rather a consequence of their fear of the Tarquin tyranny, which then inspired a defensive strategy of maintaining friendly relations with the people. In the absence of the Tarquins the nobles immediately reverted to their insolent and contemptuous ways: "As soon as the Tarquins were dead and the fear the nobles felt had departed, they began to spit out against the people the poison they had kept in their breasts, and injured them in any way they could."[36] Guicciardini similarly recounts that the generally pacific relations between patricians and plebeians under the monarchy deteriorated immediately upon its abolition, owing to the patricians' unwavering contempt for their inferiors: "All these circumstances ceased when the kings were expelled, for the patricians became masters of the city and final arbiters of everything. The plebs had no one to turn to, or anyone who might consider their interests. The leaders of the plebs could no longer hope to be elected patricians, for they were despised as ignoble. Foreigners were more likely to be elected, such as Appius Claudius."[37] Patrician insolence consequently led to the creation of the tribunes of the people, which Guicciardini acknowledges was a necessary measure: "As the plebs had a magistrate of their own they had a public leader with whom to consult and discuss their needs, and when they took their troubles to him they were no longer despised as a body without a head."[38] Desperate circumstances led to the establishment of the tribunes.

Guicciardini's analysis of *discorso* 1.6 actually critiques patrician culture more pointedly than Machiavelli's *discorso* does. Machiavelli considers whether Rome could have organized itself to avoid chronic conflict between patricians and plebeians. Contrasting Rome with Sparta and Venice, he concludes that any regime organized for martial expansion must accept popular riots, but he stops short of specifying the trigger for those riots: "So considering all these things, we see that Rome's lawgivers needed to do one of two things if Rome was to remain quiet like

[Sparta and Venice] ... either not to make use of the populace in war, like the Venetians, or not open the way to foreigners, like the Spartans. Yet they did both of these. This gave the people an increase in numbers and countless reasons for rioting."[39] Although Guicciardini disputes the larger conclusion regarding the inevitability of social conflict, his reasoning confirms Machiavelli's point while specifically identifying the patrician class's chronically oppressive conduct as the trigger:

> I believe it to be true that when the Romans wished to use the plebs in war, as they were forced to do by the small numbers of the patricians if they were to use their own national forces, it was necessary to keep the plebs satisfied. And the fact that the patricians were unwilling to do so was the cause of so many riots and plots, for they would not give them a share in the government nor would they abstain from those oppressive acts which gave the plebs cause to wish to share it. For they controlled the public wealth and were very harsh in the exaction of debts, and one may believe that in every field justice was weighted on the side of the party which held all power.[40]

While seemingly unaware of it, Guicciardini also confirms Machiavelli's axiom about the people's innate moderation. On the one hand, he routinely blames the plebeians for their destructive and undisciplined politics, blaming them entirely for the city's internal strife: "The patricians were from the first the optimates and the rest formed the plebs, which was the origin of all their seditious movements."[41] His subsequent contrast between patrician moderation and popular licence further undermines the notion that sedition might have legitimate motives: "[The tribunes of the people] did moderate the power of the nobles, [but] they did not, conversely, moderate the licence of the plebs."[42] One would expect his subsequent commentary to demonstrate numerous examples of popular licence and unreasonable sedition.

On the other hand, Guicciardini's account of Roman politics routinely portrays popular "sedition" as a reasonable, moderate reaction to a manifestly unjust conduct by the patricians, and, precisely as Machiavelli described, he shows the people as the opposite of licentious: they protest only after substantial abuse and cease protesting as soon as they attain their modest objectives. He demonstrates this in his rejection of Machiavelli's argument that the martial, expansionist power of the Roman republic critically depended on its culture of internal dissent. Guicciardini asserts the traditional view that all manifestations of disunity harm the state and are best avoided. In the Roman case in particular, he further asserts that Roman dissension could in fact have been easily avoided owing precisely to the plebeians' inherently reasonable demands: "But I repeat, that if at the beginning of freedom there had not been, as it says in the Fourth Discourse, that distinction between patrician and plebeian, or if from the first they had given the plebs office, as they were later obliged to do, there would not have been all those riots and plots among them, which ceased immediately they were given a share in government up to the time of the Gracchi."[43] He then goes on to provide a perfect illustration of Machiavelli's thesis that the people are generally unmotivated by the will to power, typical of elites, and desire only to live unmolested in the secure enjoyment of their possessions (all the while he is ostensibly disagreeing with Machiavelli): "I also maintain that if the patricians, without fully opening government to the plebs, had found the way to remedy their grievances and had opened a way by which at certain intervals the plebeian leaders could be made patricians, perhaps there would not have been those uprisings; for it was seen by experience that in the laws put forward by Publius Sextus the plebs were satisfied with measures regarding dues and property, and were not interested in office."[44]

Guicciardini's commentary on *discorso* 1.47 displays the same cognitive dissonance as aforementioned. In 1.47 Machiavelli argues that the people are rarely misinformed or deceived regarding particulars and therefore are sound electors that typically appoint competent, qualified officials. Guicciardini concludes his commentary by declaring that the people are often wrong when judging specifics – and are certainly more frequently wrong than are the few – because the multitude "believes false rumours, it acts from frivolous motives, and in fact its ignorance is much more dangerous than the decisions of the few may be."[45] Yet his preceding analysis demonstrates the opposite, supporting Machiavelli's thesis perfectly. As Guicciardini relates, the Roman people felt humiliated because they were formally excluded from consular office. After successfully fighting for the creation of the tribunes, officials with consular power who could be elected from patricians and plebeians alike, they appointed only competent people (Machiavelli specifies in fact that they only elected nobles):

> One can also see this in the example of the Romans, where the people felt it unworthy and disgraceful that they should be unable to hold office. And then feeling they had achieved enough when they succeeded in becoming eligible to the office of consul, they were largely satisfied and did not elect unsuitable people, as though they had not fought out of personal ambition to rise to that eminence, but only to remove the indignity that all the plebs should be forbidden by law to hold office. Hence Livy aptly says *contenta eo quod sui ratio habita esset.*"[46]

Not for the first time, Guicciardini aspires to reject Machiavelli's axioms about elite vice and popular virtue even while implicitly affirming them.

At times, Guicciardini's commentary – and again, apparently inadvertently – portrays the Roman people's virtue in stronger terms than do Machiavelli's original *discorsi.* For example, even though his analysis of *discorso* 1.5 rejects Machiavelli's argument that the people are superior guardians of liberty than are the elites, his subsequent discussion of *discorso* 1.40 confirms precisely that thesis. In 1.40, reflecting on Claudius Appius's failed attempt to establish a tyranny, Machiavelli concludes, consistent with major arguments in *The Prince,* that aspiring tyrants should always ally with the people against their nobles. Machiavelli employs the example of Appius merely as one example of his more universal theory that tyrannies in cities generally arise from either the excessive desire of the people for freedom or the excessive desire of elites to dominate. Guicciardini might here have chosen to turn Machiavelli's arguments against themselves: if the people possess an immoderate desire for liberty that is as likely to result in tyranny as is the nobles' immoderate desire for dominance, then it makes little sense to endow them with special prerogatives for the preservation of liberty, as Machiavelli argues in 1.5. Since Machiavelli concedes that tyrannies follow from both instincts, Guicciardini could have harnessed Machiavelli's conclusions in 1.40 to support his own reaction to 1.5 that in a proper and true mixed regime the guardianship of liberty should be equally balanced between the city's classes.

Instead, however, Guicciardini's reaction to *discorso* 1.40 confirms that the people are, in fact, singularly effective custodians of liberty, both in Rome and in Florence. Whereas Machiavelli concludes that Appius's tyrannical ambitions would have been successful had he consistently maintained popular support, Guicciardini asserts that even with the support of the plebeians no tyranny would have lasted, owing to the people's love of freedom. As evidence, he cites the case of the populist consul Manlius Capitolinus, who attacked the senate with popular backing, as Machiavelli counsels, but was undone by the people once they had perceived his kingly intent. "The first difficulty [Appius and his companions] encountered, though small, destroyed their tyranny, which I think would not have been more stable even if they had attacked the nobility with the support of the plebs, for that people was too fond of the name of liberty. And we see the example of Manlius Capitolinus who, although he acted against the senate and with purely popular means, was yet suppressed by the people itself as it was understood that he sought to destroy freedom."[47]

Without announcing it overtly (or perhaps even to himself), Guicciardini clearly suspects that tyrannies are more often the result of alliances between princes and nobles than between princes and people. From the case of Manlius and *decemviri* Machiavelli adduces the general conclusion that lasting tyrannies require popular support, citing Nabis of Sparta as his chief example. Guicciardini's general conclusion appears at first to be a familiar reiteration of his recurring critique that Machiavelli's thinking is overly formal, overly rigid, and insensitive to the power of contextual variation. He asserts that many examples exist of popular and oligarchic tyrannies and that each form has its own distinctive strengths and weaknesses, such that no "firm rule" exists – "conclusions must be drawn from the mood of the city, from the state of affairs which changes according to the state of the times, and other mutable circumstances." Yet he only offers examples of noble tyrannies: "As for the general thesis, whether it is better for one wishing to set up as a tyrant to proceed with the support of the people or to win over the nobility, there are different examples, for Sulla set up a tyranny in Rome and established it with the backing of the nobility, and in Florence the Duke of Athens was made tyrant with the support of the nobles, though he was not able to maintain his position through his imprudence and irresponsibility, which caused his early decline."[48] Guicciardini's meaning here is unclear. Perhaps he meant to write that the Duke of Athens was supported by the Florentine *popolo.* Although the duke was invited to rule at the behest of Florentine *ottimati*, his adoption of financial policies that were contrary to their interests led him aggressively to cultivate popular support to offset elite hostility. In point of fact, however, Brienne was invited and ultimately expelled by *ottimati* families, so Guicciardini may well have intended to say that that tyranny derived from noble support. Either way, the absence of a clear example of a popular-based tyranny is tellingly consistent with his earlier discussion of popular safeguards against tyranny.

Guicciardini's opening general reflections on the strengths and weaknesses of the governments of the one, the few, and the many anticipate at a theoretical level these particular internal self-doubts about the merits of aristocratic government and the limited potential for popular-based tyrannies. Regarding princely rule, Guicciardini asserts the conventional view that monarchy, under a wise and just monarch, is the best form of government but has infinite potential to degenerate under an evil or incompetent ruler into the worst form of government (hence his preference for tightly circumscribed royal power along the lines of the Venetian doge). His assessment of aristocratic rule, however, opens with a positive thesis that his subsequent explanation thoroughly undermines. In principle, because aristocratic government implies a power-sharing arrangement among many families, it benefits from stronger safeguards against tyranny than do monarchies. It benefits also from what he views as the inherent virtues of elites: they exceed the people in prudence, wisdom, and intelligence and hence govern better. But immediately upon making that declaration, Guicciardini acknowledges the opposite: aristocratic government suffers from structural instability caused by the elites' innately abusive politics and insatiable appetites. "The trouble is that as their authority is great they favour those measures useful to themselves and oppressive to the rest of the population, and as there are no bounds to men's ambition to increase their estate, they come into conflict with others like themselves, and commit acts of sedition. From this ensues the city's ruin, either through tyranny or some other means."[49] His critique of the regimes of the many features the expected denunciations of the people's capacity for judgment and of their excessive fondness for change, but acknowledges that such regimes are the most impervious to tyrannical subversion, which perhaps explains his previous omission of popular-based tyrannies: "One good thing about government by the people is that while it lasts there can be no tyranny. Laws are more powerful than men, and the proper end of all decisions is the safeguarding of universal well-being."[50]

The Relative Authority of Tradition

So far, we have considered Guicciardini's dispute with Machiavelli about the relevance of the Roman republican model for Florence and about the relative capacity for rationality of the nobles and the people. As we have seen, Guicciardini's position in both disputes was clearly informed by his aristocratic obsession with reputation, honour, and family status and his family's role as a major political actor in Florentine history. Embedded within these quarrels, however, was an even larger dispute, equally informed by the contrasting social status of Machiavelli and Guicciardini, about the role of history and the written tradition itself as a source of legitimating authority in political life. Machiavelli interpreted the tradition as a self-serving elite conspiracy while Guicciardini interpreted it as proof of the natural and timeless superiority of the few over the many.

While the two appeared to share a similar approach to history – particularly its cyclical nature and the notion of recurrence that framed historical knowledge as a form of political experience in the present – Guicciardini interpreted history in a conservative mode, and Machiavelli read his sources from a far more radically subversive position. Guicciardini generally defended his political preferences by declaring their alignment with tradition (if never identifying specific authors), whereas Machiavelli invoked the ancients but used the substance of their texts to argue against their conclusions. Much as his contemporary Martin

Luther rejected the authority of tradition, as a corrupt extension of papal tyranny, Machiavelli's *Discourses* implied that the written record itself was an elite conspiracy that disenfranchised the people, an accusation that, as we will see, Guicciardini tacitly – perhaps even unintentionally – acknowledged in his *Considerations.*

Three of Machiavelli's *discorsi* that Guicciardini engages in his *Considerations* address the complicity of history and the intellectual tradition in supporting corrupt regimes. In the first case, *discorso* 1.10, Machiavelli laments the short-sighted and self-destructive tyrannical tendencies of most princes. Such princes are not inherently corrupt or viciously inclined by nature but are rather "deceived by a false good and a false glory."[51] He concludes from his own reading of Greek and Roman history that all princely figures, whether in monarchical or republican contexts, will acquire greater security, strength, and glory by living with the laws and with the love of their people, yet few recognize that lesson. He explains why – and the source of that "deception" – by considering Julius Caesar, whose reign found many apologists both in antiquity and among the humanists of Renaissance: "Nor should anyone be deceived by the glory of Caesar, on seeing him especially celebrated by the historians, for those who praise him are bribed by his fortune and awed by the long duration of the Empire, which, being ruled under his name, did not allow writers to speak freely of him."[52] Power exerts a form of psychological slavery – explicit in the case of bribery and implicit in the case of awe – on the imaginations of the historians who write about it, and whose corrupted narratives hence lead future readers down similarly corrupted paths. As he puts it in the preface to book 2, "Most writers are so subservient to the fortune of conquerors."[53] History does offer instructive truths, but it must be read against the grain, with prudent and political inferences: "Let a reader observe too with what great praises [historians] laud Brutus, as though, unable to blame Caesar because of his power, they laud his enemy." [54] Machiavelli would use this same method when explaining the rise of the Medici family in his *Florentine Histories.*[55]

In the second case, *discorso* 1.58, on the people's superior capacity for wisdom than the princes', Machiavelli elaborates further on the written record's contribution to the enduring dominance of political culture that excludes the people, and gives a specific example of reading his source against the grain. The *discorso* opens with two episodes from Livy's history – the condemnation of Manlius Capitolinus and a succession crisis in Syracuse – that Livy uses to demonstrate the multitude's inherently mercurial character, a prejudice that Machiavelli here locates in Livy but that is a universal aspect of the historical tradition: "Nothing can be more unreliable and more inconstant than the multitude, as, like all other historians, our Titus Livius affirms."[56] Machiavelli scrutinizes Livy's examples and proceeds to demonstrate that Livy's own narrative confirms the opposite, that when in power, the Roman people demonstrated greater moderation and prudence than did the princes. The immediate quarrel is with Livy, but because Livy's anti-populism is shared by "all other historians," Machiavelli acknowledges that he is at odds with the entire historiographical tradition: "I do not know whether I am undertaking a task so hard and full of difficulties that I shall be forced to give up in disgrace or to continue with reproach when I try to defend something that, as I have said, has been condemned by all the writers."[57]

Machiavelli's explication of his method advances a universal explanation for why the multitude have always been maligned and mischaracterized, and the answer again reflects his view of the corrupting effect of power and coercion on collective memory. "I do not judge and I shall never judge it a sin to defend any opinion with arguments, without trying to use either authority or force."[58] Machiavelli offers individual elaboration of specific arguments as methodologically superior to invocation of authority. This was a provocative position, given the cherished Renaissance assumptions about the superior wisdom of the ancients. In doing so, he dismisses a mode of argumentation embraced by all his contemporaries, and particularly Guicciardini, who frequently justified their arguments by their consistency with tradition (such as this statement from the *Considerations*: "this conclusion is the one reached by all those who have written about the republics").[59] By disregarding historians' summative verdicts about the nature of people and princes, and instead by focusing on their actions, Machiavelli reaches the opposite conclusion to that of "the writers": "I say, then, about that fault of which writers accuse the multitude, that all men can individually be accused of it, and chiefly princes." He justifies his conclusion with the basic observation that "there are and have been many princes, and the good and wise ones have been few."[60] His explanation for why the historical record has inverted the inherent qualities of princes (inconstant and vicious) and people (moderate and wise) observes, simply and bluntly, that literary authority itself is a product of political intimidation and coercion: "A bad opinion about the people arises because everybody says bad things of them without fear and freely, even while they are in power. Of princes everybody speaks with a thousand fears and a thousand cautions."[61]

Guicciardini surely must have recognized Machiavelli's pre-emptive methodological challenge to sceptical readers to refute him with arguments rather than with recourse to "authority or force." Nevertheless, with one interesting exception, to be discussed next, Guicciardini's *Considerations* refused to engage with Machiavelli's provocative assertion that to extract truth from the intellectual tradition one must first acknowledge its accommodation of power and consequent elitist agenda. At a methodological level, therefore, the two were talking at cross purposes. Where Machiavelli critiques the objectivity of tradition, Guicciardini simply invokes it: "For when princes are controlled by law no one who has written on political subjects ever doubted that their rule is better than that of a mob." Guicciardini reiterates the general literary consensus: "Not without reason, the multitude is compared to the waves of the sea which, according to the winds that blow, move now here, now there, without any rule, without any firmness." Machiavelli offers one method (consider the implications of each specific case in a text and navigate independently of the path provided by its author), and Guicciardini the opposite (in the presence of a universal verdict there is no need to consider specifics): "Examples [of the weakness of popular governments] are so many and so well known that there is no point in giving details, they are such that they deservedly give rise to that universal and most ancient belief of all writers that in the multitude there is neither prudence nor constancy."[62]

As an establishment intellectual and former prince in his own right, now indignantly facing what he perceived as unjust persecution from a popular regime in Florence, Guicciardini expressed not only his own personal disdain for popular regimes but insisted also on the compatibility of his position with the entire Western tradition of political thought. And yet, intentionally or not, there is evidence in the *Considerations* that Machiavelli's *Discourses* did affect Guicciardini's thinking about the putatively unanimous consensus of the "writers" about the flaws of popular regimes. In the fifth chapter of the *Considerations* Guicciardini responds to Machiavelli's argument that in republican contexts the people make better guardians of liberty than do the nobles. Machiavelli's position involves a survey of Roman, Spartan, and Venetian practices, a valid comparison in his view because "in every republic there are rich men and men of the people."[63] Guicciardini rejects both Machiavelli's argument and his method. Machiavelli's method is flawed because he compares regimes, like Rome, in which the people and the nobles shared power with regimes that granted power to one group only, in this case Venice, which excluded the people altogether. He then disputes Machiavelli's interpretation of the Roman case. Machiavelli had identified the guardianship of liberty in Rome to the tribunes of the people, but Guicciardini observes that the tribunes were responsible not for the protection of the city's liberty overall but only for the liberty of the people. The city's collective liberty was a collective effort that included both patricians and plebeians, both of whom had the power to arraign, and that was located in the offices of consuls, dictators, and tribunes. He agrees that the Roman example is indeed the correct one to follow, not because it demonstrates the virtues of empowering the people to protect liberty, as Machiavelli mistakenly believes, but because it demonstrates the superiority of the mixed regime, the constitutional form that Guicciardini consistently championed.

Without any overt signal, Guicciardini has made a profound alteration to his own political thought: he no longer considers Venice to be an example of a mixed regime. Chapter 5 of the *Considerations* specifically rejects Venice as a mixed regime because power is exclusively in the hands of the nobles: "it is one thing to say who is to have power, the nobles or the plebs, and of this Venice is an example, for there it is so far in the hands of the nobles that all the plebs are excluded – and it is quite another thing, where all take a share in government, to say who should have special responsibility or care for the defence of liberty."[64] In all of his prior constitutional treatises he held up Venice as one of the best realizations of the classical mixed ideals, as, of course, many other Florentine aristocrats did because they resented the frequent popular challenges to their power that their Venetian counterparts had successfully finessed.[65] Only a few years earlier, in his *Dialogue on the Government of Florence*, Guicciardini defended his ideal Florentine constitution on the degree to which it emulated Venice's mixed regime:

> It seems to me that the government [outlined in book 2] is good in general and has the main features one requires in a free republic. It bears very close resemblance to the Venetian government, which, if I'm not mistaken, is the finest and best government ever enjoyed by a city, not only in our times, but also perhaps in ancient times. This is because it borrows from all the different types of government, of the one, the few and the many, and is moderated by all of them, so that it has gathered most of the good features of each and escaped most of their worst ones.[66]

Nor is Venice invoked anywhere else in the *Considerations* as a mixed regime. Guicciardini continues, as does Machiavelli, to advocate for the mixed ideal, but he now does so only on the basis of the Roman example: "I shall always praise above all others a mixed government, as described above [with respect to Roman institutions and customs]."[67] However much he may have disagreed with Machiavelli's populist reading of the Roman example, he nevertheless engaged sufficiently densely with Machiavelli's interpretation of the historical nature and contribution of the Roman plebeians that he now recognized Venice had no such popular counterpart and could not therefore be a mixed regime.

Guicciardini concludes his analysis of this *discorso* by considering a new question not previously considered either by him or by Machiavelli: if a mixed regime in which all social groups contribute to the preservation of liberty is not possible, which is superior – a government that is entirely noble or one that is entirely plebeian? Strictly speaking, Machiavelli does not raise this question in the *Discourses* because that text also advocates for a mixed regime. It seems, however, that Guicciardini interpreted that text's muscular and strident populism as an argument for the superiority of popular regimes. Guicciardini may also have raised this question as a way to critique the current regime in Florence that had come to power as a result of the circumstances of his own personal downfall and that viewed him as a traitor. In any case, his answer reiterates the superiority of a mixed regime but stresses that in its absence, government of the nobles is far superior to government by the people. His rationale reverts to his standard contrast between the two social groups: the nobles' natural capacity for prudence makes it probable that they will construct a stable regime, "whereas a people full of ignorance and confusion, and possessing many bad qualities, can only be expected to overthrow and destroy everything."[68]

To justify his preference, Guicciardini aligns himself with tradition but – again, without any overt declaration and perhaps even unintentionally – he now acknowledges that the historical record does not in fact speak with one voice in condemning popular governments. "This conclusion [popular regimes must culminate in anarchy] is the one reached by all those who have written about the republics, *and who prefer the government of the optimates to that of the mob.*"[69] In no prior text does Guicciardini ever concede a plurality of opinion in the tradition of political thought. This new tautological qualifying clause substantially diminishes the rhetorical impact of his argument, since the tradition is no longer a monolithic ally. Guicciardini now marshals the authority only of writers who shared his optimate preferences.

Further, the clause raises the question of the identity of the writers about republics who preferred governments of the people. As we have seen, the elitism of tradition was one point on which the two agreed: Machiavelli had already conceded that "all the writers" had condemned, on the surface of their texts at least, the fickleness of the multitude in favour of the prudence and rationality of princes. What text, other than Machiavelli's *Discourses*, made sustained arguments in favour of the people's prudence, stability, and judgment? In his confrontation with Machiavelli's ideas and in spite of his disagreement on many issues, the Guicciardini of the *Considerations* appears to have accepted the magnitude of Machiavelli's achievement: *The Discourses on Livy* belonged to the very canon that was its target. The fact of its existence, whether one approved or disagreed, now denied the "writers" a single voice.

The intellectual sparring evident in the interplay between these two texts, Machiavelli's *Discourses* and Guicciardini's *Considerations*, provides a sense of the magnitude of the challenge that Machiavelli faced in his advocacy of muscular populism. One would expect some formal common intellectual ground between two thinkers who were sympathetic to each other and collaborators on multiple projects. He and Guicciardini, at least during Machiavelli's last years in the 1520s, were good friends and members of a larger group of friends that included other powerful *ottimati* such as Francesco Vettori. They worked together on urgent political projects, such as protecting Florence from potential attack by Charles V and composing constitutional treatises for the Medici.[70] We have seen in Guicciardini's earlier texts considerable intellectual common ground with Machiavelli.[71] Guicciardini clearly trusted Machiavelli, since Machiavelli was his informal agent in real estate dealings and his counsellor in the marriage negotiations for Guicciardini's daughter and in strategies for extracting payment from Clement VII. Guicciardini promoted Machiavelli's literary career, arranging for the first performance of *Mandragola* before a papal audience. The sustained commentary on the *Discourses* not only in the *Considerations* but also in Guicciardini's *Dialogue on the Government of Florence* indicates Guicciardini's intellectual respect for Machiavelli's ideas.

Yet, when Guicciardini composed his formal thoughts on Machiavelli's most substantial work of political philosophy, he drew sharp lines of division on almost every page. The context surely explains at least part of Guicciardini's adversarial stance because the collapse of papal power, and therefore his own, triggered by the sack of Rome in 1527 had also led to a popular republican regime that condemned him as a leading agent of Medici tyranny and punished him with exile and confiscation of property. He wrote the *Considerations* after that persecution and after he had bloodied his hands in enforcing Medici retribution following the republic's collapse in 1530. This was hardly an environment conducive to sympathy for Machiavelli's argument about an armed people, popular tribunals, and the people's capacity for wisdom and judgment superior to that of princes. The value of tradition also must have elicited a respect from Guicciardini, being the most distinguished member of a singularly distinguished house, that prevented him from conceding the fundamental legitimacy of Machiavelli's world view and particularly his "fondness for violent and extraordinary measures." Given the degree to which the history of Florence was inextricable from the history of his family, Guicciardini could not dismiss, as Machiavelli did, the evolution of their city as a flawed, corrupt political experiment, could not view the people as solutions to a problem posed by the very existence of elites, and could not accept that the written tradition's seeming confirmation of his dim view of the people was itself the product of elite power and the fear it caused in those who were less powerful, particularly historians and philosophers seeking princely patronage.

Nevertheless, whether consciously or unconsciously, even in his strident rejection of Machiavelli, Guicciardini echoed fundamentally Machiavellian arguments about popular virtue and elite vice. His attempt to disprove Machiavelli's axiom regarding the inevitability of social conflict depended fundamentally on counterfactual historical speculation: if only the Roman patricians had been more inclined to share power with the plebeians, if only they had not routinely despised the people as a body without a head, if only they had been less harsh in the exaction of debts, then Rome might have avoided its famously factional politics. If only they had not behaved exactly as Machiavelli declared all elites behaved – abusively and arrogantly. The same applies to his characterization of the Roman plebeians and his general thoughts on populism: he routinely describes the people as irrationally fond of novelty, envious of the wealthy and excellent, incapable of prudence or moderation, and inherently licentious. Yet in his consideration of specific moments of conflict, such as the creation of the tribunes of the people, he consistently shows the people justly protesting manifest injustice, pursuing specific, reasonable objectives, and laying down their arms upon realizing those objectives – precisely as Machiavelli described all popular politics. The *Considerations*, therefore, perhaps more pointedly than any other Guicciardinian text, demonstrates the substantial overlap in the world view of the two thinkers (effectively acknowledged in Guicciardini's inclusion of *The Discourses on Livy* in the canon of "the writers").

In the next chapter we shift the focus from Guicciardini to Machiavelli, examining a long-standing controversy regarding Machiavelli's portrayal of Cesare Borgia in *The Prince*. Here too there are striking overlaps between the sentiments of Machiavelli and those of Guicciardini, both of whom esteemed Cesare Borgia's rule in the Romagna. Further, we will see that their estimation reflected the degree to which Borgia acted according to Machiavelli's populist counsel to new princes to constrain the habitual rapacity of their nobles. From a historical rather than a theoretical perspective, Guicciardini's account of Cesare Borgia was rooted in the same critique of aristocratic violence evident in all his earlier writings.

Chapter Six

Machiavelli and Guicciardini on Cesare Borgia's "Good Government": Chapter 7 of *The Prince* Revisited

For Machiavelli, outrage at and indictment of the collective failure of Italian leadership was a constant in his writing and world view. He declared his indignation outright in *The Prince*, his first formal work of political theory, which, for all its ruminations on the stratagems and tactics of an ideal prince, meditates more than anything else on the failure of Italian leadership. Reflecting on the causes of the French invasion of Italy in 1494, he invoked Savonarola but secularized the friar's influential indictment of religious corruption that had spellbound so many Florentines: "And he who used to say that the cause of it [Charles VIII's descent into Italy] was our sins told the truth, but they were not at all such as he supposed they were, but these I have mentioned; and because they were the princes' sins, the princes have suffered punishment for them."[1] He made the same denunciation against a broader historical canvas in his last major work, the *Florentine Histories*: "So if the things done by our princes, abroad and at home, cannot, like those of the ancients, be read of with wonder because of their ability and greatness, perhaps for their other qualities they will be viewed with no less wonder; for one can see how such weak and badly handled armies held in check so many splendid peoples ... I ... show with what deceptions, with what tricks and schemes, the princes, the soldiers, the heads of the republics, in order to keep that reputation which they did not deserve, carried on their affairs."[2]

By the time that Guicciardini had begun writing his own major work of history, he had embraced Machiavelli's contempt for the princes of his day. He invoked neither fortune nor the martial disparity between the Italian city states and the ultramontane national monarchies to explain the successive crises of the Italian wars, but rather zeroed in on the collective failure of peninsular leadership. He declared this outright in similarly blunt language in the prologue to the *History of Italy*:

> I have determined to write about those events which have occurred in Italy within our memory, even since French troops, summoned by our own princes, began to stir up very great dissensions here ... Thus, numerous examples will make it plainly evident how ... pernicious, almost always to themselves but always to the people, are those ill-advised measures of rulers who act solely in terms of what is in front of their eyes: either foolish or short-sighted greed. Thus by failing to take account of the frequent shifts of fortune, and misusing, to the harm of others, the power conceded to them for the common welfare, such rulers become the cause of new perturbations either through lack of prudence or excess of ambition.[3]

Like *The Prince* and the *Florentine Histories*, Guicciardini's *History of Italy* abandoned all traces of pride in the cultural and economic wealth of Renaissance culture and focused instead on its chronic political failures.

This chapter, however, focuses not on Machiavelli's and Guicciardini's condemnation of the irresponsibility of Italian leadership, but rather on the one contemporary prince whom they judged unequivocally as having earned the respect and affection of his subjects – the notorious warlord Cesare Borgia. Borgia is unique in Machiavelli's and Guicciardini's histories and political thought: he was the only prince who they declared was admired by his subjects. Guicciardini's treatment of Cesare in *The History of Florence* and *History of Italy* coincides strikingly with Machiavelli's praise of Cesare's good government in the Romagna in ways that shed new light on a long-standing controversy over the meaning of Machiavelli's enigmatic utterances on Borgia.

Machiavelli scholarship has long been and remains divided on how to interpret the meaning of the seventh chapter of *The Prince*, arguably the most paradoxical topic in the Machiavellian oeuvre that is famously characterized by paradox.[4] Machiavelli appears to idealize Cesare Borgia as a model new prince. He carefully reviews – more carefully than for any other historical figure in *The Prince* – Cesare's ambitions in Italy and stratagems for realizing them, concluding that he laid excellent foundations for his future power. On the basis of those foundations, Machiavelli declares three times in chapter 7 that new princes should model their conduct on Cesare's actions.[5] However, Machiavelli's narrative also appears to undercut his positive verdict: he praises Cesare for having acquired his own arms, but his analysis never demonstrates Cesare's military independence; he declares that Cesare won the people's affection, but also relates the hatred that his conquest of Romagna generated; he invites new princes to emulate Cesare but acknowledges both a specific catastrophic error of judgment on Cesare's part and his overall, inarguable failure to build a lasting state. Unsurprisingly, scholarship on this question generally falls into one of two camps: those who privilege Machiavelli's positive summative verdict and therefore conclude that he genuinely championed Cesare as a prudent ruler and those who privilege the apparent contradictions and therefore conclude that Machiavelli saw Cesare as an anti-hero, useful as a model for new princes of what *not* to do.[6] At stake is the larger – perhaps largest – question of whether to read *The Prince* literally or ironically. Chapter 7 is a litmus test for how to interpret all of Machiavelli's provocative utterances in *The Prince* and his political thought in general.

John Najemy explains those contradictions by arguing that they belong to Cesare rather than Niccolò. For Najemy, understanding Machiavelli's intention begins with recognizing that "[c]hapter 7's claim that ... Borgia was 'armed his own way' is the central issue."[7] His analysis surveys a variety of sources that collectively indicate not only that "Cesare never escaped dependence on mercenaries and auxiliaries" but also that Machiavelli recognized as much: "Careful reading of chapter 7 confirms that Machiavelli too saw Borgia as completely dependent on the arms of others."[8] Machiavelli's Cesare is just another mercenary adventurer fleetingly preying on the spoils of an Italy in disarray. So why then include such extreme language about Cesare's worthy methods, the nearness of his transformation into a successful founder of new modes and orders, and the dolorous lament at his exceptional bad luck? In Najemy's reading, Machiavelli's language was echoing and mimicking – mocking, really – Borgia's alternately hubristic and self-pitying world view. Via an ironic channelling of Borgia's delusional analysis of his strength, proximity to success, and extraordinary bad luck, Machiavelli was implicitly reinforcing the message of the previous chapter that only rulers truly in possession of their own arms were capable of building regimes with lasting foundations. With Machiavelli in the role of reporter of other people's words rather than as omniscient narrator, chapter 7 invites us to view the world from Cesare's eyes and laugh along with Machiavelli at the stark contrast between Cesare's vision and reality.[9]

If Machiavelli's habitually playful and ironic prose voice creates interpretive ambiguity, the same cannot be said for Francesco Guicciardini, who reiterated every aspect of Machiavelli's claims for Borgia's good government. To demonstrate the full extent of their shared vision, the first section of this chapter revisits Machiavelli's portrait of Cesare, arguing that Machiavelli's estimation of his good foundations was primarily a reference to Cesare's conception of government rather than to his military self-sufficiency.[10] Shifting the focus from Cesare's military accomplishments to the nature of the regime he built in the Romagna resolves most of chapter 7's alleged contradictions in favour of the literal reading – Machiavelli clearly esteemed Borgia's political accomplishments. In the second section I challenge the claims, frequently made in satirical readings of chapter 7, that no evidence exists for Machiavelli's claim that the Romagnol people embraced Cesare's rule. Machiavelli's legations and his narrative account of Cesare's coup against his mutinous *condottieri* at Senigallia provide several supporting examples. In the third and final section I turn to Guicciardini's assessments of Cesare's government in his *History of Florence* and *History of Italy*, demonstrating that he confirmed virtually every aspect of Borgia's government praised by Machiavelli and from a similarly populist perspective. I conclude by establishing Guicciardini's considerable credentials on this topic via examination of the parallels between Cesare's and Guicciardini's political vision for the Romagna, a region that Guicciardini also ruled on behalf of a pope.

Machiavelli's Estimation of Cesare's Regime

Najemy's analysis of chapter 7 involves demonstrating that Cesare always depended on mercenary and auxiliary troops, and concluding that Machiavelli cannot ever have believed that Cesare commanded his own forces. Having demonstrated a problematic gap on the militia question between Machiavelli's claims and historical reality, Najemy then goes on to consider further gaps between the historical record and Machiavelli's other positive claims, such as Cesare's good government, arguing that Machiavelli must have been thinking and writing in a satirical voice. In spite of Najemy's careful reconstruction of the political circumstances, however, his intervention leaves one substantial question unanswered: Why would Machiavelli choose such an oblique, subtle route to demonstrate that Cesare was a failed prince who lacked autonomy? In effect, Najemy's article offers us a variation on Straussian esoteric reading in which seeming contradictions serve as flags for readers, alerting them to the presence of implicit arguments at odds with surface claims. In the pre-Enlightenment centuries many writers engaged in esoteric writing to advance heterodox ideas, while avoiding the punishments meted out by an intolerant European-wide culture of militant orthodoxy. Many readers of Machiavelli, Leo Strauss not least among them, have long read *The Prince* esoterically to extract from the text what they view as its hidden and radically anti-democratic convictions.[11]

Why would Machiavelli need to engage in esoteric writing to condemn Cesare Borgia? The Borgias, father and son, were widely hated throughout Italy and associated with greed, cruelty, and staggeringly immoral conduct. If chapters 6 and 7 of *The Prince* are closely connected in theme, the former demonstrating the world-altering potential of rulers who rely on their own armed peoples and the latter demonstrating the fragility and transience of rulers who rely on the arms of others, who better to illustrate that thesis than Cesare, someone who, according to Najemy, Machiavelli scorned and who the rest of Italy despised? There is no evident reason, logically or rhetorically, that Machiavelli would need to invert his claims, such that he winkingly praised Borgia as a model prince to follow so that his readers would understand the opposite – and even less so in a text that otherwise took great delight in openly championing the political virtues of deceit, cruelty, and lack of faith.

A closer reading of chapter 7 reveals a different conclusion about its principal topic and the reasons for Machiavelli's praise of Cesare. I agree with Najemy that the key to understanding the chapter lies in Machiavelli's statement that "Cesare was 'armed his own way,'" but I disagree with his subsequent reflection that "[e]xactly what Machiavelli had in mind (or thought Borgia had in mind) in saying that he was 'armed his own way' is not all clear."[12] As Najemy's own analysis demonstrates, Machiavelli cannot be referring to Cesare's "own arms" in the strictly military sense of a Romagnol army conscripted by Borgia, because at that point in Machiavelli's narrative Borgia had merely added some *condottieri* formerly serving the Colonna and Orsini to his army of mercenaries and auxiliary French forces. Najemy goes on to analyse the provenance, numbers, and general strength of Borgia's army following his initial conquest of the Romagna to demonstrate that at no point did he command homegrown military forces.[13] But that analysis confirms, rather than contradicts, Machiavelli's assessment in chapter 7 for the simple reason that Machiavelli himself confirms that Borgia never achieved that objective.

Let us review what Machiavelli specifically claims about Borgia and the order in which he makes those claims. He clarifies at the outset that Borgia recognized the structural weakness caused by his dependency on mercenary forces that had been loaned by Roman baronial families and the French king. Having abandoned his territorial ambitions for Tuscany and Bologna because they conflicted with the plans of the Orsini and Louis XII, Cesare "determined not to depend further on another man's armies and Fortune."[14] So far, Machiavelli tells us only that Borgia prized and sought to acquire military autonomy – a goal rather than an accomplishment. The chapter then goes on to detail the various stratagems that Cesare employed to further that goal, including the infamous murder of his enemies at Senigallia and successfully encouraging the defection of the officer corps in the Orsini and Colonna mercenary camps: "The Duke's first act to that end was to weaken the Orsini and Colonnesi parties in Rome by winning over to himself all their adherents who were men of rank, making them his own men of rank and giving them large subsidies; and he honoured them, according to their stations, with military and civil offices, so that within a few months their hearts were emptied of all affection for the Roman parties, and it was wholly transferred to the Duke."[15] As Najemy observes, this cannot be the moment at which Cesare becomes "armed in his own way," because he has acquired only his enemies' military leadership, not troops, insufficient in itself to offset his dependence on France and his existing mercenary troops.

Machiavelli includes a brief clue here as to the significance of the defections: Cesare offers them military *and* civil offices ("*condotte e governi*"). As ruler of the Romagna, he incorporates the former Orsini and Colonnesi *condottieri* not only into his army but also into his regime, giving them a potential long-term stake in Cesare's success because they have been honoured, and presumably enriched, via both their military service and their offices in the government of the Romagna, something that will continue to generate loyalty in times of peace and encourage them to conflate their own self-interest with the prosperity of Cesare's Romagnol regime. A few sentences later, Machiavelli describes this same process as Cesare's having "changed their partisans into his friends," a claim for which both Machiavelli and Guicciardini provide specific examples, as we will see when we turn to events following the death of Borgia's father, Alexander VI. No other ruler in *The Prince*, or any other Machiavellian text for that matter, ever offered mercenaries civil positions and a stake in the fortune of the regime for which they fought. A relatively small detail, perhaps, but one that uniquely distinguishes Cesare from Machiavelli's otherwise dismal cast of egocentric and irresponsible rulers and hints at the real source of Cesare's strength and the meaning of the statement that he armed himself "in his own way."[16]

At this point, in both Machiavelli's narrative and Najemy's analysis, Cesare has not yet attained military self-sufficiency. Nevertheless, Machiavelli concludes that the foundations of Cesare's power are not only praiseworthy but complete: "Having wiped out these leaders, then, and changed their partisans into friends, the Duke had laid very good foundations for his power."[17] Earlier in the chapter, when Machiavelli introduces Cesare "the Valentino" as a virtuous ruler and explains why future princes should follow his model, he specifies not Cesare's supposed regional militia but rather those foundations: "So on examining all the steps taken by the Duke, we see that he himself laid mighty foundations for future power. To discuss these steps is not superfluous; indeed, I for my part do not see what better precepts I can give a new prince than the example of Duke Valentino's actions."[18] Machiavelli has neither reached the halfway point of the chapter's analysis of Cesare's career nor demonstrated his transcendence of reliance on other people's armies, but he has unequivocally confirmed that the foundations of the duke's power are complete. If, regarding one aspect of those foundations (military autonomy) Machiavelli's utterances are cryptic or contradictory, his language regarding the other major aspect (the introduction of new institutions that established good government in the Romagna for the first time) is unambiguous: "The Duke had laid very good foundations for his power, holding all the Romagna along with the dukedom of Urbino, especially since he believed he had made the Romagna his friend and gained the support of all those people, through their getting a taste of well-being."[19]

Regarding Cesare's introduction of good government, Machiavelli provides the reader with the first accomplishment worthy of emulation: "Because this matter is worthy of notice and of being copied by others, I shall not omit it." Assessing the region as little more than a vertically integrated criminal enterprise that preyed upon its own people, Cesare saw a double opportunity. By forcibly restraining the rapaciousness of its petty lords, he could win the persecuted people's loyalty and gratitude while destroying his rivals to power. "After the Duke had seized the Romagna and found it controlled by weak lords who had plundered their subjects rather than governed them, and had given them reason for disunion, not for union, so that the whole province was full of thefts, brawls, and every sort of excess, he judged that if he intended to make it peaceful and obedient to the ruler's arm, he must of necessity give it good government."[20] To do that, he appointed one of his Spanish captains, Ramiro de Lorqua, as his governor to whom he gave complete power to tame the region's lawless and predatory nobility. Having removed the principal obstacle to the rule of law, Cesare then introduced a constructive, representative legal innovation, the Rota: "He set up a civil court in the midst of the province, with a distinguished presiding judge, where every city had its lawyer."[21] In one of the most infamous and controversial passages in *The Prince*, Machiavelli then attributes to Cesare a notable act of cruelty well used. As Ramiro's harsh measures had generated resentment, Cesare had Ramiro executed one night, severing his erstwhile lieutenant's body in two and leaving it adjacent to a chopping block and a bloody sword in Cesena's public square.[22] Machiavelli explains Ramiro's execution as a form of public theatre designed to distance Cesare from the hostility that Ramiro's campaign of pacification had caused: "He determined to ... win them [those who hated Ramiro] over entirely by showing that any cruelty which had gone on did not originate with himself but with the harsh nature of his agent."[23] The logic of Machiavelli's paragraph includes an additional, symbolic reason for Ramiro's execution. Romero's having served his purpose of violently taming the Romagnol nobility, his execution becomes the final act of violence necessary for its cessation and the introduction of the rule of law, Cesare's region-wide centralized court of appeal.

Machiavelli goes on to identify the remaining threats to Cesare's power and his largely compelling strategies for overcoming them. In Machiavelli's estimation Cesare would have succeeded in creating a powerful and enduring new state in Italy if only his father had lived longer. Owing to Alexander's sudden death and his own illness at the same time, Cesare had resolved three of his four remaining threats. As he did not complete all his plans, Machiavelli tells us specifically, he never attained the military self-sufficiency that he, like Machiavelli, recognized as one of the indispensable sources of true security: "If he had carried out these plans (and he would have carried them out the very year when Alexander died), he would have gained such forces that he could stand by his own strength and would no longer rely on other men's Fortune and forces, but on his own vigour and ability."[24]

For Najemy, the fact that "Borgia never escaped dependence on mercenaries and auxiliaries," which Machiavelli must have known, becomes the key argument for the necessity of reading chapter 7 ironically.[25] Najemy's conclusion about Borgia's dependence is a confirmation, however, rather than a contradiction, of everything Machiavelli writes in that chapter. As we have seen, Machiavelli nowhere states in chapter 7 that Borgia had his own forces; on the contrary, he concludes the chapter by reminding his readers that Cesare to his final day relied on other people's forces. The only mention of Cesare's own forces occurs in the conditional tense: "If he had carried out these plans ... he would have gained such forces." Nor should this conclusion surprise anyone, because Machiavelli placed his lengthy analysis of Borgia's tactics in chapter 7, which is dedicated to new princedoms gained by other men's forces (where it logically belongs), rather than in chapter 6, which is dedicated to new princedoms gained by one's own arms (where it would certainly stand out as a major contradiction).

Even though, when Machiavelli examines the case of Ramiro, we are only halfway through the chapter and in the early days of Cesare's attempt to build a regime in northern Italy, he follows Ramiro's execution with the statement that Cesare was now "armed in his own way." However, we have not yet encountered an example of Borgia's amassing of a conscripted militia, and the chapter ends by telling us that he never realized that goal. The only possible explanation of Machiavelli's meaning in that statement is that Cesare was strengthened by his new strong government that enjoyed the approval of the people, his only finished act. That conclusion leaves us the question of whether this positive verdict is also sufficiently at odds with historical reality that Machiavelli's meaning must be read ironically (or esoterically, for Straussian readers) as something other than respect for Cesare's government.

Before we turn to other assessments of Cesare's government, however, let us first consider the overall narrative coherence of Machiavelli's positive assessment in chapter 7. Najemy reads Machiavelli's utterances on Cesare's alleged good government as no less contradictory than his statements about Cesare's own army, and hence further evidence that the chapter requires reading against the grain: "Machiavelli's dramatic description of the murder of messer Ramiro, whose elimination was meant to separate Borgia from the 'hatred' generated by the minister's severities, confirms that Borgia's government was not in fact winning Romagnol hearts and minds. Like Borgia's 'good foundations,' the 'friendship' of the Romagna seems more a matter of aspirations – and the duke's blinkered perception – than actual accomplishment."[26]

Machiavelli never says, however, that the people hated Ramiro, only that "past severities had generated *some* hatred [*qualche odio*] of him."[27] The subsequent statements about the psychological effect of Ramiro's execution similarly do not refer to the general population but to *those* people – presumably those who felt hate: "He determined to purge such men's [*quelli populi*, those who hated] minds and win them over entirely … The ferocity of this spectacle left those people [*quelli populi*] at the same time gratified and awe-struck."[28] If some people hated Ramiro's campaign of pacification, others evidently did not. Who are the most likely candidates to react with hatred to Cesare's innovations? In Machiavelli's narrative, Cesare's desire to establish good government was first and foremost the product of his recognition that the region was "controlled by weak lords who had plundered their subjects rather than governed them."[29] The targets of Ramiro's violence, then, must have been the feuding nobility of the Romagna, not its people, who were the chronic victims of those lords and on whose behalf Cesare unleashed his fearsome lieutenant. The "hatred" in question belongs not to the people, which would certainly undermine Machiavelli's claims that they supported Cesare, but rather to Cesare's noble rivals, who resented his attempts to curb their rapaciousness. *Their* hatred indicates that Cesare likely did improve the general lot of his Romagnol subjects.

Still leaving aside the question of the historical accuracy of Machiavelli's verdict, his account in chapter 7 is not only perfectly coherent; it also provides an historical example of major arguments advanced elsewhere in *The Prince*, *The Discourses on Livy*, and his correspondence.[30] As many people have observed, Machiavelli must have viewed Cesare's sudden destruction of Ramiro as an example of chapter 8's infamous discussion of cruelty well used – acts of violence that are swift, isolated, and, crucially, mutually beneficial to the ruler *and* his subjects: "Well used we call those … that a conqueror carries out at a single stroke, as a result of his need to secure himself, and then does not persist in, but transmutes into the greatest possible benefit to his subjects."[31] That chapter's main discussion of Liverotto da Fermo's violent treachery includes a relatively superfluous detail through which Machiavelli reminds us of the Borgia father and son. Wishing to dispose of Giovanni Fogliani and Fermo's leading citizens, Fermo invited them to a festive banquet. Once it had concluded, he shifted the topic of conversation to sensitive political issues that were best discussed in private, providing the occasion to relocate his victims to an inner chamber where assassins waited: "When the meal was finished and all the other matters customary at such banquets, Liverotto, according to plan, started certain serious discourses, talking of Pope Alexander's greatness and of Cesare his son and of their enterprises."[32] Machiavelli's mention of Cesare in Liverotto's scheming surely suggests that he wished us to think of Cesare in the context of cruelty well used (and Liverotto himself was subsequently murdered by Cesare, about which Machiavelli wrote several times).

We need not merely infer Borgia's connection to Machiavelli's estimation of the tactical benefits of cruel actions. Machiavelli opens chapter 17's famous discussion of the relative superiority of fear over love with a specific invocation of Cesare's effective use of cruelty, defined precisely in terms consistent with his portrait of Cesare in chapter 7, his high estimation of Cesare's good government, and chapter 8's criterion for cruelty "well used" – namely, that it should benefit the people.

> Cesare Borgia was thought cruel; nevertheless, that well known cruelty of his re-organized the Romagna, united it, brought it to peace and loyalty. If we look at this closely, we see that he was much more merciful than the Florentine people, who, to escape being called cruel, allowed the ruin of Pistoia. A wise prince, then, is not troubled about a reproach for cruelty by which he keeps his subjects united and loyal because, giving a very few examples of cruelty, he is more merciful than those who, through too much mercy, let evils continue, from which result murders or plunder, because the latter commonly harm a whole group, but those executions that come from the prince harm individuals only.[33]

Machiavelli's invocation of Cesare in chapter 17 not only reaffirms the essence of Cesare's good government championed in chapter 7, and specifically that it generated "loyalty," but also further clarifies the social distinction between those who appreciated Cesare's innovations (the many) and those who hated them (the few). Machiavelli here makes clear that princely "cruelty" consists of violently disciplining those who engage in murder and plunder, whereas the recipients of princely "mercy" are the people who collectively benefit from that discipline.

Chapter 17's invocation of Cesare provides a specific example of one of Machiavelli's most substantial and recurring convictions in *The Prince* and the *Discourses* regarding the contrasting nature of nobles and people. In chapter 9 of *The Prince* Machiavelli argues that, owing to the contrasting nature of nobles and people, a wise prince always allies with the latter at the expense of the former. As he explains, on the one hand, rulers can easily satisfy their people because the people wish only to live unmolested and secure in their possessions. On the other hand, the nobles not only have an innate desire to oppress others but generally consider themselves equal to their prince and are hence all potential rivals; if restrained by their prince from acting on their aggressive impulses, they conspire against him. Machiavelli offers no middle way: to make the people happy, the prince must incur the hostility of his nobles because the people's happiness depends on the prince's restraining his nobles from their involuntary, systemic, and abusive behaviour. Given a choice of the group to favour, self-preservation provides the answer: "Against a hostile people a prince can never make himself safe because they are too many; against the rich he can make himself safe because they are few."[34] Chapter 7 portrays Cesare as the embodiment of the lessons of chapters 9 and 17.

In Najemy's interpretation, in which the people hate Cesare's regime, the Romagnol people would appear to privilege means over ends. Even if Cesare's ends are good government, defined specifically as forcibly compelling its lords to govern rather than plunder their subjects, those subjects focus more on their objection to means – the violence of Ramiro's bloody campaign against those lords. As John McCormick's reconstruction of biblical allusions in chapter 7 stresses, however, Machiavelli repeatedly characterizes the people as interested in ends and outcomes, not means and methods. In a letter to Giovanbattista Soderini, Machiavelli writes: "I am looking not through your glass [of the few], in which nothing is seen but prudence, but through the glass of the many, who have to judge the end of things as they are done, and not the means by which they are done."[35] As McCormick's analysis demonstrates, chapter 7 displays a profound unity of Machiavelli, Cesare, and the Romagnol people, resulting from a common enemy in the *grandi*, persecutors of both Machiavelli and the "Romagnoli," and from resentful obstacles to Cesare's ascent: "Machiavelli hereby asserts his concerns with ends, with outcomes, over means because these are the people's chief concern. Neither Machiavelli nor the people, it would seem, can afford the luxury of fussing over means, as do the few. The direct relationship between the people and the duke – the bond between them forged by the people's appreciation for outcomes delivered by the duke – increases in importance throughout Machiavelli's account of Borgia's career in *The Prince*."[36] Given Machiavelli's larger convictions about the natures of nobles and people, the nobles are the group most likely to object to Ramiro's bloody methods, in part because a fascination with means characterizes that group in Machiavelli's mind and historically because they were the victims of those methods.

In a letter to Francesco Vettori on 31 January 1515, Machiavelli revisits and reiterates the chief claims in chapter 7 about the affection of the "Romagnoli" for Cesare. He and Vettori are discussing Pope Leo X's plans to create a new state in northern Italy to be ruled by Giuliano de' Medici, composed of Parma and Piacenza (taken from Milan) and Modena and Reggio (taken from Ferrara). In his discussion of the challenges faced by rulers of disparate territories formerly under the control of others, Machiavelli invokes Cesare in part because of the structural similarities in context – Pope Leo hoped to create a strong regional power firmly attached to the Medici family via his lieutenant Giuliano, just as Pope Alexander wished for an enduring Borgia state in Romagna via Cesare – but also because, just as he declared in *The Prince*, he judges Cesare's deeds worthy of emulation by new princes in general.[37] Machiavelli counsels against appointing a separate governor for each of the four territories in this potential northern Medicean state because it would remain "divided and devoid of prestige for him as well as unable to regard the prince with respect or fear."[38] Machiavelli instead counsels the more difficult plan of integrating the territories under central rule, offering Vettori the example of Cesare, who, faced with a similarly pluralistic regime in the Romagna, aspired to unify the territories into a single state, to popular acclaim.

Najemy interprets this letter as no less laden with irony than chapter 7's mocking praise of Cesare's "good foundations." For Najemy, the proof of Machiavelli's ironic voice stems from his apparent praise of Cesare's appointment of Ramiro de Lorqua as his governor. Machiavelli writes: "Since Duke Valentino ... was aware of this necessity, he appointed Messer Ramiro president in Romagna; this decision united those peoples and made them afraid of his authority, fond of his power, and trusting in it; all the love they felt for him, which was considerable, considering his unfamiliarity to them resulted from this decision."[39] In the discussions at the papal court about this new regional power in the making, Giuliano de' Medici was rumoured to be considering Francesco Vettori's brother Paolo as his governor. Equating Paolo in the Medici context with Ramiro in the Borgia context, Najemy concludes that Machiavelli could not have seriously recommended that, should his friend Paolo win the governor position, he model himself on Ramiro, because of Ramiro's bloody, sacrificial fate. For that reason, it follows also that Machiavelli's further statements of the region's love for Cesare are uttered with tongue firmly in cheek: "That Cesare Borgia, of all princes, should be invoked as a worthy example of power and rule based on affection, trust, and love seems in and of itself a massive irony in light of Machiavelli's own insistence, in both chapters 7 and 17, on the terror and fear inspired by Borgia's necessary cruelty."[40]

Najemy's reading, however, conflates the distinctive work that means and ends perform in Machiavelli's political world view and his correlation of the former with the many and the latter with the few. The crucial "decision" in the previous quotation that resulted in the people's love for Cesare was not Cesare's choice of means (his decision to appoint Ramiro per se as governor) but rather his choice of ends (his preference for a centralized government and the rule of law). In the absence of that distinction Najemy rightly sees a paradox – how could Machiavelli plausibly hold Cesare here as an example of "rule based on affect, trust, and love" when two years earlier in *The Prince* he had written about the "terror and fear inspired by Borgia's necessary cruelty"? But Machiavelli is concerned here less with Ramiro's bloody pacification campaign than with the good results generated by Cesare's reluctance to govern according to traditional respect for decentralized power. He established a strong, specifically popular foundation for his power, precisely what the Medici were hoping to achieve for Giuliano in the north, and precisely what Machiavelli championed in *The Prince.* The people, similarly oriented towards ends rather than means, benefited from those results. Hence, the affection that Machiavelli attributes to them here is both logical and consistent with his portrayal of Borgia in *The Prince.* Machiavelli's omission in this letter of the "terror and fear" of Cesare's rule that was allegedly implied in *The Prince* reflects only his concern with ends. The "terror and fear" caused by his means – the violent deployment of Ramiro de Lorqua – were felt not by the Romagnol people but by the Romagnol nobles who were Ramiro's target and the obstacle to that popular foundation. Cesare was simultaneously feared and loved – but not by the same constituencies.

Machiavelli's Positive Pre- and Post-*Prince* Assessments of Borgia

I hope by now to have established that Machiavelli's account of Cesare's Borgia's rise in chapter 7 is both internally consistent, in terms of logic and exposition, and consistent with Machiavelli's other lessons that he urged princes to embrace. The remaining question concerns the historical accuracy of Machiavelli's judgment of Cesare's good government and the alleged support of his subjects. In Najemy's analysis, Machiavelli's seemingly contradictory statements about Borgia signal to readers that his utterances are not his own judgments but rather sardonic mimicking of Cesare's delusional fantasies. Najemy's view explains why, elaborating on Borgia's strong foundations, Machiavelli does not declare that the people supported Cesare, but rather that it was only a matter of Cesare's perception – "it seemed to him [*parendoli*] above all that he had acquired the friendship of the people of the Romagna" – a statement apparently at odds with Machiavelli's discussion of the "hatred" generated by Ramiro's rough tactics. Najemy therefore reads Machiavelli's comments about the Romagnol people, much like his comments about Cesare's own forces, as mocking contrasts between the duke's self-portrait and reality.

Later in the chapter, however, Machiavelli returns to the people's support for Cesare, declares it in his own voice rather than the duke's, and offers historical evidence for that support. Assessing the dire situation for Cesare caused by the death of his father, Alexander VI, Machiavelli observes that Cesare had one and only one province under his control – the Romagna – with the rest of the papal states contested by multiple forces, beset by two powerful and opposed armies, and himself extremely ill. In this state of extreme vulnerability the Romagna nevertheless did not rise up against Cesare's rule but waited for over a month for Cesare to re-establish himself against his enemies, who by definition, Machiavelli implies, cannot have included the Romagnol people: "And that his foundations were good, we see; for Romagna continued waiting for him for over a month."[41] At this point it is not at all clear why, if Machiavelli's intention in the chapter was to satirize the duke's limited capacity for self-awareness, he would positively and entirely in his own voice declare the Romagnoli's supportive reaction to Cesare's sudden context of extreme weakness. Najemy discounts any relevance to that judgment on two grounds: (1) Machiavelli's early account of Ramiro and the "hatred" that he generated that appears to undermine it; and (2) a statement from a Florentine agent in the Romagna, reported by the contemporary historian Bartolomeo Cerretani, who "found the inhabitants, not only of Faenza but 'all of the Romagna,' ready to 'jump into the lap of our rule [*tutta la Romagna volta al gittarsi in grembo alla nostra signoria*]' and accept Florentine governance."[42]

Najemy concludes, consequently, that Machiavelli's assessment of Borgia's "own arms" and "good foundations" was "against all the facts, of which he was fully aware."[43] All scholars who have attributed an ironic, satirical, or esoteric voice to Machiavelli in chapter 7 stress, just as Najemy does, the degree to which Machiavelli's praise of Cesare flatly contradicted the historical record. Garrett Mattingly, for example, writes that, of Cesare's putative "good government," Machiavelli's account is contradicted by the "facts of history as reported by, among others, Machiavelli himself ... he never mentions these statesmanlike achievements ... nor do any other contemporary observers. All the indications are quite the contrary."[44] More recently, Erica Benner concurs: "Machiavelli – and many of his early readers – knew that Borgia's rule in the Romagna was unpopular."[45]

The "facts," however – defined as Machiavelli's own utterances and the conclusions of his contemporaries – are less clear than what has been implied. Analyses by Machiavelli in his legations suggest that he viewed Cesare's government as having earned the loyalty of its subjects – exactly as he had portrayed it in chapter 7. Machiavelli was an inventive, subversive, and irony-addicted author, and many of his personal writings contain startling contradictions, hence the challenge of determining whether surface statements should be read as literal expressions of his convictions. No such ambiguity, however, exists in his legations. Machiavelli's superiors in Florence expected dispassionate assessments of developments in the field, and his professional future, about which he cared more than anything, depended on their respect for those assessments. The Ten of War did not read esoterically or ironically. His reports of support for Cesare in the Romagna, therefore, cannot be dismissed as satire or irony. In addition to his legations, furthermore, his account of Cesare's murder of the *condottieri* at Senigallia and several of Francesco Guicciardini's judgments in both his *History of Florence* and his *History of Italy* provide additional evidence of Cesare's good government and the conspicuous loyalty shown to Cesare by his agents in territories under his control.[46]

Machiavelli's legations confirm, rather than contradict, chapter 7's verdict that the Romagnoli remained faithful to Cesare after the death of his father. A series of dispatches that Machiavelli wrote from Rome at the court of Julius II reveals the surprise of both Machiavelli and Julius II that, even after Cesare's arrest that put him at the pope's mercy, Julius nevertheless had to treat him warily and with feigned sympathy because of the influence that Cesare retained in the Romagna.

On 26 November 1503 Machiavelli reported that Julius had had Cesare arrested; rumours circulated that the pope had even ordered that Borgia be drowned in the Tiber. To his superiors in Florence, Machiavelli concluded that – even if Borgia were alive – his power had so diminished that his superiors in Florence need no longer concern themselves about him: "Now that Valentino is arrested, whether he is alive or dead, one can act without thinking further about this affair." The following day Machiavelli rejected the rumour of the Tiber drowning: "Of the Duke ... I know only that he is in Ostia in the Pope's power."[47]

How surprised they both must have been to learn on 28 November, when one of the pope's agents in the Romagna returned to Rome with an assessment directly at odds with that of Cerretani's Florentine agent who had reported that the Romagna was eager to accept Florentine rule. The pope's agent reported that the church had few supporters in Forlì because people there evidently preferred Cesare's rule to Caterina Sforza's, that in Imola the people remained loyal to Cesare, and that the castellan of Forlì supported Cesare unconditionally and was therefore preparing for a long siege: "Yesterday one of those men returned whom in the beginning the Pope had sent into Romagna; he reports that the Church has a very small party in Imola and Forlì, because they fear to be put back under Madonna; in Imola the people want the Duke, and the castellan of Forlì is going to fortify himself, and will keep his fidelity to the Duke as long as he lives. This account angered the Pope."[48]

Two days later Machiavelli reported that, because of Cesare's continued influence in the Romagna, the pope no longer treated him like a prisoner. Julius had changed tactics and was now sympathetically trying to negotiate – not dictate – the restoration of fortresses in the Romagna to papal control in exchange for Cesare's freedom. For Julius, it was imperative in these negotiations to maintain the fiction that he was not in fact Cesare's jailer, with power of life and death over him, because Julius feared that if it appeared to Cesare's lieutenants that the duke had acquiesced to return the fortresses only under duress, they would not cooperate: "It seems that the Pope does not yet treat Duke Valentino as a prisoner for life ... So the pope continues to soften him, and attempts to get the countersigns from him through agreement, so that it will not be learned that he has been forced to give them up, lest the castellans, in the belief that the Duke had been forced, make some trouble about turning over the castles to anyone except the Pope; and therefore he wishes to have the countersigns by agreement, as I have said."[49] At the absolute nadir of his fortunes, both Machiavelli and Julius witnessed that Cesare still commanded respect in the territories formerly under his rule.

Comments made by Machiavelli before and after those November legations align with his high estimation of Cesare's regime in chapter 7. In a dispatch of 2 November 1502 from Cesare's camp in Imola, Machiavelli views Cesare not only as a prince more than a hired general but also as a more legitimate prince than the other major participants in the conflicts in northern Italy because his regime evidently had more political substance than those of his rivals. As a result, regarding the prospect of the Florentine republic hiring Cesare, Machiavelli suggests that his station merits more an alliance, appropriate to relations with foreign states, than a contract, appropriate to the employment of mercenaries: "Third, as to this Duke's employment as general, I said to him [fictional interlocutor, not Cesare], speaking always for myself only, that his Excellency was not to be judged as are some of the other rulers, who have only the carriage, in comparison with the state he holds; but one should discuss him as a new potentate in Italy, with whom it is more proper to make a league or an alliance than an agreement as general."[50] Machiavelli's disdain here for rulers who "have only the carriage" but not the substance of government aligns with numerous laments made throughout his writings about the moral and political failings of the peninsular elite. That disdain did not apply to Cesare Borgia.

What made "the state" that Cesare "holds" sufficiently substantial that he merited being treated as a new potentate? Two passages reinforce the message of chapter 7's esteem for Cesare's good government, which consisted there of introducing a centralized circuit court of appeal for the region and forcibly restraining its thuggish barons from extorting their subjects. Evidence for the first aspect – the rule of law – is evident in Machiavelli's dispatch from Imola on 28 November 1502 in which Machiavelli praises the integrity and intelligence of the official that Cesare had appointed as the chief judge of his new court system: "Two days ago there came here the President of the Circuit Court that Duke Valentino has set up in this state, who is messer Antonio da Monte San Savino, a very learned man and of excellent character, and he resides at Cesena."[51] The fact that Borgia did not appoint one of his Spanish captains to mete out military justice but rather acquired a highly respected Italian judge suggests that Cesare took seriously the ambition to resolve the region's conflicts via peaceful, legal methods. In all his political writings and especially in *The Discourses on Livy*, the *Florentine Histories*, and the *Discourse on Florentine Affairs after the Death of Lorenzo*, Machiavelli similarly insisted on the necessity of open, public-facing mechanisms of conflict resolution.

Evidence of the second aspect – the protection of his subjects – is evident in Machiavelli's literary account of Cesare's murder of his mercenary rivals in Senigallia.[52] Having dispatched his enemies, Cesare permitted his soldiers to plunder the troops of Liverotto da Fermo, the Orsini, and the Vitelli. Cesare's forces looted Liverotto's soldiers immediately, but the forces of the Orsini and the Vitelli, owing to their further distance from the fortress of Senigallia, had time to flee. Deprived of the riches of two thirds of Cesare's enemies, Cesare's soldiers turned on Senigallia itself, commencing his fledgling lordship there with the spectre of a violent sack. Cesare, however, saved the town by violently restraining his own troops: "But the soldiers of the Duke, not being satisfied with the plunder of the followers of Liverotto, began to sack Sinigaglia; and if the Duke had not with the death of many restrained their excesses, they would have sacked it entirely ... by the end of the same day, the disturbances had been stopped."[53] According to the Perugian historian Francesco Matarazzo, cited in Najemy's critique of Borgia rule, "mercenaries flocked to Borgia because he allowed them to plunder the territories they occupied."[54] In this one instance at least, of which Machiavelli had direct experience, Cesare does precisely the opposite, protecting the people from military predation – the very first aspect of Cesare's *buon governo* praised in chapter 7 of *The Prince.*

This same text – Machiavelli's later, literary account of Cesare's murder of his mercenary enemies – also includes interesting echoes of Machiavelli's report in his legations that the castellan of Forlì would turn over the fortress keys to Cesare only. In most accounts of the murderous last supper that Borgia arranged for his enemies, Borgia is described as the architect of the plan that results in their collective assembly at Senigallia.[55] In Machiavelli's narration, however, it is the Vitelli and the Orsini, at this point notionally in Cesare's employ but clearly hostile, who propose their campaign against Senigallia, not Cesare who does. Their emissary, Liverotto da Fermo, had presented Cesare with a choice: the Orsini and the Vitelli wished either to join Cesare in a Tuscan campaign or, failing that, to besiege Senigallia: "The Duke replied that he would not begin war in Tuscany because the Florentines were his friends, but that he would be much pleased if they went to Sinigaglia."[56] Machiavelli then further specifies that it was Cesare's enemies who invited him to Senigallia, not the other way around, because the castellan of the fortress had refused to surrender the keys to anyone but Cesare: "As a result, not many days later he received a dispatch that Sinigaglia had surrendered to them, but that they had not yet captured the fortress because the castellan was determined to give it to the Duke in person and to no one else; hence they urged him to come to the city."[57]

The castellan was in fact a Genoese, Andrea Doria. Why he refused to surrender the keys to Cesare's then lieutenants is unclear. In his family biography of the Borgias, Michael Mallett reports the incident without commentary on motives.[58] In her biography of Cesare Borgia, Sarah Bradford reasons that Doria was a co-conspirator with the Vitelli and the Orsini.[59] By declaring that he would surrender the fortress to Cesare only, Doria provided the Vitelli and the Orsini with a plausible motive for summoning Cesare, presumably to his destruction amid his enemies and their collective armies. Machiavelli neither identifies Doria nor alludes to the plotting of Cesare's enemies. On the contrary, as Machiavelli reports it, the castellan's apparent loyalty to Cesare's command is the prime mover in Cesare's scheme to destroy his enemies. As a consequence of the castellan's stubbornness, Cesare's arrival in Senigallia, far from seeming potentially threatening, appears to be the result of his enemies' wishes: "To the Duke the opportunity seemed good and not such as to arouse suspicion, since he was invited by them and was not going of himself."[60]

In Bradford's interpretation, the Vitelli and the Orsini had planned to murder Cesare in Senigallia, hence the ruse of the castellan and keys requiring Cesare's physical presence in the coastal town. Machiavelli's account contradicts this interpretation, however, because he stresses multiple efforts by Cesare to keep his enemies in Senigallia, who, following the siege, had evidently planned to depart prior to Cesare's arrival: "So leaving Cesena about the middle of December, he went to Fano, where with the all crafty and prudent words he could use, he persuaded the Vitelli and Orsini to wait for him in Sinigaglia ... And though Vitellozzo was very reluctant, and the death of his brother had taught him that one ought not to injure a prince and then trust him, nonetheless, persuaded by Paolo Orsini, whom the Duke had bribed with gifts and promises, he agreed to wait for him."[61] Machiavelli, who was in Borgia's camp at the time of this episode, was a close witness to the events. The only coherent reading of his account would suggest that the castellan of the fortress was a co-conspirator in the plans of Cesare, not those of his enemies. Why would the Orsini and the Vitelli arrange for the castellan to cause Cesare's arrival to accept the fortress keys if by the time of his arrival they themselves would have already gone? However, the castellan's refusal to surrender the keys to anyone but Cesare provided crucial assistance to Cesare's scheme – by forcing the Orsini and the Vitelli to invite him to Senigallia, it camouflaged his various efforts to keep them there by implying that he was an agent of their plans, rather than vice versa.

Guicciardini's Estimation of Borgia's Regime

Francesco Guicciardini, a famously scrupulous, source-driven historian – perhaps the most thorough and careful chronicler of the *calamità d'Italia* – confirms the essence of Machiavelli's various positive statements about Cesare. His early *History of Florence*, begun in 1508, five years earlier than the composition of *The Prince* (which definitively excludes chapter 7 as an influence), analysed Cesare's prospects following the death of his father in much the same way that Machiavelli did. Guicciardini details the sudden territorial collapse of the Borgia state upon Alexander VI's death: the Vitelli reclaimed Castello; Gianpaolo Baglioni besieged Perugia with Florentine help; Guido da Montefeltro retook Urbino; and the Orsini family returned to their various territories in the papal states. The Romagna, however, continued to support Cesare. Guicciardini's explanation of their motives confirms not only Machiavelli's estimation of Cesare's good government and the popular favour towards him but also Machiavelli's view that, had Cesare not been ill at the same time that his father died, he would have succeeded in establishing permanent control of the Romagna: "Only the states of the Romagna remained firm; and if Valentino had been well, he would certainly have kept them, for the people there loved him dearly on account of the great justice and integrity with which his administrators governed."[62] Guicciardini's account even confirmed Machiavelli's report that the castellan of Forlì had refused to surrender the fortress to the pope (though he attributed it here to the self-interest of the Spanish castellan rather than to concern for Cesare, the motive that Guicciardini subsequently attributed to the castellan in his *History of Italy*, discussed next).[63]

Thirty years later, Guicciardini revisited the rise and fall of Cesare Borgia from a broader peninsular perspective in his *History of Italy*, his last, most widely read, and monumental work of history. Here, too, his account substantiated and even expanded upon Machiavelli's estimation of Borgia's government in his legations and the "good foundations" specified in chapter 7 of *The Prince*. Some of the similarity between Guicciardini's account of Cesare in his *History of Italy* and Machiavelli's in *The Prince* might be explained by the presence of *The Prince* as one of his sources (*The Prince* was first published in 1532, and Guicciardini began the *History of Italy* in 1537). Guicciardini's account of the tactical problems that Cesare faced following Alexander's death seems to invoke chapter 7. Guicciardini explains that, owing to his unexpected illness, Cesare "had much more difficulty than he had earlier imagined in carrying out this or any other of his schemes."[64] The undefined schemes in Guicciardini's account are famously itemized by Machiavelli in chapter 7, all designed to prevent any future hostile pope from acquiring enough local power to undo the Borgia state in northern Italy. This involved (1) destroying the families whose territories he had seized to eradicate a potentially vengeful fifth column; (2) making allies of the powerful Roman families; (3) making allies of the College of Cardinals; and (4) acquiring enough territory that he would be able to withstand an attack. As we saw previously, in Machiavelli's estimation, Cesare had already achieved all but the last of these schemes upon Alexander's death. After itemizing Borgia's schemes, Machiavelli then shifts from analysis to personal anecdote, inserting himself into the narrative and providing the source for his conclusion, a conversation that he had had directly with Cesare: "And [Cesare] said to me himself, on Julius II's accession-day, that he had imagined what could happen when his father died, and for everything he had found a solution, except he had never imagined that at the time of that death he too would be close to dying."[65] Guicciardini includes that private confession in his account in virtually the same words. After stressing the difficulties that Cesare faced because of his illness, Guicciardini concludes: "For this reason, he complained with the greatest indignation that although he had formerly often anticipated all the difficulties that might result from his father's death and had planned all the remedies against such troubles, it had never occurred to him that he also might happen to be impeded by a dangerous illness at the same time."[66] Perhaps Cesare complained about this so frequently that it was common knowledge. A likelier explanation, however, given the striking textual similarities, is that Guicciardini had read and agreed with Machiavelli's analysis in *The Prince* and incorporated it directly into his history.

Guicciardini's treatment of Cesare's government in the *History of Italy* not only reiterates but also expands upon his statements of Borgia "good government" in *The History of Florence*, and, again, in ways that corroborate and expand upon Machiavelli's vision in chapter 7. After detailing the swift return, following Alexander's death, of those rulers whom Cesare had ousted from their territories, Guicciardini relates that only the Romagna remained firmly in support of Cesare. His explanation for the motives for that support focuses on the advantages conferred by Cesare's centralized regime. Subjugating the region's feuding lords under Cesare's rule may have been detrimental to those lords, but it benefited their subjects because in the formerly decentralized context – the Romagnol status quo for centuries – local nobles could neither protect their subjects from external aggression nor confer material advantages. On the contrary, because of their meagre resources, they were incentivized to plunder their subjects: "The Romagna was inclined to devotion to Valentino because it had learned from experience how much more tolerable it had been for that region to serve all together under a single powerful lord than for each of those cities to remain under a particular prince, who could not defend them because of his weakness or benefit them because of his poverty, but rather was bound to oppress them inasmuch as his small revenues were insufficient for his support."[67] Of Machiavelli's twofold identification of Cesare's "good foundations," Guicciardini here confirms the first, Machiavelli's estimation in *The Prince* that via Cesare's protection the Romagnol people (not their former rulers) had begun to "taste their own well-being."[68]

Guicciardini also confirms the second foundation – Cesare's imposition of the rule of law. By establishing the Rota, the circuit court of appeals governed by the respected chief judge Antonio da Monte San Savino, Cesare introduced another innovation beneficial to the Romagnol people. Lacking a centralized court to adjudicate disputes among the region's nobles, they tended to resolve their differences through factional wars and murder, the traditional private methods that Machiavelli so frequently contrasted with the salutary public methods vital to good government. The new circuit court and its evidently capable officials channelled that violence into legal disputes, thereby providing yet another way that Cesare's rule resulted in unprecedented yet welcome physical and material security for his subjects: "The Romagnoli also remembered that as a result of Valentino's authority and greatness and because of the honest administration of justice, that country had remained at peace and been spared the factional conflicts which had previously vexed them continually and frequently resulted in assassinations."[69] Guicciardini also confirms the degree to which, as Machiavelli specified in chapter 7 about the defection of Orsini and Colonna leadership, Cesare won people over via military and civil appointments, such that – relative to the rule of Cesare's predecessors – his regime generated satisfaction: "Valentino's measures had served to make the people feel kindly disposed toward him; and similarly he had won many of them over by giving them benefits, by distributing money among picked troops, government officials and magistrates (both of his domain and of the Church), and helping ecclesiastics in matters which would be beneficial to his father: whence neither the example of the other states, where everyone was rebelling, nor the memory of their former lords, estranged them from Valentino."[70] From the corroborating testimony of Francesco Guicciardini, the period's foremost historian of the Italian wars, we see that – contrary to Mattingly, Najemy, and Benner – Machiavelli's account of Borgia's good government was not contrary to *all the facts.* Further, Guicciardini identified the very same twofold *fondamenti*: protecting the Romagnoli from their own predatory rulers and introducing the rule of law (and not a word about Cesare's "own arms"!).

Guicciardini's subsequent discussion of the wary relationship between Cesare and Julius II also confirms Machiavelli's legations indicating that, owing to the Romagna's loyalty, however much Julius had the power of life and death over Cesare, Cesare remained an independent actor whose power was respected. Following Alexander's death, Guicciardini contrasted the collapse of Borgia power in Città di Castello, Perugia, Piombino, Urbino, Pesaro, Camerino, and Senigallia with the sole loyalty of the Romagna and a discussion of the benefits Cesare conferred there. Guicciardini concludes: "Thus [owing to Romagnol support], although he was oppressed by so many difficulties, both the Spaniards and the French were making great overtures towards him with many promises and offers to join with them."[71]

Julius II, too, made similar overtures. Fearful of Venetian incursions into the Romagna caused by the collapse of the Borgia state in the northern cities of that region, Julius's initial plan was to return Cesare to Imola and reunite him there with the "one hundred men-at-arms and one hundred fifty light horse who still followed his banner" (a small force, not likely enough to counter Venice's forces but perhaps an indication of a small, inner corps of Romagnoli conscripts that Machiavelli warmed to as Cesare's "own arms").[72] Immediately regretting that he had not transferred control of the fortresses there to his own agents, Julius sent the cardinals of Volterra and Sorrento to Ostia, where Cesare was embarking on the first leg of his return to the Romagna, to persuade him to return the fortresses. Cesare refused, and "the Pope became wrathful and had him arrested on the galley" and returned to Rome, where he was surrounded by enemies: "whence he was taken to the Vatican, the entire court and all Rome rejoicing because of his arrest."[73] Just as Machiavelli reported in his legations, however, in spite of the overwhelming power disparity between the triumphant Julius and the imprisoned Cesare, the pope nevertheless had to proceed diplomatically and respectfully, given the loyalty of Cesare's agents in the Romagnol fortresses: "He was treated honourably and gently (although under a diligent guard) because the Pope feared that the castellans, despairing for his [Cesare's] safety, might not sell the fortresses to the Venetians; therefore Julius sought, by humane and peaceful means, to have the fortresses countersigned to him by Valentino."[74]

Guicciardini also confirms Machiavelli's statement in chapter 7 that Borgia was on the brink of becoming lord of Tuscany prior to his father's death, another instance in Najemy's interpretation of Machiavelli channelling Borgia's self-indulgent capacity for wishful thinking.[75] Machiavelli justifies this view with reference to the territories surrounding Tuscany that were currently in Borgia's possession and to the relative ease with which he compelled alliances with the Tuscan city states that were already resentful of Florentine rule:

> And as to further conquest, he had planned to become ruler of Tuscany, he already possessed Perugia and Piombino, and Pisa he had taken under his protection. And as soon as he no longer needed to defer to the King of France (and he would not need to do so much longer, since already the French were deprived of the Kingdom by the Spaniards, in such a way that each of them would have to buy his friendship), he would jump onto Pisa. After this, Lucca and Siena would yield at once, partly through envy of the Florentines, partly through fear. The Florentines would have no recourse.[76]

In Machiavelli's analysis, the ability of Florence to withstand Borgia's aggression depended entirely on the goodwill of the French king.

Guicciardini's *History of Florence* confirms that, without intervention from the French king, Florentines had good cause to fear Cesare's conquest of Tuscany. Regarding Cesare and Vitellozzo's campaigns near Florence, Guicciardini wrote: "The stakes then were the restoration of Piero and the rebellion of those who had expelled him; now, they were the loss of liberty and the diminution of whatever dominion we still possessed. With Arezzo and almost our whole state lost, the city was now reduced to such straits that unless the king saved it, Florence would have to agree to whatever conditions the enemy imposed ... Even the return of Piero could be considered a lesser evil to falling under the yoke of the pope and Valentino."[77]

Guicciardini's diary also lends credence to the reality of the Borgia threat, at least as understood by his family. Guicciardini explains that his father had sent him to study at the University of Ferrara in March of 1500, in part because "the affairs of Florence were very troubled at that time," a reference to conflict with Pisa and France and increasing danger from Borgia in 1501. His father's specific motive to relocate Francesco to Ferrara was to ensure a safe location to store cash in the event that Borgia did march to the city's gates: "He wished to have a safe place to send his valuables if there should arise some revolution in the city, or some threat to its liberty from without."[78] The fact that Francesco's father, Piero, swiftly funnelled funds to him in Ferrara, and Francesco's own observation about deteriorating conditions in Florence, both suggest that Machiavelli's estimation of Florence's vulnerability to Borgia aggression was grounded in sober observation rather than in satire: "When I left Florence he gave me five hundred gold ducats, and a few days later as things got worse in Florence, he sent me a further five hundred, and not long after a thousand more, and although I was young and under no one's control, I rendered him a careful account of all this."[79]

In addition to an accounting for Guicciardini's testimony from his diary and *History of Florence*, an ironic reading of Machiavelli's conclusion that Cesare nearly attained the conquest of Tuscany would also need to account for his commentary in chapter 3 of *The Prince*. Machiavelli discusses the miscalculations of the French king Louis XII, who unwisely aided Alexander VI in increasing the church's temporal power. In that chapter, in which Machiavelli does not mention Cesare by name and for which therefore no scholar has proposed an esoteric or ironic reading, Machiavelli declares that Louis was compelled to march on Italy to prevent a Borgia conquest of Tuscany: "Nor did he understand that by this policy [initial support for Alexander VI] he was making himself weak – by getting rid of his friends and those who had thrown themselves into his arms – and the Church strong, by adding to the spiritual power which gives her such great influence, so much temporal power. Yet having made his first mistake, he was forced to go on until, to put an end to Alexander's ambition and keep him from becoming ruler of Tuscany, the King was forced to come into Italy."[80] Given that Cesare was always Alexander's political instrument in the exercise of secular rule, Machiavelli effectively declares here that, were it not for French intervention, Cesare would likely have become lord of Tuscany. To conclude otherwise, one would have to provide a plausible motive for an ironic reading of Machiavelli's interpretation of Louis XII's judgment.

However authoritative Machiavelli and Guicciardini were as historians (and they were two of the greatest – perhaps the greatest – historians produced by Renaissance culture), one still has to explain why so few contemporary sources align with their positive assessments of Borgia's rule. As Garrett Mattingly, the Borgia debate's most thorough reader of diplomatic correspondence, observed, not one report from the French, Spanish, Sienese, and Venetian ambassadors to Borgia's camp mentions popular esteem for his Romagnol regime, and, as Najemy noted, contemporary historians such as Piero Parenti, Bartolomeo Cerretani, and the anonymous Perugian chronicler all recorded variations of local hostility towards Cesare's government.

Michael Mallett's discussion of Cesare's government provides the crucial insight that helps explain why Machiavelli and Guicciardini seized on details omitted by the vastly more ubiquitous condemnations of Borgia rule. Mallett recognizes that, before one can assess the historical legitimacy of Machiavelli's claims about Cesare's "good government," one must first establish how contemporaries would have understood that term. As he elaborates, Machiavelli's conception of good government differed substantially from conventional expectations (unsurprising, of course, given how frequently he deviated from the conventional pieties of his contemporaries). The pre-existing conception of good government, typical of decentralized regions throughout medieval and early modern Europe, consisted first and foremost in respect for and protection of traditional local and group privileges, as well as "fair administration of a traditional justice, relief from taxes, the establishment of order so that the old pattern of Romagnol society could live on undisturbed. Such a conception of *buon governo* was essentially conservative."[81] At times, Cesare certainly embraced this vision. As Mallett explains, he did so for reasons of expediency and pragmatism because it "was the key to general popularity and a *quick* restoration of a certain stability and order."[82] The traditional, conservative notion of *buon governo,* as Mallett stresses, fundamentally obstructed innovation in general, and centralization in particular, always anathema to local elites.

Cesare also had his own distinctive conception of good government that was directly at odds with the tradition. His ultimate goal involved a longer-term, novel, and vastly more ambitious conception of centralized government in the region that would ultimately abolish local jurisdictions to create a single state powerful enough to equal the peninsula's other major powers such as Florence, Venice, Naples, and Milan. In pursuit of that vision of good government – his own, not the region's – Cesare violently curbed the nobility's predatory excesses and resolved their private quarrels via public institutions, in this case his new circuit court of appeals, the "good foundations" praised by Machiavelli in chapter 7. Much like Cesare's other similarly ambitious but ultimately failed project to acquire a formidable army composed entirely of Romagnol conscripts loyal to him only, the reach of Cesare here exceeded his grasp. Even if the grasp failed, however, as Mallett observes, the attempt to acquire it – his reach – "was not likely to be popular with a majority of the local population."[83] Indeed! For the region's numerous lords, powerful enough only to plunder their own inhabitants and long accustomed to a weak papacy that routinely confirmed their right to do so in exchange for notional promises of fealty, Cesare's vision of good government posed an existential, extinction-level threat.

Why would the people of the Romagna – subjects, not rulers – object to Cesare's new, centralized political vision in their lands? As Machiavelli declared numerous times in an axiom at the heart of his political thought, the people wish only to live unmolested and secure in the possession of their property and material goods. All accounts from this period, Machiavelli's and Guicciardini's included, speak with one voice about the Romagna prior to Cesare (and in Guicciardini's case, afterwards, as we will see shortly): it was, to use an anachronistic term, a failed state, characterized by chronic violence among its governing elites and funded by the equally chronic extortion of their subjects' wealth. If the Romagnol people felt hatred towards those above them, it surely must have been directed at the region's traditional, notable families, Cesare's opponents. If, as Machiavelli wrote to Soderini, the people were generally concerned with ends rather than means, they also surely must have recognized that their overriding collective desire – security of life and material wealth – was the immediate by-product of Cesare's ends, that is, a centralized state with impartial and effective administration of justice. In short, the Romagnol people were the chief beneficiaries of Cesare's temporary pacification of the region and of his new institutions. As Machiavelli alludes in chapter 7, it was Cesare's means, not ends, that generated hatred, particularly Ramiro de Lorqua's effective campaign of pacification aimed specifically at the region's nobility. For all his rough violence, Ramiro was clearly engaged in something different from the Romagna's traditional conflicts. Rather than raising funds for Cesare by plundering the region, Ramiro was breaking the political will and power of the traditional plunderers themselves.

It should come as no surprise that the historical record contains few references to popular favour towards Cesare and abundant assertions of the contrary. Cesare's enemies monopolize the written record.[84] His campaigns in Tuscany had alienated the Florentines, whose hatred of Cesare is so abundantly clear in the histories of Piero Parenti and Bartolomeo Cerretani. The Venetian republic had its own territorial ambitions in the Romagna that would have been unrealizable were Cesare to succeed in unifying the region under his command – hence the many declarations of disdain for his rule in the *relazioni* of their ambassadors.[85] At the papal court in Rome, Italian cardinals widely resented Spanish usurpation of the papacy. And all the baronial families who had long considered prelacies in church government and even the papal tiara itself to be a birthright were the very same families targeted by Ramiro in the Romagna: the Orsini, the Colonna, and the Della Rovere. Small wonder, then, that positive assessments are few and far between.

Machiavelli's estimation of Cesare's "good foundations" resulted not from contact with written testimony but rather from his eyewitness sense of matters on the ground as he travelled throughout the region in Cesare's camp. Given what we know about Cesare's plans and who stood to gain and lose from their implementation, Machiavelli's statement that Cesare had gained the people's affection seems altogether more plausible than the opposite. And given his larger political project of defending the rationality of the multitude from the judgments of his aristocratic peers and of "all the writers," there is even less wonder that the perspective of the Romagnol people counted for more with Machiavelli – designated a secretary rather than an ambassador because he lacked the requisite distinguished family for that title – than it did for the ambassadors in Cesare's camp.

If Machiavelli's self-identification with the many rather than the few helps explain the contrast between his assessment and the general trend of diplomatic chatter about Cesare, what explains Guicciardini's multiple statements of Cesare's popularity among the Romagnoli and the integrity of his judicial system? Guicciardini was a proud aristocrat, conspicuously aware of his family's high status, and therefore far more likely to respect the verdicts of ambassadors, who were presumably drawn from the ranks of the experienced, prudential few whom he so frequently praised. Like Parenti, Cerretani, and other Florentine historians, at a personal level he loathed the Borgia father and son. The vast majority of his utterances, whether in the early *History of Florence* or the later *History of Italy*, express high-minded moral outrage at the bottomless depths of Borgia depravity. In *The History of Florence* he asserts that it was "firmly believed" that Rodrigo and Cesare shared an incestuous relationship with Lucrezia, the former's daughter and the latter's sister, and that Cesare, having conquered Faenza, betrayed a promise of safety and freedom to the city's boy ruler, Astorre Manfredi; Cesare instead imprisoned, raped, and murdered him.[86] Narrating the great joy taken in Rome by Alexander's death, Guicciardini writes: "All Rome thronged with incredible rejoicing to see the dead body of Alexander in Saint Peter's, unable to satiate their eyes enough with seeing spent that serpent who in his boundless ambition and pestiferous perfidy, and with all his examples of horrible cruelty and monstrous sensuality and unheard-of avarice, selling without distinction sacred and profane things, had envenomed the entire world."[87] As we saw previously, the *History of Italy*, in its inclusion of Machiavelli's personal anecdote about Cesare lamenting the consequences of his unforeseen illness, may have drawn on *The Prince* as a source, which in turn might explain Guicciardini's discussion of Cesare's good government. Guicciardini did not, however, simply reiterate Machiavelli's brief remarks in chapter 7 but expanded on them in greater detail. He also praised Cesare's good government in *The History of Florence*, written prior to *The Prince* and Guicciardini's friendship with Machiavelli, categorically ruling out Machiavelli as a source for that early positive verdict. Nor did Machiavelli discuss Cesare with Guicciardini in their correspondence.

Even though he did not have Machiavelli's first-hand view of Borgia's interactions with the Romagnoli, Guicciardini had direct, personal experiences that made him arguably the most informed judge on the question of the effectiveness of Borgia's government. In 1524 Clement VII appointed Guicciardini the president of the Romagna, charged with the very same task that Alexander had charged Cesare by appointing him Duke of the Romagna roughly twenty years earlier. Cesare and Guicciardini both set out forcibly to remake Romagnol government from the vision upheld by local elites – a dense, pluralistic patchwork quilt of regional autonomy and unique privileges – into the innovative vision of strong, centralized papal government. For both, implementing that vision meant war with the region's bellicose and lawless families.[88] During his presidency Guicciardini was compelled to see the world through Cesare's eyes: both owed their power to papal appointments, and both served as papal lieutenants, and in their own and the world's eyes the confidence that their papal masters had in them was evident in the difficulty of the job with which they had been entrusted – taming the Romagna, "proverbially the most factious in Italy."[89]

Like Cesare, Guicciardini was immensely ambitious and aspired to complete Cesare's unfinished agenda of unity and rule of law. Perhaps better than any Renaissance contemporary, Guicciardini appreciated the challenges that Cesare faced. On 19 June 1521 he confessed to Clement: "I cannot do otherwise than curse every day a thousand times the hour in which I came to this province, and surely if His Holiness wished it to be governed in this manner, he should have sent someone else."[90] Arriving in the medium-term aftermath of the collapse of the Borgia state there, Guicciardini, much like Ramiro, had been obliged to mete out particularly rough justice. A few years later he expressed repeated concern in his letters to the Roman court for papal absolution for his frequent imprisonment, torture, and execution of the region's numerous uncooperative papal vicars – rough means indeed in pursuit of the ends of centralized papal government.[91] Twenty-one years had elapsed between Alexander's death in 1503 and Guicciardini's appointment as president of the Romagna in 1524 – not a long enough interregnum that Guicciardini would not have been surrounded by Cesare's living memory, and against whose rule he surely must have compared his own. If he hated the family at a personal level for their moral failings, by the time he had begun composing the *History of Italy*, his experience of holding Cesare's former job led him to acknowledge that Cesare had ruled with impartial and respected justice and that he had repressed the region's marauding nobles sufficiently effectively to win the affection and appreciation of the Romagnol people.

By way of conclusion, I propose a solution to two venerable questions at the heart of the Machiavelli-Borgia controversy: (1) why, if Machiavelli believed that Cesare had acquired his own arms, did he assign Cesare to chapter 7 rather than to chapter 6, on the topic of those who come to power with their own arms? And (2) why, given the general disfavour towards Cesare in Italy and his ultimate failure, would Machiavelli advocate to his hoped-for Medici readers that they model themselves on Cesare's actions?

The answers lie in the style and habits of Machiavelli's way of thinking. The vision held by Machiavelli, as an intellectual, historian, and philosopher, often gravitated towards fascination with mythological ideal types from which he derived abstract and universal principles. We see this Machiavelli in his address to Vettori in which he famously describes himself donning the vestments of court and palace and conversing nocturnally with the ancients. The vision of Machiavelli, a civil servant, de facto ambassador, and seeker of Medici employment, equally gravitated towards applied, rather than theoretical, possibilities – towards what limited gains one could make under adverse and often swiftly changing circumstances.

Machiavelli alludes to these two ways of thinking in the dedication when he announces his credentials as an adviser: "my lengthy experience with recent matters and my continual reading on ancient ones."[92] Both visions are abundantly evident in *The Prince* and, although at times they appear to conflict, they both represent Machiavelli's convictions.

Chapter 6 of *The Prince*, which famously discusses the virtue of rulers who come to power via their own arms and ability, reflects Machiavelli the visionary. It deals primarily with founder figures whose stature and role in history seamlessly blend history and myth: the demigod Theseus who founded Athens; Romulus, founder of the Roman empire; Cyrus, founder of the Persian empire; and Moses, a major prophet of the semitic religions. Machiavelli had no contemporaries about whom he could plausibly suggest parallels with such world-altering figures. Even if Machiavelli had discerned people of such potential among the princes of Italy in his day, they would not belong in chapter 6 for the simple reason that none of the rulers of Italy had established arms of their own; with the sole, brief exception of Machiavelli's failed militia experiment in Florence, every Italian power relied on mercenary forces. This explains why the only contemporary that Machiavelli invokes – Girolamo Savonarola – is deployed as a contrast, the failed modern version of the armed prophet Moses.

Chapters 7 and 8, however, reflect Machiavelli the adviser and tactician. There he begins to invoke his contemporaries, such as Francesco Sforza and Liverotto da Fermo, in terms of instructive lessons worth emulating, even if his examples fall short of the theoretical ideal outlined in chapter 6. In chapters 7 and 8 Machiavelli holds up as examples people who at least recognized the value of what he wrote at the outset of chapter 6: "Since men almost always walk in the paths beaten by others and carry on their affairs by imitating – even though it is not possible to keep wholly in the paths of others or to attain the ability of those you imitate – a prudent man will always choose to take paths beaten by great men and to imitate those who have been especially admirable, in order that if his ability does not reach theirs, at least it may offer some suggestion of it."[93] None of his contemporaries was suitable for comparison on the basis of achievement with the mythological heroes of antiquity, but he could find examples of those with virtuous aspirations, whose actions might offer "some suggestion" of the true founders of new modes and orders.

Machiavelli must have seen Cesare Borgia in these terms and identified him as someone who shared many convictions that Machiavelli had distilled from his experiences and his reading of ancient history. The entire vision of Cesare in *The Prince* is essentially present, fully formed, in Machiavelli's dispatch of 13 November 1502 from Cesare's camp in

Imola: "And the way to keep [what he has conquered] is to continue to be armed with his own arms, to gain his subjects' favour, and to make allies of his neighbours. That is [Cesare's] intention."[94] Machiavelli was interested less in the fact of Cesare's failure than in the potential of his intentions. Who else among the warring potentates of Italy in Machiavelli's day aspired to military autonomy? Who else introduced new modes and orders in the territories under their control, centralizing their states and replacing violent feuds with public-facing legal institutions? Who shared Machiavelli's view that a prudent prince should dispense with noble support and instead make allies of his people? Cesare was certainly more successful at building a new regime than he was at establishing military self-sufficiency, but Machiavelli was not interested in that distinction: his portrait and praise of Cesare reflected his sense of the soundness of Cesare's aspirations.

In terms of pragmatic, realizable objectives, the example of Cesare – unlike that of Moses or Theseus – resonated in the Medici context in precise, applicable ways. Both Cesare and the Medici had come to power by force of Spanish arms. Both ruled territories on behalf of a pope. Machiavelli had already counselled the Medici not to incur the people's hostility and to be wary of the aristocrats who had helped arrange the family's return to the city, whose long-term hostility was vastly more significant than their fleeting support.[95] Cesare recognized in the approval of Romagnol subjects a significant source of stability and power, to the direct detriment of the region's noble families, whose relationship to Cesare was not dissimilar to that of the Florentine *ottimati* to the Medici. He aspired to arm his people and defend himself with the affections of his armed subjects, precisely what Machiavelli advocated numerous times. By emphasizing the strength and stability that Cesare enjoyed as a result of popular favour, Machiavelli was not only counselling the Medici not to count on *ottimati* support but also implicitly reminding them of the people's rationality and dependability, provided that the ends of Medici rule benefited them.

Given the disaster that befell sixteenth-century Italy, all its princes were failures, Cesare included. The failure of Cesare, however, unlike every other political actor in the Italian wars, occurred despite his ambitions, not because of them, a point that Machiavelli and Guicciardini both recognized and respected.

Conclusion

Given how close Machiavelli and Guicciardini were personally and professionally, scholarship on their political thought is surprisingly divided in its portrayal of their intellectual relationship, one camp portraying them as a study in opposites and the other as champions of a shared vision.

Scholars such as Quentin Skinner and John Pocock, and the many others loosely associated with the Cambridge school of political thought, interpret Machiavelli as a canonical member of the republican, mixed-constitution tradition.[1] While acknowledging the novelty of his praise of tumults, they nevertheless define him as a conventional republican thinker, part of a tradition linking ancient Greece and Rome, early modern Italy and Britain, and anti-monarchists of the Enlightenment and revolutionary eras.[2] As a consequence of that conventional interpretation, their accounts of Renaissance political thought portray Machiavelli and Guicciardini as fundamentally similar thinkers, with only passing recognition of Guicciardini's traditional praise of unity in contrast to Machiavelli's minor, idiosyncratic praise of conflict.[3] Scholars such as John McCormick and Yves Winter, by contrast, privilege Machiavelli's praise of conflict and the muscular populism that it legitimates, as the defining feature of his political thought. Their accounts of Machiavelli's politics stress the degree to which he was the only thinker in an otherwise thoroughly elitist tradition who granted the people an active role in political life and empowered them to discipline violently their social betters when necessary.[4]

Both camps, however, share a common understanding of Guicciardini, who functions as a static counterpart to contrasting interpretations of Machiavelli's political thought that portray Machiavelli as either a fundamentally traditional thinker or a violent innovator. Guicciardini is the unwavering champion of a senatorial mixed republican constitution.

As Felix Gilbert expressed it in his 1965 classic, "Guicciardini had the aristocratic conviction that his class knew better than anyone else how to rule because they had been trained and schooled in the art of government."[5] John Najemy recently expresses the same view: "Guicciardini never relinquished his nostalgia for [the Albizzi oligarchy], which was, after all, the only instance in the century and a half from 1382 to the 1520s of a Florentine government entirely in the hands of those 'men of worth' – like himself – to whom he always attributed the qualities he believed to be necessary to save the republic from both (Medici) tyranny and broad-based popular government."[6] Both camps also devote considerably more attention to reconstructing the nuances of Machiavelli's political thought than they do interrogating Guicciardini – unsurprising, perhaps, given that discussion of the two's relationship is effectively a method for situating Machiavelli in the tradition.

I have taken a different approach and addressed the question of how their writings intersect based on a close reading of Guicciardini, with a largely static Machiavelli in the background (except for the latter's chapter 7). First a clarification about the presentation of Machiavelli is required. As my focus is on Guicciardini, the book does not take up the question invoked in the introduction of how to interpret Machiavelli's new, seemingly aristocratic claims about the extremism and ingratitude of the people in his last major work, the *Florentine Histories.* In my various summaries and recapitulations of Machiavelli's political thought I have presented him as a violent populist and therefore as a radical critic of the political tradition. I think that position best captures the essence and major purpose of his political writings, and it certainly captures the most immediate and substantial contrast between the accounts of Machiavelli and most (arguably all) accounts of Guicciardini. Guicciardini, however, does receive close scrutiny, and the book addresses, in detail, the changes in his thinking over time and the seeming contradictions between his theoretical pronouncements in favour of an elite, senatorial order and his historical observations about the political profiles of nobles and people that appear to undercut those pronouncements.

As we have seen, in spite of Guicciardini's frequent theoretical pronouncements in favour of government by the aristocratic few, he harboured lifelong doubts about the actual viability of those regimes to rule with prudence and wisdom and about their ability in practice not to abuse the privileged position assigned them by his constitutions. As we saw in chapter 2, these doubts were fully formed in Guicciardini's mind prior to any sustained contact with Machiavelli's political thought. When reflecting on the social implications of competing electoral strategies under consideration by the 1494 republic, he analysed Florentine politics in terms that would later define the building blocks of Machiavelli's populism, particularly the biological assumption that elites were instinctually inclined towards domination and people towards non-domination.

In chapter 3's reading of Guicciardini's *Ricordi*, we saw that Guicciardini not only shared many of Machiavelli's most controversial ethical arguments from *The Prince* but also defended them using assumptions about the many and the few that echoed Machiavelli. The chapter therefore implicitly suggests that Guicciardini's innate intellectual profile and method of reasoning and argumentation, if not outright conclusions, shared considerable structural similarities with Machiavelli.

Chapters 4–6 looked at Machiavelli's direct textual influence on Guicciardini. Chapter 4 examined Machiavellian themes in Guicciardini's *Dialogue on the Government of Florence*, his most substantial work of constitutional analysis. Given Guicciardini's sustained rejection of the Roman military model and the utility of citizen militia in book 2 of that text, the *Dialogue* plays a canonical role in the scholarship as evidence of Guicciardini's overarching rejection of Machiavelli's *Discourses on Livy*. We saw, however, that the *Dialogue* continued to display Guicciardini's doubts about the viability of elite rule and, further, that he had begun to express those doubts using explicitly Machiavellian language, and even incorporated Machiavelli's critiques of the Albizzi regime from his *Discourse on Florentine Affairs after the Death of Lorenzo* and his *Florentine Histories*.

Chapter 5 addressed the only text that Guicciardini dedicated exclusively to engagement with Machiavelli's republican theory, his *Considerations on the "Discourses" of Machiavelli*. The *Considerations* ostensibly refuted all the major axioms of Machiavelli's republican theory, from its critique of mercenaries, to its assumption of universally flawed human nature, and especially to its praise of tumults and convictions about elites and people upon which Machiavelli defended that theory. The *Considerations* stands out in the Guicciardinian canon for its exclusive and transparent focus on Machiavelli and for the stridency of its rejection of the *Discourses*. For that reason it plays the single largest role in arguments that we should interpret these two thinkers, despite their friendship, as intellectual antagonists. Following John McCormick, chapter 5 attributed the *Considerations* less to Guicciardini's considered rejection of Machiavellian ideas than to its context: Guicciardini had experienced the first major political setback of his life, following a career of staggering success, and persecution by a regime defined by two of Machiavelli's major causes – the Great Council and a citizen militia. An additional and substantial argument for understanding that text as the product more of context than of intrinsic disagreement is the continued presence of Guicciardini's implicit recognition of Machiavelli's binary view of nobles and people. In every instance of Guicciardini's analysis of early Roman history, despite his surface claims to the contrary, he reaffirms Machiavelli's contrast between the insolence and domineering instincts of Roman senators and the moderation and prudence of the city's plebeians.

The sixth and final chapter shifted the focus to Machiavelli and the controversies surrounding his enigmatic utterances about Cesare Borgia in chapter 7 of *The Prince.* Contrary to many interpretations of chapter 7 that argue for an ironic or satirical reading, my chapter 6 demonstrated that Machiavelli admired Cesare Borgia and that his observations in *The Prince* are both internally consistent and externally consistent with his other remarks about Cesare in his legations and in his correspondence. Chapter 6 herein also challenged the widespread claim that Machiavelli was alone in praising Cesare and that no other contemporary claim can be found for the existence of Cesare's "good government" in the Romagna. As we saw, Guicciardini had extensive knowledge of the Romagnol context, owing to his appointment by Clement VII as president of the Romagna, the same post that Cesare had held twenty years earlier. In Guicciardini's *History of Florence,* his first major text, and his *History of Italy,* his last and most substantial text, he affirmed every aspect of Machiavelli's praise of Cesare. For both Machiavelli and Guicciardini, Cesare was a rare – arguably unique – Renaissance prince because he alone had earned the affection of his subjects. For both, he did so by enacting Machiavelli's advice in *The Prince* to ally with the people and demonstrate his good faith by violently repressing their abusive noble rulers. However much Guicciardini may have praised unity and concord in his theoretical constitutional writings, his verdicts about Cesare implicitly validated Machiavelli's populist politics.

Two larger conclusions about these arguments immediately stand out. The first concerns the basic question of how to relate the political philosophies of these two writers. By focusing primarily on Guicciardini rather than on Machiavelli, the argument presented here synthesizes the two major camps outlined at the beginning of the conclusion into a single interpretation. It does so by demonstrating that Machiavelli was not alone, contrary to his claim in *discorso* 1.58, in defending the wisdom and constancy of the many. Machiavelli's allegedly solitary voice defending the many against the few is the single most important factor for scholars who interpret the two as fundamentally antagonistic champions of mutually exclusive ideal regimes. Even for scholars who dispute that Machiavelli genuinely championed populism, he remains the only writer even to attribute positive surface arguments to the people. As Leo Strauss wrote, "It may easily appear that Machiavelli was the first philosopher who questioned in the name of the multitude or of democracy the aristocratic prejudice or the aristocratic premise which informed classical philosophy."[7] This is not the place to wade into the substantial controversies regarding Machiavelli's surface statements and whether they contradicted or confirmed his more detailed, historical elaborations on them. Suffice to say here that I generally agree with John McCormick's various arguments in favour of the fundamental internal consistency in Machiavelli's claims about nobles and people. Given the lesser role Guicciardini plays in discussion of the relationship between the two, few scholars have paused to consider at length the substantial discrepancies between Guicciardini's surface claims about both the superiority of the aristocratic capacity for wisdom and the unique virtues of regimes of the few and his actual commentary about the conducts of elites and people in Florentine and Roman history. Guicciardini may have overtly and consistently championed an aristocratic senatorial order, but at every stage of his life he engaged in reasoning that made precisely the same claims as did Machiavelli about the moderation of the people and the absolute certainty with which elites could be counted on to behave abusively, egotistically, and destructively. Even if his constitutional proposals did not create populist regimes, he nevertheless made populist claims that were every bit as detailed and historically informed as those of Machiavelli. As a result of that observation, we should, just as the Cambridge school urges us, view the two as fellow travellers whose visions were predicated upon shared assumptions about how nobles and people behaved both in theory and in history. We should also recognize their separation from the tradition, contrary to the major works of Skinner and Pocock that situate the two within a longue durée of republican theory. That is, of course, relatively easy to do with Machiavelli because he tells us explicitly that he disputes the canon. But Guicciardini, however much he wished to agree with the humanists and ancient writers, levelled the same critiques and in as sustained a manner as did Machiavelli about the improbability that prudential elites would ever rule in the interests of the common good, or that such a concept could even plausibly be said to exist.

The second concerns the legacy of Renaissance republicanism, as understood in terms of the contributions of Machiavelli and Guicciardini. Skinner and Pocock have influentially interpreted the two as essentially conventional, classical or neo-Roman, republican theorists linking ancient political thought to the English civil war, the Atlantic republican tradition, and colonial political thought. As McCormick has argued, however, Machiavelli should be severed from that tradition because his praise of conflict and its commitment to empowering the people at the expense of wealthy elites puts him at direct odds with a tradition that was vastly more preoccupied with justifying elite privilege.

By downplaying that aspect of Machiavelli's thinking, Pocock assimilated Machiavelli into a long tradition that he famously labelled "the Machiavellian moment." McCormick went on to argue that that moment would be more aptly termed "the Guicciardinian moment" because subsequent writers and the "tradition" as it unfolded followed Guicciardini's senatorial model rather than Machiavelli's violent populism. That tradition was dominated by writers who upheld the senatorial, electorally based republican model, such as Jean-Jacques Rousseau and James Madison, all of whom claimed Machiavelli as a source but only after seriously diminishing the implications of his anti-aristocratic politics. The various arguments advanced here suggest, somewhat counter-intuitively, that the "Machiavellian moment" may remain a useful term to convey the contribution of these two to the subsequent tradition. One author argued overtly against the aristocratic bias of the tradition, while the other proclaimed its virtue even while demonstrating in detail that its pieties could not withstand historical analysis. As a result, even if one recognizes that subsequent political thought (and the various regimes legitimated by it) followed the elitist tradition, Guicciardini's contribution was a Trojan horse: it appeared to confirm the tradition even while affirming every aspect of Machiavelli's critique of it.

Notes

Introduction

1 Black, 2013, 6–10.
2 Najemy, 1990, 101–18.
3 Skinner, 1978, 1:161. For this aspect of Guicciardini's outlook in the *Dialogue on the Government of Florence* see Silvano. For Machiavelli see McCormick, 2011 ; McCormick, 2001.
4 Ridolfi, 1963, 187–8.
5 Najemy, 2010, 2.
6 Jurdjevic, 2014.
7 For arguments in favour of Machiavelli's later adoption of establishment views see Black, 2013; Black, 2022; Bausi, 2005; Ascoli, 2013. For arguments against, see McCormick, 2018, 269–105; McCormick, 2017; *Najemy*, 2022, 295–318.
8 Black, 2013, 190–1.
9 *The Many and the Few* is more about Guicciardini than Machiavelli, so I do not engage Black's thesis that Machiavelli's intellectual trajectory reflects "radical to reactionary," which is surely overstated. *A Great and Wretched City*, despite its passages reconstructing Machiavelli's new critical views of the Florentine people, argued that Machiavelli continued to pursue a provocative and radical strain of republican theory even while serving the Medici. If Machiavelli were indeed championing an aristocratic, establishment version of the mixed constitution during the years of his new friendship with Guicciardini, why would Guicciardini write to him *after* Machiavelli's constitutional proposal, allegedly espousing an oligarchic regime, stating: "You have always been considered exceedingly extravagant in your opinions by most people, and the inventor of new and outlandish things" (Guicciardini quoted in Machiavelli, 1996a, 339. On the dating of the proposal, see Black, 2013, 232. Machiavelli certainly never lost his

instinct for provocation or his disdain for the Florentine elite class. My position is that his new vocabulary in the *Florentine Histories* and *Discursus* was imposed on him by the social complexities of Florence's urban industrial and banking economy, a context that did not lend itself to the binary perspective of his earlier theory.

10 Machiavelli, 1996a, 382. "Voi sapete et sallo ciascuno che sa ragionare di questo mondo, come i popoli sono varii et sciocchi; nondimeno, così fatti come sono, dicono molte volte che si fa quello che si doverrebbe fare" (Machiavelli, 1971, 1229).
11 Machiavelli, 1996a, 387. "Voi sapete quante occasioni si sono perdute: non perdete questa né confidate più nello starvi, rimettendovi alla Fortuna et al tempo, perché con il tempo non vengono sempre quelle medesime cose, né la Fortune é sempre quella medesima. Io direi più oltre, se io parlassi con huomo che non intendesse i segreti o non conoscesse il mondo. Liberate diuturna cura Italiam, extirpate has immanes belluas, quae hominis, preter faciem et vocem, nichil habent" (Machiavelli, 1971, 1232).
12 Black, 2013, 266.
13 Guicciardini quoted in Machiavelli, 1996a, 339.
14 Machiavelli, 1996a, 351. "Ho atteso et attendo in villa a scrivere la historia, et pagherei dieci soldi soldi, non voglio dir più, che voi fosse in lato, perché, havendo a venire a certi particulari, harei bisogno di intendere da voi se offendo troppo o con lo esaltare o con lo abbassare le cose" (Machiavelli, 1971, 1212).
15 Machiavelli, 1996a, 371. "Comincio hora a scrivere di nuovo, et mi sfogo accusando i principi, che hanno fatto tutti ogni cosa per condurci qui" (Machiavelli, 1971, 1224).
16 Guicciardini quoted in Machiavelli, 1996a, 339.
17 Guicciardini quoted in Machiavelli, 362–3.
18 Guicciardini quoted in Machiavelli, 363–4, 367–8, 372–3, 377–9.
19 Guicciardini quoted in Machiavelli, 373.
20 An English translation of Guicciardini's *Considerations* is published in Guicciardini, 1965.
21 Najemy, 1990.
22 Sasso, 1984, 49, 74; on the impact of Guicciardini's legal training on this aspect of his prose style, see Carta, 2008.
23 The *Discorso di Logrogno* is also known as "On the Mode of Reordering the Popular Government" (English translation in Jurdjevic, Piano, and McCormick, 2019) and "How the Popular Government Should Be Reformed" in Guicciardini, 1997.
24 Guicciardini, 1997, 216–17. "E se bene questo è pasto da infiammare pochi, non è però questo infiammarli inutile, perché in ogni republica bene ordinata e in ogni tempo si è sempre veduto che la virtù di pochi cittadini è

quella che ha retto e regge le republiche, e le opere gloriose e effetti grandi sono sempre nati da pochi e per mano di pochi, perché a volere guidare cose grande e essere capi del governo in una città libera, bisogna moltissime parte e virtù che in pochissimi si coniungono" (Guicciardini, 1970a, 1:274).

25 Guicciardini, 1997, 217. "Ma non ha una discretiva sottile e minuta ... dove sedranno tutti li uomini savi e prudenti" (Guicciardini, 1970a, 1:275). Guicciardini, 219. "E in effetto tutto 'l pondo del governo si reduce alla fine in sulle spalle di molti pochi, e così fu sempre in ogni republica e a' tempi antichi e a' moderni" (Guicciardini, 1970a, 1:277).

26 McCormick, 2018, 144–75.

27 Leo Strauss quoted in McCormick, 2018, 146.

1 Machiavelli and Guicciardini

1 On the conflict and the Machiavelli family's administration of churches around Sant'Andrea in Percussina see Brucker, 2010.

2 Machiavelli, 1996a, 7. "In hoc te virum exibeas rogo totasque effundas vires. Nam si pigmei gigantes aggredimur, multo major nobis quam illis paratur victoria: illis enim sicut contendere turpe est, sic erit cedere turpissimum; nos non tantum vinci ignominiosum, quam decorum contendisse ducimus, praesertim competitorem habentes, cujus nutu istic omnia fiunt: propterea quacumque fuerimus usi fortuna, talibus nos hujuscemodi excidisse ausis non poenitebit" (Machiavelli, 1971, 1009).

3 Machiavelli, 1996a, 7. "Et chi volessi la famiglia nostra et quella de' Pazi iusto lance perpendere, se in ogni altra cosa pari ci iudicassi, in liberalità et virtù d'animo molto superiori ci iudicherà" (Machiavelli, 1971, 1010).

4 Machiavelli, 2019, 102. "Pur, se credessi alcun, dicendo male, tenerlo pe' capegli, e sbigottirlo o ritirarlo in parte, io l'ammonisco, e dico a questo tale che sa dir male anch'egli, e come questa fu la suo prim'arte, e come in ogni parte del mondo, ove el 'sì' sona, non istima persona, ancor che facci sergieri a colui, che può portar miglior mantel che lui" (Machiavelli, 1971, 869).

5 Guicciardini, 1965, 129–50.

6 Guicciardini, 133. "[E]d ebbi più condizione assai che non si aspettava alla età mia ed al numero de' dottori che erano in Firenze ed alle poche cause che ci erano rispetto a' tempi avversi che correvano, ed a comparazione ancora degli altri dottori giovani" (Guicciardini, 1961, 8).

7 Guicciardini, 1965, 134. "[N]ondimeno io mi dirizzai a volerla tòrre, perché allora Alamanno ed Iacopo di parentadi, ricchezza, benivolenzia e riputazione avanzavano ogni cittadino privato che fussi in Firenze ed io ero vòlto a queste cose assai, e per questi rispetti gli volevo a ogni modo per parenti" (Guicciardini, 1961, 9).

8 Guicciardini, 1965, 137. “Io fui chiamato alla pratica insieme con più dottori e con molti de’ primi cittadini di Firenze, fra’ quali etiam fu mio padre; e non vi fu nessuno che non avessi almeno dieci anni più di me” (Guicciardini, 1961, 12).

9 Guicciardini, 1965, 139. “La quale elezione, benché lo uficio fussi di poco momento, fu onorevole rispetto alla qualità degli uomini in compagnia di chi avevo a essere, che erano Domenico Mazzinghi, Pietro Lenzi, Giovacchino Guasconi, Niccolò del Nero, Alessandro Mannelli, Bartolommeo Benci, Giovan Batista Bartolini, Alamanno Salviati, e questi furono presenti alla elezione” (Guicciardini, 1961, 14).

10 Guicciardini, 1965, 146. “E benché io stessi molto sospeso dello accettare, parendomi gita da non avanzare e dare disturbo allo esercizio mio, nel quale mi trovavo rispetto alla età mia molto aviato, e mi pareva che lo stare a Firenze ancora due o tre anni fussi per assodarmivi meglio; pure per consiglio di Piero mio padre al quale ne scrissi, che si trovava a Montepulciano commessario, accettai; perché a lui parve che mi fussi suto fatto onore grande, rispetto allo essere la legazione molto onorevole per le qualità di quello re, e tanto più nella età mia, che non era memoria a Firenze fussi mai più stato eletto in una simile legazione uno sì giovane solo” (Guicciardini, 1961, 20).

11 Guicciardini, 1965, 140. “Fu cosa di poco utile ma molto onorevole per la qualità del luogo, per esservi stati sempre e’ primi dottori di Firenze, ed andoronvi a partito messer Antonio Strozzi, messer Francesco Gualterotti e molti altri dottori” (Guicciardini, 1961, 14–15).

12 Celli, 2019, 15.

13 Black, 2013, 263–87.

14 Black, 77–8.

15 Guicciardini returned to Florence in 1514; in March 1514 he was appointed to the Seventeen Reformers, in August to the Otto di guardia, and in September, to the Signoria. Guicciardini, 1994a, xxx.

16 Guicciardini’s *History of Florence* relates in detail the degree to which the Guicciardini family was in the inner circle of Cosimo, Piero, and Lorenzo’s allies.

17 Celli, 2019, 20.

18 Guicciardini, 1994a, xxx.

19 On which see Najemy, 2006, 446–64; Roth, 1925.

20 Guicciardini, 1970b, 17.

21 Najemy, 2006, 463–8.

22 On which see Jurdjevic, 2014, 132–205.

23 Guicciardini quoted in Machiavelli, 1996a, 353.

24 Black, 2013, 270–3.

25 Machiavelli, 1996a, 54. "[E] circa le cose di costà non ho da dirvi altro, se non che seguitiate come avete fatto insino a ora, che mi pare satisfacciate a tutti" (Machiavelli, 1999, 52).
26 Machiavelli, 1996a, 189. "Se voi scrivete a messer Francesco vostro, ditegli che mi raccomandi a la combriccola" (Machiavelli, 1999, 203).
27 See discussion by Sasso, 1984, 51–2.
28 Machiavelli, 1996a, 208. "E' mi pare vedere el Casa e Francesco e Luigi venirvi a trar di casa apresso lo arrivar vostro, e menarvi a un solino o in Santa Maria del Fiore per votarvi et intendere tutte le cose di qua" (Machiavelli, 1999, 224).
29 Machiavelli, 1996a, 263. "E Fruosino in spezie mandò per certe cataste senza dirmi nulla, et al pagamento mil voleva rattenere 10 lire, che dice aveva avere da me quattro anno sono, che mi vinse a cricca in casa Antonio Guicciardini … Batista Guicciardini, Filippo Ginori, Tommaso del Bene e certi altri cittadini, quando quella tramontana soffiava, ognuno me ne prese una catasta … Di modo che, veduto in chi era guadagno, ho detto agl'altri che io non ho più legne; e tutti ne hanno fatto capo grosso, et in spezie Batista, che connumera questa tra l'altre sciagure di Prato" (Machiavelli, 1999, 295).
30 *Sasso*,, 52–3.
31 Najemy, 2006, 375–413.
32 Guicciardini, 1970b, 248. "[U]omini di meno cervello e qualità" (Guicciardini, 1999, 204).
33 Machiavelli, 2007, 376. "Et se voi ricercherete bene chi sono questi che fanno quest calca, voi conoscerete essere vero quello che io vi dico, perché pare loro avere adquistato uno odio grande con lo universale, sendo stati nimici di Piero, se non si truova che sia un tristo, et che lo meriti. Et vorrebbono purgare questo odio per fare el facto loro, non quello de' Medici" (Machiavelli, 1997, 88).
34 Butters, 2010, 66; Rubinstein, 1954, 161–3.
35 On this view of Machiavelli and Soderini see Black (2013, 38–48), who offers a persuasive rebuttal.
36 Black, 2013, 42–5; Najemy, 2007, 407–13; Najemy, 1990. For a different view see Black, 2014.
37 Guicciardini, 1970b, 253. "Erane stato tutto il verno grandissimo disparere, pignendola il Gonfaloniere, per satisfare al Cardinale, che si diceva averlo loro promesso e cominciato di già a dare e' danari" (Guicciardini, 1999, 208).
38 Guicciardini, 1970b, 304. On Machiavelli's early attempts to secure Salviati patronage see Butters, 65–8; Black, 2013, 39–40.
39 Guicciardini, 1970b, 253. "Vi mandorono e' dieci mandatario Ruberto di Donato Acciaiuoli, avendone pero fatto conclusione con grandissima

difficultà; perché el gonfaloniere vi si opponeva, e per avervi uno uomo suo intrinseco, vi voleva mandare Niccolò Machiavelli, cancelliere de' dieci, in chi si confidava assai" (Guicciardini, 1999, 208).

40 Sasso, 1984, 65–7.

41 Guicciardini, 1970b, 257. "[E] perché dubitava che se si metteva in pratica de' dieci, e' cittadini non la acconsentissino, fece prima destramente tentare dal Machiavello, cancelliere, lo animo de messer Francesco Gualterotti, Giovan Batista Ridolfi, Piero Guicciardini e di alcuno de' primi" (Guicciardini, 1999, 211).

42 Guicciardini, 1970b, 258. "[E] dubitando, come era vero, che la pratica non vi concorrerebbe, cominciò el gonfaloniere, sanza fare consulta" (Guicciardini, 1999, 211).

43 Guicciardini, 1970b, 257. "Ebbone e' cittadini di qualità grande alterazione, dubitando che questa voglia di avere don Michele non fussi fondata in su qualche cattivo disegno e che questo instrumento non avessi a servire o per desiderio di occupare la tirannide o, quando fussi in qualche angustia, per levarsi dinanzi e' cittadini inimici sua" (Guicciardini, 1999, 211; Najemy, 2007, 411–13).

44 Guicciardini, 1970b, 271. "E fu eletto per opera del gonfaloniere, che vi voleva uno di chi e' si potessi fidare, el Machiavello" (Guicciardini, 1999, 219).

45 Najemy, 1993, 76–8.

46 Guicciardini, 1970b, 275. "Però el gonfaloniere, che desiderava avervi uno dì che e' si potessi fidare e credergli, e fare forse non meno e' fatti sua che della città, introdusse ne' dieci che, per dubio che le lettere non capitassino male, sarebbe bene mandarvi uno che riferissi a bocca; e così non sendo chi si opponessi, ottenne che vi fussi mandato el Machiavello" (Guicciardini, 1999, 222).

47 Black, 2013, 266–8.

48 Guicciardini quoted in Machiavelli, 1996a, 335.

49 Guicciardini quoted in Machiavelli, 1996a, 338.

50 Guicciardini quoted in Machiavelli, 1996a, 386.

2 Populist Perspectives in Guicciardini's *On the Method of Electing Offices in the Great Council*

1 Sasso, 1984.

2 Hankins, 2019, 41.

3 Gilbert, 1939, 263.

4 Rubinstein, 1954; Rubinstein, 1960.

5 Guicciardini, 2019, 236. "El primo e principale, che le siano ordinate in modo che ciascuno cittadino abbia a stare equalmente sotto le legge,

ed in questo non si faccia distinzione dal ricco al povero, dal potente a l'impotente ... El secondo fine che ha a avere si è che e' benifici della republica, cioè gli onori e gli utili publichi che ha, si allarghino in ognuno quanto si può ed in modo che tutti e' cittadini ne participino el piú che sia possibile" (Guicciardini, 1932, 175–6).

6 Guicciardini, 2019, 237. "E nel mettere ordine al modo del distribuire, fu avuto l'altro rispetto che la città avessi a essere bene governata, con fare che gli ufici si eleggono per le più fave, acciò che e' magistrati fussino più scelti che fussi possibile. Perchè non è dubio che se sono qui cento uomini a dare giudicio se uno cittadini è buono per uno uficio o no, che communemente sarà più sicuro quello giudicio a che si accorderanno, verbigrazia, sessanta, che quello a che si accorderanno solamente cinquanta" (Guicciardini, 1932, 177).

7 Guicciardini, 2019, 237. "Ma poi che le sono loro che distribuiscono gli ufici a chi e come gli pare, né ci è strettezza o larghezza se non quella che fanno loro medesime" (Guicciardini, 1932, 178).

8 Guicciardini, 2019, 238. "[P]er intervenire piú numero può essere manco sospetto di corruzione, che non interviene in uno numero minore?" (Guicciardini, 1932, 178).

9 Guicciardini, 2019, 238. "Se uno merita, non s'ha a stare a giudicio de' particulari ma del popolo, el quale ha migliore giudicio che nessuno altro, perché è el principe ed è sanza passione ... Lui cognosce meglio ognuno di noi che non facciamo noi stessi, né ha altro fine se non di distribuire le cose in chi gli pare che meriti" (Guicciardini, 1932, 179).

10 Machiavelli, 1965, 1:294. "Credo ancora, che si possa conchiudere, che mai un uomo prudente non debba fuggire il giudicio populare nelle cose particulari, circa le distribuzioni de' gradi e delle dignità: perché solo in questo il popolo non s'inganna; e se s'inganna qualche volta, sia sì rado, che s'inganneranno piú volte i pochi uomini che avessono a fare simili distribuzioni" (Machiavelli, 1971, 130).

11 Guicciardini, 2019, 238. "[E] che alla giornata sempre si limeranno e se ne fará manco, perché quanto si andrá piú in lá, sará ogni di piú cognosciuto quello che pesa ognuno, perché si vedranno oggi le azione di questo, e domani di quello, ed el popolo che ha cominciato a porsi a bottega a questo consiglio, e cognoscere che el governo è suo, porrà piú mente agli andamenti e costumi di ognuno, che non faceva prima, in modo che ogni dí sará migliore giudice di quello che meritino gli uomini ... e si cognoscono alla giornata meglio le cose, in modo che possiamo credere che sempre si andrá migliorando" (Guicciardini, 1932, 179).

12 Guicciardini, 2019, 239. "E se non girano in tanto numero quanto molti desiderano, questo non è inconveniente, poi che piace al popolo; el quale non merita essere biasimato né lacerate, se desidera commettere le

faccende sue a persone cittá sua che è di tanta importanza, quell oche fa ognuno di avere miglioti ministri che potete … E se a qualcuno pare strano vedere che a uno medesimo siano date molte volte gli ufici e degnitá, non pare cosi al popolo che cerca che la sua cittá ed el suo dominio sia bene governato" (Guicciardini, 1932, 180).

13 Guicciardini, 2019, 239. See also discussion in chapter 4 for examples from his *Discorso di Logrogno* and *Dialogue on the Government of Florence*.

14 Guicciardini, 1970a, 127.

15 Guicciardini, 127.

16 Guicciardini, 128.

17 Guicciardini, 127.

18 Guicciardini, 128.

19 Guicciardini, 2019, 242. "[S]uscitano tanto romore; biasimano el giudicio del Popolo da chi hanno la sicurtá e la libertá" (Guicciardini, 1932, 184).

20 Guicciardini, 1970b, 29–30. "Non è el frutto delle libertà, né el fine al quale le furono trovate, che ognuno governi (perché non debbe governare se non chi è atto e lo merita)" (Guicciardini, 1994b, 53).

21 Guicciardini, 2019, 240. "[I]ntrantano ognî Cittadino gode el frutto principale delle libertá, che è di non temere di essere oppressato se non quanto dispongono le legge vostre; non avere altro superior che e'magistrati; non s'avere a cavere la berretta a persona; e nel distribuire gli onori ed utili della cittá, avere tanta autoritá quanta ha el piú ricco ed el piú potentente che ci sia" (Guicciardini, 1932, 181).

22 McCormick 2001; McCormick, 2011.

23 Guicciardini, 1965, 65. "[E] se sono ottimati per successione e non per elezione, di prudenti e buoni vengono presto le cose in mano di imprudenti e cattivi. Bisogna, a trarre di questa spezie di governo quel che si può di bene e fuggire el male, che gli ottimati non siano sempre le medesime linee e famiglie, ma che di tutto el corpo della città, cioè di tutti quegli che secondo le legge sono abili a participare de' magistrati, si elegga uno senato che abbia a trattare le cose ardue, cioè che sia el fiore degli uomini prudenti, nobili e ricchi della città" (Guicciardini, 1970c, 611).

24 Guicciardini, 2019, 255. "Di poi la elezione de' magistrati, se bene importa, non è tanto difficile al giudicarla: volgevisi el populo secondo la riputazione e esistimazione che ha degli uomini, che nasce più tosto da una voce commune di tutti che da giudicio proprio di ciascuno … Non interviene così nelle legge che richieggono considerazione di uomini savi, e le quali quando sono guidate dallo appetito della multitudine, si vede che sono quasi sempre or dannose o vane" (Guicciardini, 1970c, 258). He makes a similar point in the *Dialogue on the Government of Florence*: "The first [good], that important deliberations are in the hands of those who understand them and aren't decided by the arbitrary will of the populace, which is the

first danger to be feared from popular government" (Guicciardini, 1994a, 114).

25 Guicciardini, 2019, 243. "Perché se tr alcuni girassino sempre e'magistrati ed el governo, gli altri non ne sentissino mai, chi dubita che la riputazione e la grandezza sarebbe in quegli, e che le cose loro sarebbono ne'giudici e ne'magistrati trattate con grandissimo rispetto, in modo che in ogni caso sarebbe tra una sorte di uomini ed una altra grandissimo disavantaggio?" (Guicciardini, 1932, 187).

26 Guicciardini, 2019, 243.

27 Guicciardini, 2019, 247. "Né sará mai o rare volte che la metá del consiglio si inganni a giudicare sufficiente uno che non sia, né concorreranno tanti rispetti privati in uno, che gli possino fare avere tanto partito" (Guicciardini, 1932, 192).

28 Guicciardini, 2019, 247. "[E]'nostri pari che fanno piú tosto professione di essere governati che di governare, e volentieri si rapportano a chi sa piú" (Guicciardini, 1932, 193).

29 Guicciardini, 2019, 245. "Molti amatori della libertá quanto loro e forse piú che loro; perché noi non speriamo luogo se non in uno vivere libero, loro sperano d'avere in uno stato stretto ed aspresso a'tiranni parte come hanno avuto per el passato" (Guicciardini, 1932, 189–90).

30 Guicciardini, 2019, 26. "E se e'passati vostri sono stati cittadini modesti, ed atteso agli esercizi loro, né cercato di farsi innanzi con questio modi, non per questo siate da manco di loro né dovete avere minore parte nella cittá; anzi e'vostri maggiori hanno fatto, quando è accaduto, bene alla republica e non mai male, come hanno fatto e'maggiori di molti di loro, che sono stati ministri di stati stretti e si sono ingranditi con queste arte" (Guicciardini, 1932, 190).

31 Guicciardini, 2019, 248. "Se s'ha a attendere chi sa piú atto al governo, cosi abbiamo spirito, cosi sentimento, cosi lingua come loro, e forse manco voglie e manco passione, dalle quali si corrompe el giudicio, che non hanno loro" (Guicciardini, 1932, 193).

32 McCormick, 2018, 69–108.

33 Guicciardini, 2019, 243.

34 Guicciardini, 2019, 243–4. "In modo che non solo è giusto che ora abbiamo la parte nostra, ma sarebbe ancora giusto che noi ora participassimo tanto piú che gli altri, che ci ragguagliassimo del tempo passato" (Guicciardini, 1932, 187).

35 Guicciardini, 2019, 244. "Che voi vi contentiate, lasciata la memoria del passato, avere di presente la vostra parte, ed in questo è laudabile la modestia" (Guicciardini, 1932, 187).

36 Guicciardini, 2019, 245. "Si fanno favore tra loro medesimi quando vanno a partito, ed a'nostri pari, cioè al tre, dua ed asso, non danno mai se non fave

bianche" (Guicciardini, 1932, 189). A white bean is a negative vote; black is positive.

37 Guicciardini, 2019, 245. "E questa è la ragione vera che ancora che uno pare nostro sia d'assai e sufficiente a ogni impresa, nondimeno per le piú fave non ha mai nulla, se non forse qualche volta e bene di rado, per compassione o per disgrazia; perché bisogna che di necessitá le piú fave siano di questi dal quattro in su, che hanno favore da'loro pari ed anche da noi altri; ma noi al piú abbiamo favore solamente da'nostri, e da loro tutte fave bianche" (Guicciardini, 1932, 189).

38 Guicciardini, 2019, 247. "Bisognerebbe … o veramente che noi del tre, dua, asso, facessimo come fanno loro, che non rendessimo fave se non a'medesimi, che certo essendo maggiore numero che non sono loro, gli faremo presto accorgere che cosa sia favorire e'suoi simili e disfavorire gli altri" (Guicciardini, 1932, 192).

39 Guicciardini, 2019, 249. "Alla quale bisogna provedere o co'modi violenti e scandalosi, il che potremo fare facilmente perché siamo molti piú" (Guicciardini, 1932, 194).

40 Guicciardini, 2019, 247. "El secondo potrebbe essere scandaloso e principio di dividere la cittá" (Guicciardini, 1932, 192).

41 Guicciardini, 2019, 245. "[P]erché ancora che uno di noi fussi virtuosissimo che fussi uno Aristotile o uno Salamone" (Guicciardini, 1932, 189).

42 Guicciardini, 2019, 247. "Anzi se ci sará disavantaggio, sará a vostro danno, perch. Molti di noi si lasciano spesso tanto abbagliare da queste loro condizione, che non considerano quanto bisogna la loro sufficienzia; dove a'nostri pari non interverrá cosi, che se non saranno portati dall virtù, non aggiugneranno mai a questo partito" (Guicciardini, 1932, 192).

43 Guicciardini, 2019, 248. "[N]on dicono come la sta" (Guicciardini, 1932, 193).

44 Guicciardini, 2019, 248. "Perché feciono come due partu della cittá, cioè el sei, cinque e quattro, ed el tre, dua, asso; ed ordinorono per legge che gli ufici si dividessino, cioè che ognuna delle parte n'avessi la metá" (Guicciardini, 1932, 193).

45 Guicciardini, 2019, 248.

46 McCormick, 2018, 68–108.

47 Guicciardini, 2019, 247. "La quale vincendosi, potrete sperare ancora voi di entrare qualche volta in quelle borse, e poi stare alla sorte" (Guicciardini, 1932, 192).

48 Guicciardini, 1965, 96. "E quanto alla invidia, cade più facilmente negli uomini popolari, a'quali ogni grandezza punto eminente o di nobilità o di ricchezze o di virtù o di riputazione è ordinariamente molesta; né cosa alcuna dispiace loro che vedere altri cittadini che abbino più qualità di loro, e questi sempre desiderano abbassare" (Guicciardini, 1970c, 645).

49 Guicciardini, 2019, 245; emphasis mine. "Però mi pare a proposito dirne qualche cosa, non in quello modo che n'hanno parlato molti scirttori, ma secondo e'termini della cittá nostra e la natura" (Guicciardini, 1932, 190).

50 Machiavelli, 1965, 1:313 (emphasis mine). "Io non so se io mi prenderò una provincia dura e piena di tanta difficultà, che mi convenga o abandonarla con vergogna, o seguirla concarico; volendo difendere una cosa, la quale, come ho detto, da tutti gli scrittori è accusata" (Machiavelli, 1971, 140).

51 Guicciardini, 2019, 246. "Però non la virtù ma ragione estraordinarie gli hanno tirati in questa altezza, delle quali voi non dovete tenere conto" (Guicciardini, 1932, 190).

52 Najemy, 2010, 12.

53 Guicciardini, 2019, 246. "[P]er ... fortuna e per favore di tempi" (Guicciardini, 1932, 190).

54 Guicciardini, 2019, 246. "Perché se hanno avuto corso, è stato ... delle volte tirannici o perché è stato tra loro qualche uomo ricco, che hanno avuto modo a imparentarsi altamente e nobilitarsi con la ricchezza; ed alcuni hanno acquistato favore da chi reggeva gli stati con cagione vergognose a dirlo" (Guicciardini, 1932, 190).

55 Guicciardini, 2019, 246–7. "[S]ulle virtú, in su'meriti, in sulla prudenzia, ma in cose di fortuna, di favori e di guadagni illeciti ... Sono altri che per essere ricchi entrano in questo numero ... ma molte volte è acquistata con usure o con altre arte inoneste e vituperose, e quegli che per avere guadagnato la roba ingiustamente meriterebbono essere puniti" (Guicciardini, 1932, 191).

56 Guicciardini, 1970b, 103. "La malignità ne' poveri può facilmente procedere per accidente, ne'ricchi è più spesso per natura. Però ordinariamente è da biasimare più in uno ricco che in uno povero" (Guicciardini, 1961, 146).

57 Guicciardini, 2019, 246. "Chiamano sé medesimi uomini da bene, come se noi fussimo uomini da male ed usi a rapinare ed primere gli altri" (Guicciardini, 1932, 191).

58 Guicciardini, 2019, 244. "Perché ci è una sorte di uomini, cioè quelli che sono dal quattro in su, che per essere piú ricchi, tenuti piú nobili, o che hanno fresca nello stato la riputazione de'padri e degli avoli, pare loro che a lore propri si appartenga lo stato, e che e'nostri pari cioè el tre, dua, asso, non meritino le degnitá ma che ci dobbiamo contentare con qualche uficiuzzo, e del resto portare la soma come abbiamo fatto per el passato" (Guicciardini, 1932, 188).

59 Guicciardini, 2019, 245. "[Q]uasi appropriato lo stato con queste prosunzione ed opinione false" (Guicciardini, 1932, 190).

60 Guicciardini, 2019, 249. "Ed augumenterete in modo la arroganzia di costoro che vi terranno per loro famigli e vi tratteranno, che vi

costrigneranno a desiderare di provedervi a quelche tempo, ma sará forse tardi" (Guicciardini, 1932, 195).

61 Guicciardini, 2019, 245–7. "Ma ci tengono affogati con queste loro nobilitá, con queste loro riputazione, che portano seco uno certo splendore, che ancora noi altri ne restiamo abbagliati … quello che è peggio chiamati uomini da bene … E nondimanco noi siamo si grossi, che ne tegnamo piú conto che di noi medisimi" (Guicciardini, 1932, 191).

62 Guicciardini, 2019, 243. "Che siate da essere imputati che voi vi governate bene spesso con troppo rispetto e con troppa modestia, e che gli intervenga a voi come a uno che è stato lungamente in servitú, che benché gli sia renduto la libertá, nondimanco può tanto in lui l'abito del servire, che procede nelle azione sue timidamente e con lo animo abietto, ritenendo ancora la memoria ed e'vestigi della antica servitú" (Guicciardini, 1932, 186).

63 Guicciardini, 2019, 249. "[N]on solo vi sará danno ma vergogna grandissima … Però vi conforto, mentre che el bene ed el male vostro è in mano vostra, e che a voi sta o ridurvi e col nome e con gli effetti in una vera libertá e godere e'frutti di quella, overo confinarvi sotto nome di falsa libertá in una vera servitú" (Guicciardini, 1932, 195).

64 Machiavelli, 1988, 122–3. "Né vi sbigottisca quella antichità del sangue che ei ci rimproverano; perché tutti gli uomini, avendo avuto uno medesimo principio, sono ugualmente antichi, e da la natura sono stati fatti ad uno modo. Spogliateci tutti ignudi: voi ci vedrete simili; rivestite noi delle veste loro ed eglino delle nostre: noi senza dubio nobili ed eglino ignobili parranno; perché solo la povertà e le ricchezze ci disaguagliano. Duoimi bene che io sento come molti di voi delle cose fatte, per conscienza, si pentono, e delle nuove si vogliono astenere … E della conscienza noi non dobbiamo tenere conto; perché dove è, come è in noi, la paura della fame e delle carcere, non può né debbe quella dello inferno capere. Ma se voi noterete il modo del procedere degli uomini, vedrete tutti quelli che a ricchezze grandi e a grande potenza pervengono o con frode o con forza esservi pervenuti; e quelle cose, di poi, eh' eglino hanno o con inganno o con violenza usurpate, per celare la bruttezza dello acquisto, quello sotto falso titolo di guadagno adonestano. E quelli i quali, o per poca prudenza o per troppa sciocchezza, fuggono questi modi, nella servitù sempre e nella povertà affogono; perché i fedeli servi sempre sono servi, e gli uomini buoni sempre sono poveri; né mai escono di servitù se non gli infedeli e audaci, e di povertà se non i rapaci e frodolenti" (Machiavelli, 1971, 701).

65 Winter, 2018, 176.

66 McCormick, 2018, 176–206.

67 Sasso, 1984, 91.

68 Najemy, 1996, 124.

69 Najemy, 2009, 87.
70 Najemy, 87; Guicciardini, 2019, 245.
71 Najemy, 2009, 88.
72 Najemy, 88.
73 Guicciardini, 1970b, 65–6. "La ragione di questo detto può essere che e pochi e non e molti danno communemente el moto alle cose del mondo, e e fini di questi sono quasi sempre diversi da' fini de' molti, e però partoriscono diversi effetti da quello che molti desiderano" (Guicciardini, 1994b, 48–9).

3 Radical *Virtù* in *The Prince* and the *Ricordi*

1 Felix Gilbert, 1939, argued that Guicciardini never read *The Prince.* For Gilbert and Sasso, because Guicciardini's political outlook – an elitist preference for a mixed regime centred around an aristocratic senate – was already fully formed in his first two texts (*The History of Florence* and *Discorso di Logrogno,* both written prior to *The Prince*), they largely omit consideration of Guicciardini's relationship to *The Prince.*
2 Machiavelli, 1989, 1:57. "E perché io so che molti di questo hanno scritto, dubito, scrivendone ancora io, non essere tenuto presuntuoso, partendomi massime, nel disputare questa materia, dagli ordini degli altri. Ma sendo l'intento mio scrivere cosa utile a chi la intende, mi è parso più conveniente andare drieto alla verità effettuale della cosa, che alla imaginazione di essa" (Machiavelli, 1971, 280).
3 Machiavelli, 1989, 1:57–8. "[E] molti si sono imaginati republiche e principati che non si sono mai visti né conosciuti essere in vero; perché egli è tanto discosto da come si vive a come si doverrebbe vivere, che colui che lascia quello che si fa per quello che si doverrebbe fare impara piuttosto la ruina che la perservazione sua: perché uno uomo che voglia fare in tutte le parte professione di buono, conviene rovini infra tanti che non sono buoni" (Machiavelli, 1971, 280).
4 Guicciardini, 1970b, 54. "Non si può tenere stati secondo conscienza, perché – chi considera la origine loro – tutti sono violenti, da quelli delle republiche nella patria propria in fuora, e non altrove" (Guicciardini, 1994b, 310. As chapters 2 and 4 show, there were certainly contexts within a republic's walls that Guicciardini considered violently oppressive.
5 Guicciardini, 1970b, 54. "E da questa regola non eccettuo lo imperadore e manco e preti, la violenza de' quali è doppia, perché ci sforzano con le arme temporale e con le spirituale" (Guicciardini, 1994b, 31).
6 Guicciardini, 1970b, 86. "[N]on essendo più el mondo e e prìncipi fatti come doverrebbono, ma come sono" (Guicciardini, 1994b, 77).
7 Hankins, 2019, 31–62.

8 Machiavelli, 2005b, 54–5. "E però, a volersi mantenere infra gli uomini el nome del liberale, è necessario non lasciare indrieto alcuna qualità di suntuosità; talmente che sempre uno principe così fatto consumerà in simili opere tutte le sue facultà, e sarà necessitato alla fine, se si vorrà mantenere el nome del liberale, gravare e' populi estraordinariamente ed essere fiscale, e fare tutte quelle cose che si possano fare per avere danari. Il che comincerà a farlo odioso con sudditi, e poco stimare da nessuno, diventando povero" (Machiavelli, 1971, 280–1).
9 Machiavelli, 2005b, 56. "E non ci è cosa che consumi se stessa quanto la liberalità: la quale mentre che tu usi, perdi la facultà di usarla, e diventi o povero e contennendo, o, per fuggire la povertà, rapace e odioso" (Machiavelli, 1971, 281).
10 Machiavelli, 2005b, 55. "[I]n modo che, con questa sua liberalità, avendo offeso gli assai e premiato e' pochi, sente ogni primo disagio" (Machiavelli, 1971, 281).
11 Machiavelli, 2005b, 62. "E gli uomini, in universali, iudicano più agli occhi che alle mani; perché tocca a vedere a ognuno, a sentire i pochi" (Machiavelli, 1971, 284).
12 Machiavelli, 2005b, 55. "Perché col tempo sarà tenuto sempre più liberale, veggendo che con la sua parsimonia le sua intrate li bastano, può defendersi da chi li fa guerra, può fare imprese sanza gravare e' populi; talmente che viene a usare liberalità a tutti quelli a chi non toglie, che sono infiniti, e miseria a tutti coloro a chi non dà, che sono pochi" (Machiavelli, 1971, 281).
13 Guicciardini, 1970b, 84–5. "[P]iù detestabile e più pernizioso e in uno principe la prodigalità che la parsimonia, perché, non potendo quella essere sanza tôrre a molti, è più ingiurioso a sudditi el tôrre che el non dare" (Guicciardini, 1994b, 74).
14 Guicciardini, 1970b, 114. "[P]erché el prodigo è necessitate fare estorsione e rapine, lo stretto non toglie a nessuno; più sono quelli che patiscono dalle gravezze del prodigo che quelli che hanno beneficio della sua larghezza" (Guicciardini, 1994b, 75).
15 Guicciardini, 1970b, 114. "Piace sanza dubio più uno principe che abbia del prodigo che uno che abbia dello stretto; e pure doverrebbe essere el contrario" (Guicciardini, 1994b, 75).
16 Guicciardini, 1970b, 85. "[N]on potendo quella essere sanza tôrre a molti, è più ingiurioso a sudditi el tôrre che el non dare. E nondimeno pare che a' popoli piaccia più el principe prodigo che lo avaro" (Guicciardini, 1994b, 74–5).
17 Guicciardini, 1970b, 85. "La ragione è che, ancora che pochi siano quegli a chi dà el prodigo a comparazione di coloro a chi toglie – che di necessità sono molti – pure, come è detto altre volte, può tanto più negli uomini la speranza

che el timore, che facilmente si spera essere più presto di quegli pochi a chi è dato che di quegli molti a chi è tolto" (Guicciardini, 1994b, 74–5).

18 Guicciardini, 1970b, 100. "Quella generosità che piace a' populi si truova rarissime volte negli uomini veramente savi; però non è così laudabile chi pare che abbia del generoso come chi ha del maturo" (Guicciardini, 1961, 145).

19 Guicciardini, 1970b, 42. "Se gli uomini fussino discreti o grati a bastanza, doverrebbe uno padrone, in ogni occasione che n'ha, beneficare quanto potessi e suoi servidori; ma perché la esperienza mostra – e io l'ho sentito da' miei servidori in me medesimo – che spesso come sono pieni, o come al padrone manca occasione di potergli trattare bene come ha fatto per el passato, lo piantano, chi pensa al profitto suo debbe procedere con la mano stretta, e con loro inclinare più presto nella scarsità che nella larghezza" (Guicciardini, 1961, 98).

20 Guicciardini, 1970b, 42. "Intrattenendogli più con la speranza che con gli effetti; la quale perché gli possa ingannare, è necessario beneficarne talvolta qualcuno largamente, e questo basta; perché è naturale degli uomini che in loro possa ordinariamente tanto più la speranza che el timore, che più gli conforta e intrattiene lo essemplo di uno che veggono benificato che non gli spaventa el vedersene innanzi agli occhi molti che non sono stati bene trattati" (Guicciardini, 1961, 98).

21 On violence as a foundational order in Machiavelli's political thought see Winter, 2018.

22 On Agathocles see McCormick, 2015; McCormick, 2016.

23 Machiavelli, 1998, 37–8. "Credo che questo avvenga dalle crudeltà male usate o bene usate. Bene usate si possono chiamare quelle (se del male è licito dire bene) che si fanno a uno tratto, per la necessità dello assicurarsi, e di poi non vi si insiste drento, ma si convertiscono in più utilità de' sudditi che si può" (Machiavelli, 1971, 270).

24 Guicciardini, 1970b, 60. "Né Alessandro Magno, né Cesare, né gli altri che sono stati celebrati in questa laude, usorono mai clemenza per la quale conoscessino guastare o mettere in pericolo lo effetto della sua vittoria, perché sarebbe forse più presto demenza; ma solo in quegli casi ne' quali lo usarla non diminuiva loro sicurtà e gli faceva più ammirabili" (Guicciardini, 1994b, 39).

25 Guicciardini, 1970b, 58. "Non procede sempre el vendicarsi da odio o da mala natura, ma è tal volta necessario perché con questo essemplo gli altri imparino a non ti offendere: e sta molto bene questo che uno si vendichi e *tamen* non abbia rancore di animo contro a colui di chi fa vendetta" (Guicciardini, 1961, 113).

26 Machiavelli, 1998, 66–8. "E gli uomini hanno meno respetto a offendere uno che si facci amare, che uno che si facci temere; perché l'amore è

tenuto da uno vinculo di obligo, il quale, per essere gli uomini tristi, da ogni occasione di propria utilità è rotto; ma il timore è tenuto da una paura di pena che non ti abbandona mai ... Concludo ... che, amando gli uomini a posta loro, e temendo a posta del principe, debbe uno principe savio fondarsi in su quello che è suo, non in su quello che è d'altri: debbe solamente ingegnarsi di fuggire l'odio, come è detto" (Machiavelli, 1971, 282–3).

27 Guicciardini, 1970b, 116. "Non si possono governare e sudditi bene sanza severità, perché la malignità degli uomini ricercar così" (Guicciardini, 1994b, 25).

28 Guicciardini, 1970b, 116–17. "Ma si vuole mescolare destrezza e fare ogni dimostrazione perché si creda che la crudeltà non ti piaccia, ma che tu la usi per necessità e per salute publica" (Guicciardini, 1994b, 25).

29 Machiavelli, 2005b, 58. "Perché degli uomini si può dire questo generalmente: che sieno ingrati, volubili, simulatori e dissimulatori, fuggitori de'pericoli, cupidi di guadagno" (Machiavelli, 1971, 282).

30 Guicciardini, 1970b, 52–3. "Se gli uomini fussino buoni e prudenti, chi è preposto a altri legittimamente arebbe a usare più la dolcezza che la severità; ma essendo la più parte o poco buoni o poco prudenti, bisogna fondarsi più in sulla severità: e chi la intende altrimenti, si inganna. Confesso bene che, chi potessi mescolare e condire bene l'una con l'altra, farebbe quello ammirabile concento e quella armonia, della quale nessuna è più suave: ma sono grazie che a pochi el cielo largo destina e forse a nessuno" (Guicciardini, 1994b, 25).

31 Guicciardini, 1970b, 53. "Non mi piacque mai ne' miei governi la crudeltà e le pene eccessive, e anche non sono necessarie, perché da certi casi essemplari in fuora, basta, a mantenere el terrore, el punire e delitti a 15 soldi per lira: pure che si pigli regola di punirgli tutti" (Guicciardini, 1994b, 27).

32 Guicciardini, 1970b, 124–5. "Non è gran cosa che uno governatore, usando spesso asprezza e effetti di severità, si faccia temere, perché e sudditi facilmente hanno paura di chi gli può sforzare e rovinare e viene facilmente alle essecuzione. Ma laudo io quelli governatori che, con fare poche severità e essecuzione, sanno acquistare e conservare el nome del terribile" (Guicciardini, 1994b, 25).

33 Machiavelli, 1965, 1:229. "Italia ... è stata sotto più principi e signori, da' quali è nata tanta disunione e tanta debolezza, che la si è condotta a essere stata preda, non solamente de' barbari potenti, ma di qualunque l'assalta. Di che noi altri Italiani abbiamo obbligo con la Chiesa, e non con altri" (Machiavelli, 1971, 96).

34 Guicciardini, 1965, 81. "Ed anche credo sia vero che la grandezza della Chiesa, cioè la autorità che gli ha data la religione, sia stata causa che

Italia non sia caduta in una monarchia; perché da un canto ha avuto tanto credito che ha potuto farsi capo, e convocare quando è bisognato principi esterni contro a chi era per opprimere Italia, da altro essendo spogliata di arme proprie, non ha avuto tante forze che abbia potuto stabilire dominio temporale, altro che quello che volontariamente gli è stato dato da altri" (Guicciardini, 1961, 340).

35 Guicciardini, 1970b, 127. "E Viniziani hanno avuto a pigliare terre use a servire, le quali non hanno ostinazione né nel difendersi né nel ribellarsi ... Di poi la vicinità della Chiesa è stata e è grandissimo ostaculo, la quale, per avere le barbe tanto fondate quanto ha, ha impedito assai el corso del dominio nostro" (Guicciardini, 1994b, 17).

36 Guicciardini, 1970b, 49. "Hanno di poi la Chiesa vicina, che è potente e non muore mai, in modo che se qualche volta travaglia, risurge alla fine el suo diritto più fresco che prima. e per vicini hanno avuto principi secolari, la vita e la memoria de' quali non è perpetua" (Guicciardini, 1994b, 17).

37 Machiavelli, 1965, 1:44. "Perché sono sustentati dagli ordini antiquati nella religione, quali sono suti tanto potenti e di qualità che tengono e' loro principi in stato, in qualunque modo si procedino e vivino. Costoro soli hanno stati, e non li defendano; sudditi, e non li governano: e li stati, per essere indifesi, non sono loro tolti" (Machiavelli, 1971, 273–4).

38 Guicciardini, 1969, 398. "Esempio certamente molto considerabile e forse non mai, da poi che la Chiesa fu grande, accaduto: uno pontefice, caduto di tanta potenza e riverenza, essere custodito prigione, perduta Roma, e tutto lo stato ridotto in potestà d'altri: il medesimo, in spazio di pochi mesi, restituito alla libertà, rilasciatogli lo stato occupato, e in brevissimo tempo poi ritornato alla pristina grandezza. Tanta è appresso a' prìncipi cristiani l'autorità del pontificato, e il rispetto che da tutti gli è avuto" (Guicciardini, 2013, 2248).

39 Machiavelli, 1996b, 131. "La nostra religione ha glorificato più gli uomini umili e contemplativi, che gli attivi. Ha dipoi posto il sommo bene nella umiltà, abiezione, e nel dispregio delle cose umane; quell'altra lo poneva nella grandezza dello animo, nella fortezza del corpo, ed in tutte le altre cose atte a fare gli uomini fortissimi ... Questo modo di vivere, adunque, pare che abbi renduto il mondo debole" (Machiavelli, 1971, 150).

40 Guicciardini, 1970b, 104. "[F]u detto veramente che la troppa religione guasta el mondo, perché effemmina gli animi, aviluppa gli uomini in mille errori e divertisceli da molte imprese generose e virile" (Guicciardini, 1961, 146).

41 Guicciardini, 1970b, 104. "Né voglio per questo derogare alla fede cristiana e al culto divino, anzi confermarlo e augmentarlo, discernendo el troppo da quello che basta e eccitando gli ingegni a bene considerare quello

di che si debbe tenere conto e quello che sicuramente si può sprezzare" (Guicciardini, 1961, 146).

42 Machiavelli, 1996b, 131–2. "E benché paia che si sia effeminato il mondo, e disarmato il Cielo, nasce più sanza dubbio dalla viltà degli uomini, che hanno interpretato la nostra religione secondo l'ozio, e non secondo la virtù" (Machiavelli, 1971, 150).

43 Guicciardini, 1970b, 104. "[N]on combattete mai con la religione, né con le cose che pare che dependino da Dio; perché questo obietto ha troppa forza nella mente degli sciocchi" (Guicciardini, 1961, 146).

44 Machiavelli, 1965, 1:90. "Questa opinione è suta più creduta ne' nostri tempi, per la variazione grande delle cose che si sono viste e veggonsi ogni dì, fuora di ogni umana coniettura. A che pensando, io, qualche volta, mi sono in qualche parte inclinato nella opinione loro" (Machiavelli, 1971, 295.

45 Machiavelli, 1965, 1:90. "Credo, ancora, che sia felice quello che riscontra el modo del procedere suo con le qualità de' tempi, e similmente sia infelice quello che con il procedere suo si discordano e' tempi" (Machiavelli, 1971, 295–6).

46 In a famous metaphor, he personified Fortune as a woman who shows a preference for the young and the daring.

47 Guicciardini, 1970b, 56. "Quanto disse bene el filosofo: 'De futuris contingentibus non est determinata veritas'! Aggirati quanto tu vuoi, che quanto più ti aggiri, tanto più truovi questo detto verissimo" (Guicciardini, 1994b, 32).

48 Guicciardini, 1970b, 138. "Chi facessi in su qualche accidente giudicare a uno uomo savio gli effetti che nasceranno e scrivessi el giudicio suo, troverrebbe, tornandolo a vedere in progresso di tempo, sì poche cose verificate, come si truova a capo d'anno nel giudicio degli astrologi: perché le cose del mondo sono troppo varie" (Guicciardini, 1961, 151).

49 Guicciardini, 1970b, 61. "Le cose medesime che, tentate in tempo, sono facile a riuscire, anzi caggiono quasi per loro medesime, tentate innanzi al tempo, non solo non riescono allora, ma ti tolgono ancora spesso quella facilità che avevano di riuscire al tempo suo: però non correte furiosi alle cose, non le precipitate, aspettate la sua maturità, la sua stagione" (Guicciardini, 1961, 114).

50 Guicciardini, 1970b, 65. "È antico proverbio che tutti e savi sono timidi, perché conoscono tutti e pericoli, e però temono assai. Io credo che questo proverbio sia falso … Però più presto si può chiamare savio uno animoso che uno timido; e presupposto che tutt'a dua vegghino assai, la differenza dall'uno all'altro nasce perché el timido mette a entrata tutti e pericoli che conosce che possono essere, e presuppone sempre el peggio de' peggi; l'animoso, che ancora lui gli conosce tutti, considerando quanti se ne possino schifare dalla industria degli uomini, quanti ne fa smarrire el caso

per se stesso, non si lascia confondere da tutti, ma entra nelle imprese con fondamento e con speranza che non tutto quello che può essere abbia a essere" (Guicciardini, 1961, 117).

51 Guicciardini, 1970b, 47. "[L]e cose future sono tanto fallace e sottoposte a tanti accidenti, che el più delle volte coloro ancora che sono bene savî se ne ingannano … Però lasciare uno bene presente per paura di uno male futuro è el più delle volte pazzia, quando el male non sia molto certo o propinquo o molto grande a comparazione del bene" (Guicciardini, 1961, 102).

52 Machiavelli, 1965, 1:91. "Da questo ancora depende la variazione del bene; perché, se uno che si governa con respetti e pazienzia, e' tempi e le cose girono in modo che il governo suo sia buono, e' viene felicitando; ma, se li tempi e le cose si mutano, e' rovina, perché non muta modo di procedere" (Machiavelli, 1971, 296).

53 Machiavelli, 1965, 1:91. "Né si truova uomo sì prudente che si sappi accomodare a questo; sì perché non si può deviare da quello a che la natura lo inclina; sì etiam perché, avendo sempre uno prosperato caminando per una via, non si può persuadere partirsi da quella. E però l'uomo respettivo, quando egli è tempo di venire allo impeto, non lo sa fare; donde rovina" (Machiavelli, 1971, 296). On the improbability of virtuous reformers in *The Prince* and *The Discourses* see Jurdjevic, 2014, 53–80.

54 Guicciardini, 1970b, 109. "Coloro ancora che, attribuendo el tutto alla prudenza e virtù, escludono quanto possono la potestà della fortuna, bisogna almanco confessino che importa assai abattersi o nascere in tempo che le virtù o qualità per le quali tu ti stimi siano in prezzo" (Guicciardini, 1961, 104).

55 Guicciardini, 1970b, 49. "Si può porre lo essemplo di Fabio Massimo, al quale lo essere di natura cunctabundo dette tanta riputazione, perché si riscontrò in una spezie di guerra, nella quale la caldezza era perniziosa, la tardità utile; in un altro tempo sarebbe potuto essere el contrario. Però la fortuna sua consisté in questo, che e tempi suoi avessino bisogno di quella qualità che era in lui" (Guicciardini, 1961, 104).

56 Guicciardini, 1970b, 49. "Ma chi potessi variare la natura sua secondo le condizione de' tempi, il che è difficillimo e forse impossibile, sarebbe tanto manco dominato dalla fortuna" (Guicciardini, 1961, 104).

57 Martinez, 2010.

58 Machiavelli, 1965, 1:65. "Non partirsi dal bene, potendo, ma sapere intrare nel male, necessitato … E quello che ha saputo meglio usare la golpe, è meglio capitato. Ma è necessario questa natura saperla bene colorire, ed essere gran simulatore e dissimulatore" (Machiavelli, 1971, 283–4).

59 Machiavelli, 2005b, 61. "[C]olui che inganna, troverrà sempre chi si lascerà ingannare" (Machiavelli, 1971, 283).

60 Guicciardini, 1970b, 107. "Piace universalmente chi è di natura vera e libera: e è cosa generosa, ma talvolta nuoce. Da altro canto la simulazione è utile e anche spesso necessaria per male nature degli altri: ma è odiata e ha del brutto" (Guicciardini, 1994b, 51).

61 Guicciardini, 1970b, 107. "Cioè nel corso tuo ordinario e commune di vivere usare la prima, in modo che acquisti el nome di persona libera; e nondimanco in certi casi importanti e rari usare la simulazione, la quale a chi vive così è tanto più utile e succede meglio, quanto, per avere nome del contrario, ti è più facilmente creduto" (Guicciardini, 1994b, 51).

62 Guicciardini, 1970b, 67. "Per le ragione di sopra non laudo chi vive sempre con simulazione e con arte, ma escuso chi qualche volta la usa ... E é odiosa, la simulazione, ma è molto piu utile a se medesimo; e quella realità giova più presto a altri che a sé" (Guicciardini, 1994b, 51).

63 Machiavelli, 1965, 1:65. "Alessandro VI non fece mai altro, non pensò mai ad altro, che a ingannare uomini: e sempre trovò subietto da poterlo fare. E non fu mai uomo che avessi maggiore efficacia in asseverare, e con maggiori giuramenti affermassi una cosa, che la osservassi meno" (Machiavelli, 1971, 283–4).

64 Guicciardini, 1970b, 67. "Ancora che uno abbia nome di simulatore o di ingannatore, si vede che pure qualche volta gli inganni suoi truovano fede. Pare strano a dirlo, ma è verissimo; e io mi ricordo el re Catolico più che tutti gli altri uomini essere in questo concetto, e nondimeno ne suoi maneggi non gli mancava mai chi gli credessi più che el debito" (Guicciardini, 1994b, 52).

65 Machiavelli, 2005b, 61.

66 Guicciardini, 1970b, 67–8. "[E] questo bisogna che proceda o dalla semplicità o dalla cupidità degli uomini: questi per credere facilmente quello desiderano, quelli per non conoscere" (Guicciardini, 1994b, 52).

67 Guicciardini, 1970b, 92. "Sempre, quando con altri volete simulare o dissimulare una vostra inclinazione, affaticatevi a mostrargli, con più potente e efficace ragione che voi potete, che voi avete in animo el contrario" (Guicciardini, 1994b, 84).

68 Guicciardini, 1970b, 101. "È molto utile el governare le cose sue segretamente, ma più utile in chi si ingegna può di non parere con gli amici: perché molti, come poco stimati, si sdegnono quando veggono che uno recusa di conferirgli le cose sue" (Guicciardini, 1994b, 80).

69 Guicciardini, 1970b, 128. "Nessuno conosce peggio e servidori suoi che el padrone, e proporzionamente el superiore e sudditi; perché non se gli apresentano innanzi tali quali si apresentano agli altri, anzi cercano coprirsi a lui e parergli di altra sorte che in verità non sono" (Guicciardini, 1994b, 72).

70 Machiavelli, 1965, 1:58. "[P]erché uno uomo che voglia fare in tutte le parte professione di buono, conviene rovini infra tanti che non sono buoni" (Machiavelli, 1971, 280).

71 Guicciardini, 1970b, 97. "[C]ome in una commedia o tragedia non é più in prezzo chi porta la persona del padrone e del re chi porta quella di uno servo, ma solamente si attende chi la porta meglio" (Guicciardini, 1994b, 90).

72 Guicciardini, 1970b, 63. "Chi è in maneggi grandi o tende a grandezza, cuopri sempre le cose che gli dispiacciono, amplifichi quelle che gli sono favorevole. È una spezie di ciurmeria e assai contro alla natura mia; ma, dependendo el traino di costoro più spesso dalla openione degli uomini che dagli effetti, el farsi fama che le cose ti vadino prospere ti giova, el contrario ti nuoce" (Guicciardini, 1994b, 43–4).

73 Guicciardini, 1970b, 108. "Lo ignorarsi e tuoi pensieri fa che gli uomini stanno sempre attoniti e sospesi a osservare le tue azione: e in su ogni tuo minimo moto si fanno mille commenti, il che ti fa grandissima riputazione" (Guicciardini, 1994b, 45).

74 Guicciardini, 1970b, 63. "Così, non si sapendo da chi ti è intorno né da' sudditi e fatti tuoi, stanno sempre gli uomini sospesi e quasi attoniti, e ogni tuo piccolo moto e passo è osservato" (Guicciardini, 1994b, 44).

75 Machiavelli, 1965, 1:81. "E così sempre ha fatte e ordite cose grandi, le quali sempre hanno tenuto sospesi e ammirati gli animi de' sudditi e occupati nello evento di esse" (Machiavelli, 1971, 291).

76 See Hankins's critique of Machiavelli's logic in Hankins, 2019, 449–75.

77 Machiavelli, 2005b, 58. "Perché degli uomini si può dire questo generalmente: che sieno ingrati, volubili, simulatori e dissimulatori, fuggitori de' pericoli, cupidi di guadagno" (Machiavelli, 1971, 282).

78 Machiavelli, 2005b, 58. "Perché l'amore è tenuto da uno vinculo di obligo, il quale, per essere gli uomini tristi, da ogni occasioni di propria utilità è rotto" (Machiavelli, 1971, 282).

79 Machiavelli, 2005b, 60–1. "E se gli uomini fussino tutti buoni, questo precetto non sarebbe buono; ma perché sono tristi, e non la osservarebbono a te, tu etiam non l'hai ad osservare a loro" (Machiavelli, 1971, 283).

80 Guicciardini, 1970b, 81. "Non è bene vendicarsi nome di essere sospettoso, di essere sfiducciato; nondimeno l'uomo è tanto fallace, tanto insidioso, procede con tante arte sì indirette, sì profonde, è tanto cupido dello interesse suo, tanto poco respettivo a quello di altri che non si può errare a credere poco, a fidarsi poco" (Guicciardini, 1994b, 70)

81 Guicciardini, 1970b, 108. "Perché si fanno schiavi di coloro a chi gli communicano, oltre a tutti gli altri mali che el sapersi può portare. E se pure la necessità vi strigne a dirgli, metteteli in altri per manco

tempo potete, perché nel tempo assai nascono mille pensamenti cattivi" (Guicciardini, 1994b, 79).

82 Guicciardini, 1970b, 48. "[P]erché quelle sicurtà che sono fondate in sulla voluntà e discrezione di altri sono fallace, atteso quanto poca bontà e fede si truova negli uomini" (Guicciardini, 1994b, 14).

83 Guicciardini, 1970b, 91. "[P]erché in loro communemente può più el rispetto del suo interesse o la sua mala natura che non può la ragione, e meriti tuoi, o le obligazione che avessino teco" (Guicciardini, 1994b, 83).

84 Machiavelli, 2005b, 58. "[E] mentre fai loro bene, sono tutti tua, offeronti el sangue, la roba, la vita, e'figliuoli, come di sopra dissi, quando il bisogno é discosto; ma, quando ti si appressa, e' si rivoltano ... perché gli uomini sdimenticano più presto la morte del padre che la perdita del patrimonio" (Machiavelli, 1971, 282).

85 Machiavelli, 2005b, 30. "E chi crede che ne' personaggi grandi e' benefizii nuovi faccino dimenticare le iniurie vecchie, s'inganna. Errò, adunque, el duca in questa elezione; e fu cagione dell'ultima ruina sua" (Machiavelli, 1971, 269).

86 Guicciardini, 1970b, 106. "Più fondamento potete fare in uno che abbia bisogno di voi o che nel caso che corre abbia lo interesse commune, che in uno beneficato da voi, perché gli uomini communemente non sono grati; però, se non volete ingannarvi, fate e calculi vostri con questa misura" (Guicciardini, 1994b, 15).

87 Guicciardini, 1970b, 47–8. "Guardatevi da fare quelli piaceri agli uomini che non si possono fare sanza fare equale dispiacere a altri: perché chi è ingiuriato non dimentica, anzi reputa la ingiuria maggiore; chi è beneficato non se ne ricorda o gli pare essere beneficato manco che non è. Però, presupposte le altre cose pari, se ne disavanza più di gran lunga che non si avanza" (Guicciardini, 1994b, 15).

88 Guicciardini, 1970b, 79. "Non basti a farvi fidare o rimettere in uomini ingiuriati da voi el conoscere che di quello negocio medesimo risulterebbe, conducendolo bene, anche utilità e onore a loro; perché può in certi uomini per natura tanto la memoria delle ingiurie che gli tira a vendicarsi contro al proprio commodo: o perché stimino più quella satisfazione o perché la passione gli acciechi in modo che non vi discernino drento quello che sarebbe l'onore e utile suo. E tenete a mente questo ricordo, perché molti ci errano" (Guicciardini, 1994b, 67).

89 Hankins, 2019, 432.

90 Hankins, 463.

91 Guicciardini, 1970b, 42, 88, 144. Guicciardini even acknowledged the irony of writing a book that contained a lesson regarding the inadequacy of the written word for many lessons. "These ricordi are rules that can be written in books. But particular cases have different circumstances and must be

treated differently. Such cases can hardly be written anywhere but in the book of discretion" (Guicciardini, 1970b, 105).

92 Guicciardini, 1970b, 94–5. "La scienza delle legge è ridotta oggi in luogo che se nella decisione di una causa è da uno canto qualche viva ragione, dall'altro la autorità di uno dottore che abbia scritto, più si attende nel giudicare la autorità. Però e dottori che praticano sono necessitati volere vedere ognuno che scrive; e così quello tempo che s'arebbe a mettere in speculare, si consuma in leggere libri con stracchezza di animo e di corpo, in modo che l'ha quasi più similitudine a una fatica di facchini che di dotti" (Guicciardini, 1994b, 87).

4 Deconstructing Regimes of the Few in Guicciardini's *Dialogue on the Government of Florence*

1 On the *Dialogue*, see Brown's introduction to Guicciardini, 1994a, vii–xxvii; Pocock, 2003, 219–71; Cadoni, 1999, 59–139; Cadoni, 1994, 187–234; Cadoni, 1983; Sasso, 1984, 181–253; Focher, 2000; Fournel; Tafuro, 2005; Palumbo, 2007.

2 These dates are from Brown's introduction to Guicciardini, 1994a, xxix–xxx. On the dating of the *Dialogue*, see Ridolfi, 1960, 150–2, 210–14, 462–3, 470–1; Focher, 1996, 19.

3 For a "political philological" reading of the relationship between Guicciardini's political and historical vocabulary (and to a lesser extent that of Machiavelli) and the crisis of the Italian wars, see Fournel and Zancarini, 2009.

4 Vincent Luciani raised this same question, arguing, on the basis of Guicciardini's renewed praise of the Albizzean oligarchy in the Cose fiorentine that he began in 1527, that the *Dialogue*'s uncharacteristic criticism was insincere, the result of "the pressure of circumstances." Given his larger argument that Machiavelli had a negligible impact at best on Guicciardini, his dismissal is not surprising. To evaluate the strength of his argument we need a discussion of the nature of the contextual circumstances, but he provides none (Luciani, 1950, 114). Given that Guicciardini was writing in a Florence under renewed Medici power and served the Medici pope Clement VII, his criticism in the *Dialogue* may have been calculated flattery designed to please his masters, whose distinguished ancestor Cosimo il vecchio de' Medici first rose to power in Florence by toppling the Albizzi regime. This explanation, however, does not explain Bernardo del Nero's larger theoretical condemnation of aristocratic regimes in general.

5 Sasso, 1984, 74–6, 82–90. Giorgio Cadoni reads the *Dialogue*'s multiple contradictory voices as similarly expressing inner and irresolvable conflicts within Guicciardini's thought (Cadoni, 1983, 187–234).

6 Sasso, 1984, 75.
7 Sasso, 55, 65–7, 80–1.
8 Sasso, 97.
9 Sasso, 90–2 (my translation).
10 See discussion by Rubinstein, 1960, 163–7.
11 Prohibiting repeated re-election.
12 Guicciardini, 1970b, 2. "Finalmente con uno parlamento si fermò lo stato nel 93, sendo gonfaloniere di giustizia messer Maso degli Albizzi ... e rimase el governo in mano di uomini da bene e savi, e con grandissima unione e sicurtà si continuò insino presso al 1420; e non fa maraviglia, perché gli uomini erano tanti stracchi delle turbulenzie passate, che abattendosi a uno vivere ordinato, tutti volentieri si riposorono. E veramente in quegli tempi si dimostrò quanta fussi la potenzia della città nostra quando era unita" (Guicciardini, 1999, 51–2).
13 Guicciardini, 1970b, 3. "E finalmente ebbono tanti successi, e nella città che si conservò libera, unita e governata da uomini da bene e buoni e valenti, e fuora, che si difesono da inimici potentissimi ed ampliorono assai lo imperio, che meritamente si dice che quello è stato el più savio, el più glorioso, el più felice governo che mai per alcuno tempo abbi avuto la città nostra" (Guicciardini, 1999, 52).
14 Guicciardini, 1970b, 4. "[P]er sicurtà dello stato cacciò di Firenze in grandissimo numero tutti gli avversari sua, che furono molte famiglie nobilissime e ricchissime, e in luogo di quelle cominciò a tirare su di molti uomini bassi e di vile condizione" (Guicciardini, 1970c, 64).
15 Guicciardini, 1970b, 25. "[E] dando favore a quegli uomini d' quali non gli pareva potere temere, per essere spogliati di parenti e credito, come fu in quel tempo uno messer Bernardo Buongirolami, uno Antonio di Puccio" (Guicciardini, 1970c, 84).
16 Guicciardini, 1970b, 29. "El quale, benché apresso di sé avessi un numero di cittadini nobili e prudenti ne' quali si distribuivano gli onori della città e si trattavano le cose di importanza, nondimeno in molte cose seguitava solo el suo consiglio e parere contro alla voluntà degli altri e teneva precipua cura che nella città non si facessi alcuno sì potente che lui avessi cagione da temerne" (Guicciardini, 1970c, 89).
17 Guicciardini, 1970b, 79–96.
18 Guicciardini, 36. "E questo è el fine delle divisione e discordie civile: lo esterminio di una parte; el capo dell'altra diventa signore della città; e' fautori e aderenti sua, di compagni quasi sudditi; el popolo e lo universale ne rimane schiavo; vanne lo stato per eredità e spesse volte di uno savio viene in uno pazzo che poi dà l'ultimo tuffo alla città" (Guicciardini, 1970a, 99).
19 Guicciardini, 1970b, 219. "Non possono essere el più delle volte se non uomini deboli e di poca qualità ed esperienzia degli stati; in modo che se

e' non prestano fede a' cittadini savi ed esperti, anzi vogliono procedere di loro capo ed autorità, come interveniva allora perché avevano sospetto che e' primi cittadini non volessino mutare lo stato, impossibile è che la città non vadia in perdizione" (Guicciardini, 1999, 185–6).

20 Guicciardini, 1970b, 220. "E però e' savi cittadini e di riputazione, vedute queste cattive cagione, né vi potendo riparare perché subito si gridava che volevano mutare el governo, stavano male contenti e disperati e si erano in tutto alienati dallo stato; ed erano el più di loro la maggiore parte a specchio, né volevano esercitare commessarie o legazione se non per forza e quando non potevano fare altro; perché sendo necessario pe' nostri disordini che di ogni cosa seguitassi cattivo effetto, non volevano avere addosso el carico e grido del popolo sanza loro colpa" (Guicciardini, 1999, 186).

21 Guicciardini, 1970b, 220–1. "Questi modi dispiacevano tanto a' cittadini savi e che solevano avere autorità, che erano quasi stracchi del vivere; perché e' vedevano la città rovinare ed andarne all 'ngiù cento miglia per ora, vedevano essere spogliati di ogni riputazione e potere; il che doleva loro e per rispetto proprio e perché in effetto quando gli uomini di qualità non hanno, io non dico la tirannide, ma quello grado che si conviene loro, la città patisce. Aggiugnevasi che ogni volta che nasceva qualche scompiglio, el popolo pigliava sospetto di loro e portava pericolo che non corressi loro a casa, in modo che ogni dì pareva loro essere in sul tavoliere; e però sommamente desideravano che el governo presente si mutassi o meno si riformassi, in modo che la città fussi bene governata" (Guicciardini, 1999, 186).

22 Guicciardini, 1970b, 221. "[A]llo universale della città, che erano gli uomini di case basse e che conoscevano che negli stati stretti le case loro non arebbono condizione, erano gli uomini di buone case, ma che avevano consorti di più autorità e qualità di loro e però vedevano che in uno vivere stretto rimarrebbono adrieto" (Guicciardini, 1999, 187).

23 Guicciardini, 1970b, 221. "[S]i faceva poca distinzione da uomo a uomo presente e da casa a casa; e con tutto intendessino vi era qualche difetto, pure ne erano tanto gelosi e tanto dubio avevano che non fussi loro tolto, che come si ragionava di mutare ed emendare nulla, vi si opponevano" (Guicciardini, 1999, 187).

24 See discussion by Sasso, 1984, 76–82; Rubinstein, 1960, 167–72; and Moulakis, 2000, 200–22.

25 Guicciardini, 1997, 202. "Non essere aperta via agli uomini virtuosi e valenti di mostrare e esercitare la virtù loro, non proposti premi a quegli che facessino buone opere per la republica, una ambizione universale in ognuno a tutti li onori, e una presunzione di volersi ingerire in tutte le cose publiche di qualunque importanza; gli animi degli uomini effeminati

e enervati e vòlti a uno vivere delicato e, rispetto alle facultà nostre, suntuoso; poco amore della gloria e onore vero, assai alle richezze e danari" (Guicciardini, 1970c, 1:250).

26 Guicciardini, 1997, 216–17. "E se bene questo è pasto da infiammare pochi, non è però questo infiammarli inutile, perché in ogni republica bene ordinata e in ogni tempo si è sempre veduto che la virtù di pochi cittadini è quella che ha retto e regge le republiche, e le opere gloriose e effetti grandi sono sempre nati da pochi e per mano di pochi, perché a volere guidare cose grande e essere capi del governo in una città libera, bisogna moltissime parte e virtù che in pochissimi si coniungono" (Guicciardini, 1970c, 1:274).

27 Guicciardini, 1997, 217. "[È] adunche bene per eccitare questa onesta ambizione nelli spiriti grandi e dare loro occasione di operare cose glorioso, mostrare questo luogo e questa commodità di potere venire a uno grado che non può essere maggiore in una città libera" (Guicciardini, 1970c, 1:274).

28 Guicciardini, 1997, 217. "[M]a non ha una discretiva sottile e minuta … dove sedranno tutti li uomini savi e prudenti" (Guicciardini, 1970c, 1:275).

29 Guicciardini, 1997, 219. "[E] in effetto tutto 'l pondo del governo si reduce alla fine in sulle spalle di molti pochi, e così fu sempre in ogni republica e a' tempi antichi e a' moderni" (Guicciardini, 1970c, 1:277).

30 Guicciardini, 1997, 218. "[Q]uel consiglio … abbi a coniungere, abbi a essere el timone della città e moderatore di ogni cosa che occorra" (Guicciardini, 1970c, 1:276).

31 Guicciardini, 1997, 226. "Felice le republiche che sono piene di questa ambizione, perché li è necesario che vi fiorischino quelle arte che conducono a questi gradi, cioè le virtù e opere buone, sievi uno appetito ardente di fare opere grande e generose a beneficio della patria e in coloro che desiderano venire in questà autorità, e in quelli che già vi sono. La grandeza e reputazione de' quali non è contraria né nociva alla libertà" (Guicciardini, 1970c, 1:287).

32 On Guicciardini's relationship to the humanist historical tradition see Wilcox, 1984, 19–33. For an intriguing discussion of Guicciardini's and Machiavelli's contrasting assessments of Paolo Vitelli see Chiappelli, 1984, 53–63.

33 Black, 2013, 263.

34 Machiavelli, 1996a, 339. "Vedi che, mutati solum e visi delli uomini et e colori estrinseci, le cose medesime tutte ritornano; nè vediamo accidente alcuno che a altri tempi non sia stato veduto. Ma el mutare nomi e figure alle cose fa che soli e prudenti le riconoscono: e però è buona et utile la storia, perché ti mette innanzi e ti fa riconoscere e rivedere quello che mai non avevi conosciuto né veduto. Di che seguita un sillogismo fratesco: che molto è da comendare chi vi ha dato la cura di scrivere annali; e da esortare

voi che con diligenza esequiate lo officio commesso" (Machiavelli, 1999, 377).

35 Machiavelli, 1996a, 351. "Ho atteso et attendo in villa a scrivere la istoria, e pagherei dieci soldi, non voglio di più, che voi fosse in lato che io vi potessi mostrare dove io sono, perché, avendo a venire a certi particulari, arei bisogno di intendere da voi se offendo troppo o con lo esaltare o con lo abbassare le cose" (Machiavelli, 1999, 389).

36 Machiavelli, 1996a, 371. "Io ebbi quello augmento insino in cento ducati per la Istoria. Comincio ora a scrivere di nuovo, e mi sfogo accusando i príncipi, che hanno fatto tutti ogni cosa per condurci qui" (Machiavelli, 1999, 411).

37 Guicciardini, 1970b, 3–4. "Cacciato Cosimo, rimasono capi del governo messer Rinaldo degli Albizzi, Niccolò Barbadori, Peruzzi, Bischeri, Guadagni, Castellani, Strozzi ed altri simili, ma poco lo seppono tenere" (Guicciardini, 1999, 52).

38 Guicciardini, 1994a, 21. "Fu pure, a tempo di messer Maso degli Albizzi, di Gino mio bisavolo, di Niccolò da Uzzano e di quegli altri, uno stato in mano de' cittadini principali e di più qualità, né però stretto in modo che la città non fussi libera; durò unito molti anni, e si governorono drento e fuora con grandissima riputazione, perché tennono la città sanza mutazione, e non solo si difesono da inimici potentissimi che cercorono in quel tempo di opprimerci, ma ancora acquistorono Pisa e molti altri luoghi, ed augumentorono assai el dominio e la riputazione della città, in modo che, secondo la opinione di ognuno che ha parlato o scritte in queste cose, non fu mai stato in Firenze che l'abbia meglio governata e più onorata di quello" (Guicciardini, 1999, 339).

39 Sasso, 1984, 86.

40 Guicciardini, 1994a, 18. "La intenzione nostra fu cavare la città dalla potenzia di uno e riducerla in libertà, come si è fatto. Vero è che desideravamo non mettere el governo assolutamente nel popolo, ma in mano di cittadini principali e di più qualità, in modo che fussi più tosto uno stato di uomini da bene che tutto populare" (Guicciardini, 1999, 337).

41 Guicciardini, 1994a, 21. "E però non avevamo a disperarci che ciò che fu allora potessi tornare un'altra volta, massime che eravamo per accostarci, e già avavamo comminciato, a quella forma di vivere el più che avessimo potuto" (Guicciardini, 1999, 339).

42 Guicciardini, 1994a, 22. "Né voglio che vi inganni lo esemplo di quello stato che fu a tempo di messer Maso e delli altri … e così io ho udito molte volte da' più vecchi, che due condizioni che estraordinariamente vi concorsono, furono cagione di tenerlo più unito che non erano soliti a essere e' governi che erano stati innanzi" (Guicciardini, 1999, 340).

43 Guicciardini, 1994a, 22. "La seconda, che alla città non furono mai fatte più pericolose guerre né più lunghe né da più potenti inimici; perché

avemo la guerra gravissima col conte di Virtù, che durò dodici anni, e poi col re Ladislao, che furono di tanto peso e di tanto pericolo, che molto più furono forzati, lasciato da canto le gare, attendere con ogni studio alla conservazione della città" (Guicciardini, 1999, 340).

44 Guicciardini, 1994a, 22–3. "E nondimeno, leggete e considerate bene le vostre chroniche, quello non fu governo libero, perché ogni cosa fu in mano di pochi cittadini, ed el popolo non vi ebbe, si può dire, parte alcuna; né fu anche pacifico, perché vi furono spesso novità e travagli; né a pena ebbono finito di assicurarlo e stabilirlo che vennono tra loro in nuove divisioni, e sursono quelle parte donde poi nacque el 33 ed el 34. Però vi dico che, considerato bene tutto questo discorso, quello governo non fu tale, né durò tanto che voi dovessi contentarvi, se bene ne avessi introdotto uno simile" (Guicciardini, 1999, 340).

45 Guicciardini, 1994a, 134–5. "Pochi cittadini hanno potuto nella città, come fu dalla ruina di messer Giorgio Scali insino al 34, e prima in molti altri tempi, che in fatto hanno oppressi e tenuti in servitù gli altri con mille ingiurie ed insolenzie, e tra loro medesimi sono stati pieni di sedizioni in modo che si sono cacciati, decapitati, rovinati l'uno l'altro, e fatto peggio a questa povera patria che non feciono mai gli inimici" (Guicciardini, 1999, 410).

46 On Machiavelli's view of the Albizzi regime see Jurdjevic, 2014, 132–48.

47 Machiavelli, 1988, 146–7. "Dico pertanto che lo stato il quale in Firenze dalla morte di messer Giorgio Scali ebbe nel 1381 il principio suo, fu prima dalla virtù di messer Maso degli Albizzi, di poi da quella di Niccolò da Uzano sostenuto … Le parti che nacquono per la discordia degli Albizzi e de' Ricci, e che furono di poi da messer Salvestro dei Medici con tanto scandolo riuscitate, mai non si spensono … Vero è che gli spessi parlamenti e le continue persecuzioni fatte contro a' capi di quella dallo '81 al 400, la redussono quasi che a niente … Rinfrescando adunque costoro con I lori sinistri modi ogni dì l'odio nello universale, e non vigilando le cose nocive per non le temere, or nutrendole per invidia l'uno dell' altro, feciono che la famiglia de' Medici riprsese autorità" (Machiavelli, 2005, 474–5).

48 Machiavelli, 1965, 1:101–2. "E cominciandosi dalla riforma fatta in detto tempo da messer Maso degli Albizzi, si vedrà come allora le volleno dar forma di repubblica governata da ottimati, e come in essa fu tanti difetti che la non passò quaranta anni, e sarebbe durata meno se le guerre dei Visconti non fussono seguite, le quali la tenevano unita" (Machiavelli, 1997, 733).

49 Machiavelli, 1965, 1:102. "Aveva ancora la signoria poca riputazione e troppa autorità, potendo disporre senza appello della vita e della roba dei cittadini, e potendo chiamare il popolo a parlamento; in modo che la veniva ad essere non defensitrice dello stato, ma instrumento di farlo perdere" (Machiavelli, 2005, 733).

50 Guicciardini, 1994a, 22–3; Machiavelli, 1965, 1:102. "Le quali cose tutte insieme facevano infiniti disordini, e se, come ho detto, le guerre esterne non l'avessino tenuta ferma, la rovinava più presto che la non rovinò" (Machiavelli, 2005, 734).

51 Guicciardini, 1965, 64–5. "Nel governo degli ottimati è questo bene ... essendo e' più qualificati uomini della città, la governano con più intelletto e con più prudenza che non farebbe una moltitudine; ed essendo honorati, hanno manco causa di travagliarla, come essendo mal contenti potrebbono fare facilmente. El male è, che trovandosi la autorità grande, favoriscono quelle cose che sono utile a loro e deprimono el populo; e non avendo termine la ambizione degli uomini, per accrescere le condizione loro, si rompono insieme e fanno sedizione, donde nasce o per via della tirannide o per altro modo la ruina della città" (Guicciardini, 1999, 461).

52 Guicciardini, 1994a, 19. "Questo me lo ha insegnato la esperienzia de' tempi passati, ne' quali tutti, quando lo stato è venuto in mano di pochi cittadini, la città sempre è stata piena di discordie: ogni dì se è fatto mutazione e parlamenti; pochissimi sono stati grandi in quelli modi di governi che non siano stati decapitati or mandati in esilio; e finalmente in breve spazio di tempo lo stato uscito di mano di quelli pochi, o si è ristretto in uno solo o è ritornato alla larghezza. Li esempli sono sì spessi e sì noti che io non voglio perdere tempo in raccontargli" (Guicciardini, 1999, 338).

53 Guicciardini, 1994a, 19–20. "[E]d inoltre e' cervelli nostri hanno per sua proprietà lo essere appetitosi ed inquieti, e questa seconda ragione fa che quelli pochi che hanno la stato in mano sono discordi e disuniti, e per appetito di prevalere l'uno a l'altro tirano chi in qua chi in là, in modo che per difetto loro viene a indebolirsi tanto più la sua potenzia. Ed el non amare gli altri la superiorità di alcuno, fa che a ogni occasione che venga, vanno in terra; perché dispiacendo naturalmente a Firenze a ognuno che non è nel cerchio la grandezza d'altri, è impossibile che la duri se la non ha uno fondamento ed una spall ache la sostenga. E come vi può essere questa spalla e questo fondamento, se coloro che reggono non sono d'acordo?" (Guicciardini, 1999, 338).

54 Guicciardini, 1994a, 81. "Perché come in una republica e' cittadini principali, che poi a l'ultimo sono quegli che sono potissima causa del bene e del male della città, si propongono certi fini, e quando non vi possono arrivare cercono di travagliare ogni cosa per condurvisi e pensano più alla ambizione ed appetiti loro che alla quiete della città, allora surgono le discordie e le divisioni, allora si fanno autori di cose nuove, dove loro spesso rovinano e la città patisce sempre; e' travagli della quale, mossi dalle discordie civil, partoriscano o tirannide nuova o ritorno del tiranno vecchio, o una dissoluzione e licencia di popolo e di plebe che tumultuosamente conquassa la città. La signoria del duca di Atene, el ritorno e la grandeza di

Cosimo, la tempesta de' Ciompi, non ebbono altri fondamenti che questi" (Guicciardini, 1999, 376).

55 Guicciardini, 1994a, 18. "[C]hé come dice el nostro proverbio, le some si acconciano tra via" (Guicciardini, 1999, 338).

56 Guicciardini, 1994a, 91. "E quegli ingegni più elevati che sentono più che gli altri el gusto della vera gloria ed onore, aranno occasione e libertà di dimostrare ed esercitare più le sue virtù. Di che io tengo conto non per satisfare o fomentare la ambizione loro, ma per beneficio della città, la quale, se si discorre bene e' progressi di ogni età ed antica e moderna, si troverrà che sempre si regge in su la virtù di pochi, perché pochi sono capaci di impresa sì alta, che sono quegli che la natura ha dotati di più ingegno e' giudicio che gli altri. E' quali … si dirizzano tutti a conseguire la gloria ed onore vero, che consiste totalmente in fare opere generose e laudabili in beneficio ed esaltazione della sua patria ed utilità degli altri cittadini … Legghinsi bene le istorie de' greci e de' romani ed anche le nostre croniche: troverassi che sempre in ogni vivere ordinato, el pondo della città si è posato in su le spalle di questi tali, e' quali in ogni età sono stati pochi, né mai le cose grandi e gloriose si sono mosse e condotte per altre mani" (Guicciardini, 1999, 383).

57 Guicciardini, 1994a, 95. "[E]d ogni stato che ha del violento non può essere che di necessità non abbia seco di molti mali nella cose sustanziali" (Guicciardini, 1999, 385).

58 Guicciardini, 1994a, 96. "[È] lodato in secondo luogo quelli di pochi … si chiamono ottimati; governo che a giudicio mio in ogni luogo ha molte difficultà a essere buono, ma a Firenze sopra tutti gli altri, perché da l'una casa a l'altra non è tanto eccesso, né ci sono qualità sì rilevate, che questa distinzione possi farsi se non per forza. La equalità ci è naturale e contrarissimo el vedere tanti capi; sanza che, per infinite cagioni nascerebbono tra loro emulazioni e discordie, e sarebbe impossibile che on si riducessino presto con disordine o in una tirannide o in una licenzia populare; in modo che io reputo che questo degli ottimati sia el peggiore governo che possa avere la nostra città, peggiore anche che quello che uno, perché arebbe come quello tutti e' mali che procedano da essere el governo violento, e di più quegli che nascono dalle dissensioni e discordie civili" (Guicciardini, 1999, 385–6).

59 Guicciardini, 1994a, 96. "Resta adunque pensare al governo popolare, el quale poi che è proprio e naturale, si può sperare che si ordini in modo che sia buono, massime che con tutte le tirannide e stati stretti che a' tempi passati have avuto questa città, non è mai stato spento quello che suole essere el fondamento della libertà, anzi è conservato non altrimenti che se la città fussi stata sempre libera; e questo è la equalità de' cittadini, che è el subietto proprio atto a ricevere la libertà" (Guicciardini, 1999, 386).

60 Guicciardini, 1994a, 97. "[Q]uanto per mostrare che, ancora che la libertà sia gratissima alla città, che non basta avere introdotto uno stato libero, perché e sotto quello possono nascere molti errori e disordini, ma bisogna sia ordinato di sorte che si sentino e' frutti della libertà, altrimenti el nome sarà buonoe piacevole, ma gli effetti molto spesso simili a quegli del tiranno" (Guicciardini, 1999, 386).

61 Guicciardini, 1994a, 102. "[A] me pare che el governo viniziano per una città disarmata sia così bello come forse mai avessi alcuna republica libera" (Guicciardini, 1999, 390).

62 Gilbert, 1968.

63 Guicciardini, 1994a, 103. "E se la plebe non vi participa, la non participa anche a noi, perché infiniti artefici, abitatori nuovi ed altri simili, non entrano nel nostro consiglio. Ed anchora che a Vinegia gli inabili siano abilitati con più difficultà agli uffici che non si fa a noi, questo non nasce perché la spezie del governo sia diversa, ma perché in una spezie medesima hanno ordini diversi" (Guicciardini, 1999, 390).

64 Guicciardini, 1994a, 103. "E però se noi chiamassimo gentiluomini e' nostri, e questo nome appresso a noi non si dessi se non a chi è abile agli uffici, troveresti che el governo di Vinegia è populare come el nostro e che el nostro non è manco governo di ottimati che sia el loro" (Guicciardini, 1999, 390).

65 Arrighi, 1990.

66 Najemy, 2006, 282, 365.

67 Guicciardini, 1994a, 9.

68 Brown, in Guicciardini, 1994a, xxi–xxii.

69 Najemy, 2006, 436–7.

70 Sasso, 1984, 86–7.

71 Machiavelli, 1965, 57. "[A]ndare dreto alla verità effettuale della cosa che alla immaginazione di essa" (Machiavelli, 1997, 159).

72 Machiavelli, 1996, 539. "Honorando cognato" (Machiavelli, 2005, 387).

73 Machiavelli, 1996, 541.

74 Machiavelli, 1996, 349–50, 354, 356, 366.

75 Machiavelli, 1996, 392. "Onorando in luogo di padre" (Machiavelli, 2005, 433).

76 On their financial activity for Clement VII, see Bullard, 1980, 121, 136, 147–58.

77 Black, 2013, 266.

78 Machiavelli, 1996, 416. "Io amo messer Francesco Guicciardini, amo la patria mia" (Machiavelli, 1999, 459).

79 Black, 2013, 213–87; Jurdjevic, 2014, 81–131; Hankins, 2017.

80 McCormick, 2018, 72; see also McCormick 2015. For Machiavelli's *terminus a quo* on nobles and people see McCormick, 2011.

81 Black, 2013, 260.
82 Polizzotto, 1994, 318–19; Jurdjevic, 2014, 45–8.
83 Book 7, chapters 1–2 of the *Florentine Histories.*
84 Jurdjevic, 2014, 149–78; Najemy, 1982; Najemy, 2006, 437.
85 Dionisotti, 1980, 392.
86 Black, 2013, 303.

5 Cognitive Dissonance in Guicciardini's *Considerations on the "Discourses of Machiavelli"*

1 Guicciardini, 1994a, xxix–xxxi.
2 Guicciardini, 1969, xvii.
3 Najemy, 2006, 448.
4 Najemy, 450–2.
5 Celli, 2019, 26–30.
6 Guicciardini, 1965, 78–9. "Lo esemplo si può porre nella nostra città dove, doppo la mutazione dello stato del '26, sono stati perseguitati e conculcati alcuni cittadini buoni e bene qualificati, e in ultimo nella venuta del principe di Oranges, necessitati o disubidire a' commandamenti fatti dalli otto di fermarsi in Firenze sotto pena [di] rebellione, o restare con pericolo di essere amazzati, e almanco con certezza di essere sostenuti come sospetti. E'quali la necessità ha condotti o a desiderare la mutazione di uno stato che sotto nome di libertà è tirannico e distrutore della patria, o tacitament lasciarsi con somma ingiugiustizia tôrre la patria e le facultà" (Guicciardini, 1970c, 626).
7 Guicciardini, 1965, 85. "[E]l perseguitare doppe el '26 acerbamente sanza distinzione quelli che erano stati amici loro, hanno fatto desiderare da molti la ritornata loro, che altrimenti l'arebonno aborrita non manco che gli altri" (Guicciardini, 1970c, 634).
8 Najemy, 2006, 462; Ridolfi, 1968, 211.
9 Quoted in Najemy, 2006, 462.
10 Machiavelli, 1965, 1:203. "In ogni republica due umori diversi, quello del popolo, e quello de'grandi; e ... tutte le leggi che si fanno in favore della libertà, nascano dalla disunione loro" (Machiavelli, 1971, 82).
11 Guicciardini, 1965, 68. "La causa delle disunione di Roma tra patrizi e plebei fu dallo essere divisi gli ordini della città, cioè che una parte fussino patrizi, l'altra plebei ... Ché se da principio o non fussi stata questa distinzione tra patrizi e plebei ... non nascevano quelle divisione" (Guicciardini, 1970c, 615).
12 Guicciardini, 1965, 69. "[R]are volte, o forse non mai, è addacuto che una republica abbia avuto da principo la sua ordinazione perfetta" (Guicciardini, 1970c, 617).

13 Machiavelli, 1989, 209. "[Q]uelle inimicizie che intra il popolo ed il senato nascessino, tollerarle, pigliandole per uno inconveniente necessario a pervenire all romana grandezza" (Machiavelli, 1971, 86–7).

14 Guicciardini, 1965, 72. "Non veggo adunche che a'romani fussi impossibile ordinare el governo in modo che tra'l senato e la plebe non avessino a essere quelli tumulti e sedizione, anzi lo giudico molto facile" (Guicciardini, 1970c, 620).

15 Guicciardini, 1965, 71. "Vorrò che la guardia della libertà contro a chi volessi opprimere la republica appartenga a tutti, fuggendo sempre quanto si possa la distinxione tra nobili e plebei" (Guicciardini, 1970c, 618).

16 Guicciardini, 1965, 65. "E se ono ottimati per successione e non per elezione, di prudenti e buoni vengono presto le cose in mano di imprudente e cattivi" (Guicciardini, 1970c, 611).

17 Guicciardini, 1965, 65. "[N]on siano sempre le medesime linee e famiglie, ma che di tutto el corpo della città, cioè di tutti quegli che secondo le legge sono abili a participare de'magistrati ... siano molti in numero acciò che più facilmente siano tollerati dagli altri, e'quali aranno continua speranza che loro o case loro succedino in luogo di quelli che alla giornata mancassino; e anche perché, essendo el numero largo, si potrà sperare vi entri ciascuno che lo meriti" (Guicciardini, 1970c, 611).

18 Guicciardini, 1965, 65. "Ebbono e'lacedemòni gli ottimati in questo modo, cioè non di particulare sorte di uomini, ma di tutto el corpo della città; ebbongli e'romani ma con distinzione, perché apresso a loro e'patrizi da'princìpi erano gli ottimati, gli altri erano plebei, che fu causa di tutte le loro sedizione" (Guicciardini, 1970c, 612).

19 Machiavelli's definitions are unambiguous in *The Prince* and the *Discourses*. There is debate about the degree to which he modified his views in his later writing. See Jurdjevic, 2014; Black, 2022.

20 Machiavelli, 1989, 40. "[N]on si può con onestà satisfare a'grandi e sanza iniuria d'altri, ma sì bene al populo: perché quello del populo è più onesto fine che quello de'grandi ... non essere oppresso" (Machiavelli, 1971, 271).

21 Guicciardini, 1965, 64. "Nel governo degli ottimati è questo bene, che essendo più, non possono così facilmente fare una tirannide come uno sole; essendo e'più qualificati uomini della città, la governano con più prudenza che non farebbe una moltitudine" (Guicciardini 1970c, 611).

22 Guicciardini, 1965, 71. "Ma quando fussi necessitato mettere in una città o uno governo meramente di nobili; perché essendovi più prudenza e avendo più qualità" (Guicciardini, 1970c, 618).

23 Guicciardini, 1965, 65. "[M]a appartenga a loro el consultare e deliberare di quelle cose a che è più necessaria la prudenza degli uomini, cioè le guerre, le pace, le pratiche co'prìncipi, e tutte le cose sustanziale alla conservazione e augumento del dominio" (Guicciardini, 1970c, 612).

24 Guicciardini, 1965, 66. "[E]l popolo per la ignoranza sua non è capace di deliberare le cose importante ... e però facile a essere mosso e ingannato dagli uomini ambiziosi e sediziosi" (Guicciardini, 1970c, 612).
25 Guicciardini, 1965, 73. "[E]l quale non intende né esamina le cose bene, e [è] facile muoversi a'romori e calunnie false" (Guicciardini 1970c, 621).
26 Guicciardini, 1965, 103. "[N]é esamina o distingue sottilmente, in modo che si inganna spesso ... crede a'romori falsi, muovesi per fondamenti leggieri, e in effetto quanto alla ignoranza è molto più pericoloso che el giudicio di pochi" (Guicciardini, 1970c, 654).
27 Guicciardini, 1965, 96. "E quanto alla invidia, cade più facilmente negli uomini popolari, a'quali ogni grandezza punto eminente o di nobilità o di ricchezze o di virtù o di riputazione è ordinariamente molesta; né cosa alcuna dispiace loro che vedere altri cittadini che abbino più qualità di loro, e questi sempre desiderano abbassare" (Guicciardini, 1970c, 645).
28 Guicciardini, 1965, 66. "[B]atte volentieri e'cittadini qualificati, che gli necessita a cercare novità e turbazione" (Guicciardini, 1970c, 612).
29 Guicciardini, 1965, 73. "Ma bisogna anche avertire che siano ordinati in modo che gli innocenti non siano facilmente vessati o puniti. Perché oltre a essere ingiusto è anche pernizioso alla città, perché andando questo pericolo sopra gli uomini nobili e di più qualità, vivendo loro con questo continuo sospetto, diventano di necessità malcontenti, e la mala contentezza de'più potenti diventa in molti modi pericolosa alla republica" (Guicciardini, 1970c, 620–1).
30 Guicciardini, 1965, 117–18. "Quando sono bene trattai amassino el principe suo, io confesso che quanto a loro sarebbono, a ogni principe che governassi bene, inutile le fortezze ... Ma considerato quanto molte volte e'popoli eziandio bene trattati, sono spesso poco ragionevoli in loro la memoria dello antico principe se ora sono sotto uno imperio nuovo, quanto lo appetito della libertà se sono usati a averla, e quanto spesso per questo e per altri rispetti uno principe o tiranno è sforzato governare e'cittadini o sudditi suoi con qualche ingiuria ... è necessario fare qualche fondamento in sulla forza, in sul tenere e'popoli suoi in qualche terrore; altrimenti sarebbe troppo spesso in preda ... della malignità" (Guicciardini, 1970c, 669–70).
31 McCormick, 2022.
32 McCormick.
33 Guicciardini, 1965, 68. "Ma dico in conclusione che la causa delle disunione di Roma tra patrizi e plebei fu dallo essere divisi gli ordini della città, cioè che una parte fussino patrizi, l'altra plebei, e che tutti e'magistrati fussino de'patrizi, esclusa la plebe, e tolta a'plebei ogni speranza di potergli conseguire. Ché se da principio o non fussi stata questa distinzione tra patrizi e plebei, o se almanco si fussi data la metà degli onori alla plebe,

come si fece poi, non nascevano quelle divisione" (Guicciardini, 1970c, 615).

34 Guicciardini, 1965, 68. "Molto utile alla grandezza sua che e'patrizi più presto cedessino alla voluntà della plebe, che entrassino in pensare modo di non avere bisogno della plebe" (Guicciardini, 1970c, 616).

35 Guicciardini, 1965, 69. "Ma sotto e're non noceva perché essendo la autorità ne're, non poteva el senato per sé medesimo opprimere le plebe; e quello che non faceva el senato di pensare a'commodi, lo facevano e're, etiam ... usavano ancora di eleggere talvolta de'plebei ne'patrizi, che faceva che gli altri tolleravano più facilmente quello grado al quale ancora loro speravano potere pervenire" (Guicciardini, 1970c, 616).

36 Machiavelli, 1989, 201. "Ma, come prima ei furono morti i Tarquinii, e che ai Nobili fu la paura fuggita, cominciarono a sputare contro alla Plebe petto, ed in tutti I modi che potevano la offendevano" (Machiavelli, 1971, 82).

37 Guicciardini, 1965, 69. "Le quali ragione tutte cessorono quando e'refurono cacciati, perché e'patrizi diventorono padroni della città e arbitri di ogni cosa: non aveva la plebe a chi fuggire né chi pensassi a'commodi suoi; né e'capi della plebe più speranza di essere eletti ne' patrizi, perché da loro erano fastiditi come ignobili, e più presto eletti e'forestieri come fu Appio Claudio" (Guicciardini, 1970c, 616).

38 Guicciardini, 1965, 67. "Che avendo la plebe uno magistrato particulare veniva a avere uno capo publico, col quale si poteva consultare e trattare e'commodi suoi, e a chi avendo la plebe ricorso, non era disprezzata come corpo che non avessi capo" (Guicciardini, 1970c, 614).

39 Machiavelli, 1989, 209. "Considerando adunque tutte queste cose, si vede come a'legislatori di Roma era necessario fare una delle due cose, a volere che Roma stesse quieta come le sopradette republiche: o non adoperare la plebe in guerre, come i Viniziani; o non aprire la via a'forestieri, come gli Spartani. E loro feciono l'una e l'altra; il che dette alla plebe forze ed augumento, ed infinite occasioni di tumultuare" (Machiavelli, 1971, 85).

40 Guicciardini, 1965, 71–2. "Io credo essere vero che volendo e'romani adoperare la plebe alla guerra, come per el piccolo numero de'patrizi erano necessitati, volendo adoperare le arme proprie, che era necessario tenerla contenta; e el non volere fare questo e'patrizi, fu causa di tanti tumulti e sedizione, perché né gli volevano ammettere nel governo, né si astanevano da quelle ingiurie che davano causa alla plebe di desiderare di participarne; perché occupavano le possessione publiche e erano molto rigidi nella esazione de'debiti, e si può credere che in tutte le altre cose la giustizia fussi inequale in favore di quella parte che aveva in mano tutta la autorità" (Guicciardini, 1970c, 619).

41 Guicciardini, 1965, 65. "Patrizi da'princìpi erano gli ottimati, gli altri erano plebei, che fu causa di tutte le loro sedizione" (Guicciardini, 1970c, 612).

42 Guicciardini, 1965, 67.

43 Guicciardini, 1965, 72. "Ma dico bene, che se nel principio della libertà non fussi stata, come è detto nel quarto Discorso, la distinzione tra patrizi e la plebe; o come si fece poi per necessità, si fussi da principio communicati gli onori, che non sarebbono stati tra loro quelli tumulti e sedizioni, e'quali cessorono subito che el governo fu communicato, insino al temp de'Gracchi" (Guicciardini, 1970c, 619).

44 Guicciardini, 1965, 72. "Dico ancora che se e'patrizi, sanza communicare interamente el governo alla plebe, avessino saputo porre qualche buono ordine alla ingiurie, e avessino aperta la via per la quale a certi tempi e'plebei principali potessino essere stati fatti patrizi, che forse non sarebbono stati quelli tumulti; perché si vedde per esperienza che nelle legge proposte da Publio Sestio, la plebe si contentava di provedere a'deviti e a'benu occupati" (Guicciardini, 1970c, 619–20).

45 Guicciardini, 1965,103. "[C]rede a' romori falsi, muovesi per fondamenti leggieri, e in effetto quanto alla ignoranza è molto più pericoloso che el giudicio di pochi" (Guicciardini, 1970c, 654).

46 Guicciardini, 1965, 102.

47 Guicciardini, 1965, 101. "El primo accidente benché piccolo distrusse la loro tirannide, la quale non credo fussi stata più stabile, se bene si fussino vòlti a battere col favore della plebe la nobilità, perché quello populo era troppo amicissimo del nome della libertà" (Guicciardini, 1970c, 651). Machiavelli also discusses Manlius Capitolinus in *discorso* 1.58.

48 Guicciardini, 1965, 101. "E quanto dottrina generale, quale sia meglio a chi vuole occupare la tirannide, o procedere col favore del popolo o farsi amica la nobilità, gli esempli si truovano diversi; perché e Silla occupò la tirannide a Roma e la stabili con le spalle della nobilità, e a Firenze el duca d'Atene fu fatto tiranno col favore de'nobili, e'quali per la sua imprudenza e levità non si seppe mantenere, il che fu causa di farnelo cadere presto" (Guicciardini, 1970c, 652).

49 Guicciardini, 1965, 64–5. "El male è, che trovandosi la autorità grande, favoriscono quelle cose che sono utile a loro e deprimono el populo; e non avendo termine la ambizione degli uomini, per accrescere le condizione loro, si rompono insieme e fanno sedizione, donde nasce o per via della tirannide o per altro modo la ruina delle città" (Guicciardini, 1970c, 611).

50 Guicciardini, 1965, 65–6. "Nel governo del poplo è di buono, che mentre dura non vi è tirannide; possono più le legge che gli uomini; e el fine di tutte le deliberazione è riguardare al bene universale" (Guicciardini, 1970c, 612).

51 Machiavelli, 1989, 220. "[I]ngannati da uno falso bene e da una falsa gloria" (Machiavelli, 1971, 92).

52 Machiavelli, 1989, 221. "Né sia alcuno che s'inganni, per la gloria di Cesare, sentendolo, massime, celebrare dagli scrittori: perché quegli che lo

laudano, sono corrotti dalla fortuna sua, e spautiti lunghezza dello imperio, il quale, reggendosi sotto quel nome, non permetteva che gli scrittori parlassono liberamente di lui" (Machiavelli, 1971, 92).

53 Machiavelli 1989, 321. "Perché il più, degli scrittori in modo alla fortuna de'vincitori ubbidiscano" Machiavelli, 1971, 144. Machiavelli makes a similar point in the preface in explaining his choice of citizens as dedicatees, rather than of a prince: "I have got away from the common custom of those who write, who always address their works to some prince and, blinded by ambition and avarice, praise him for all the worthy traits, when they ought to blame him for every quality that can be censured" (Machiavelli 1989, 188).

54 Machiavelli 1989, 221. "Vegga ancora con quante laude ei celebrano Bruto; talché, non potendo biasimare quello per la sua potenza, ei celebravano il nimico suo" (Machiavelli, 1971, 92).

55 As Machiavelli explained in a letter to Donato Giannotti regarding the composition of the *Florentine Histories,* he communicated his own thoughts about the Medici family via the speeches of their enemies.

56 Machiavelli 1989, 313. "Nessuna cosa essere più vana e più incostante che la moltitudine, così Tito Livio nostro, come tutti gli altri istorici affermano" (Machiavelli, 1971, 140).

57 Machiavelli 1989, 313. "Io non so se io mi prenderò una pronvincia dura e piena di tanta difficultà, che mi convenga o abandonarla con vergogna, o seguirla con carico; volendo difendere una cosa, la quale, coe ho detto, da tutti gli scrittori è accusata" (Machiavelli, 1971, 140).

58 Machiavelli, 1989, 313–14. "Io no giudico né giudicherò mai essere difetto difendere alcuna opinione con le ragioni, sanza volervi usare o l'autorità o la forza" (Machiavelli, 1971, 140).

59 Guicciardini, 1965, 71.

60 Machiavelli, 1989, 314. "Dico, adunque, come di quello difetto di che accusano gli scrittori la moltitudine, se ne possono accusare tutti gli uomini particularmente, e massime i principi" (Machiavelli, 1971, 140); Guicciardini, 1965, 71.

61 Machiavelli, 1989, 318. "Ma la opinione contro ai popoli nasce perché de'popoli ciascuno dice male sanza paura e liberamente, ancora mentre che regnano: de'principi si parla sempre con mille paure e mille rispetti" (Machiavelli, 1971, 142).

62 Guicciardini, 1965, 105. "Gli esempli sono tanti e si noti che non accade replicargli, e tali che meritamente hanno partorito quella opinione antichissima e commune di tutti gli scrittori, che nella moltitudine non sia né prudenza né constanza" (Guicciardini, 1970c, 656).

63 Machiavelli, 1989, 204. "[E] perché in ogni republica sono uomini grandi e popolari" (Machiavelli, 1971, 83).

64 Guicciardini, 1965, 70. "[A]ltro è a dire in chi ha a essere el governo, o ne' grandi o nella plebe, e a questo serve lo esemplo di Vinegia, perché è in modo ne' nobili che la plebe tutta ne è esclusa, altro è dire, participando ognuno del governo, una autorità o cura particulare per difesa della libertà in chi ha a essere" (Guicciardini, 1970c, 617).

65 Gilbert, 1968; Rubinstein, 1954; Rubinstein, 1960.

66 Guicciardini, 1994a, 134. "Parmi bene che in genere el governo sia buono e che abbia quelle parte principali che si ricercano in una republica libera, ed ha grandissima similitudine col governo viniziano, el quale, se io non mi inganno, è el più bello ed el migliore governo non solo de' tempi nostri, ma ancora che forse avessi mai a' tempi antichi alcuna città, perché participa di tutte le spezie de' governi, di uno, di pochi e di molti, ed è temperato di tutti in modo che ha raccolta la maggiore parte de' beni che ha in sé qualunche governo e fuggiti la più parte de' mali" (Guicciardini, 1961, 297).

67 Guicciardini, 1965, 71. "Ma quanto al titolo della quistione, io loderò sempre più che tutti gli altri governi uno governo misto come di sopra" (Guicciardini, 1970c, 618).

68 Guicciardini, 1965, 71. "[C]he in una plebe la quale essendo piena di ignoranza e di confusione e di molte male qualità, non si può sperare se non che precipiti e conquassi ogni cosa" (Guicciardini, 1970c, 618).

69 Guicciardini, 1965, 71; emphasis mine. "E questa conclusion è secondo la sentenza di tutti quelli che hanno scritto delle republiche, che prepongono el governo degli ottimati a quello della moltitudine" (Guicciardini, 1970c, 619).

70 Guicciardini must have been thinking of Machiavelli's *Discourse on Florentine Affairs,* a text that urged the Medici to establish a republic and abandon any hope of ruling the city directly, when he wrote the following: "Hence these ideas that tyrants should abandon their tyranny and kings find a wise system for their realms, depriving their heirs of the succession, are more easily given form in books and in men's imaginations than carried into effect; rather, though private citizens have frequently discussed them, real examples are extremely rare" (Guicciardini, 1965, 79).

71 Explored in chapters 2 and 3 herein.

6 Machiavelli and Guicciardini on Cesare Borgia's "Good Government"

1 Machiavelli, 1965, 1:47. "E chi diceva come e' n'erano cagione e' peccati nostri, diceva il vero; ma non erano già quelli che credeva, ma questi che io ho narrati: e perché elli erano peccati de' principi, ne hanno patito la pena ancora loro" (Machiavelli, 1971, 275).

2 Machiavelli, 1965, 3:1233. "E se le cose fatte dai principi nostri, fuori e in casa, non fieno, come quelle degli antichi, con ammirazione per la

loro virtù e grandezza lette, fieno forse per le altre loro qualità, con non minore ammirazione considerate, vedendo come tanti nobilissimi popoli da sì deboli e male amministrate armi fussino tenuti in freno ... si vedrà con quali inganni, con quali astuzie e arti, i principi, i soldati e i capi delle repubbliche, per mantenersi quella reputazione che non avevono meritata, si governavano" (Machiavelli, 1971, 739).

3 Guicciardini, 1969, 3. "Io ho deliberato di scrivere le cose accadute alla memoria nostra in Italia, dappoi che l'armi de' franzesi, chiamate da' nostri prìncipi medesimi, cominciorono con grandissimo movimento a perturbarla ... onde per innumerabili esempli evidentemente apparirà ... quanto siano perniciosi, quasi sempre a se stessi ma sempre a' popoli, i consigli male misurati di color oche dominano, quando, avendo solamente innanzi agli occhi o errori vani o le cupidità presenti, non si ricordando delle spesse variazioni della fortuna, e convertendo in detriment altrui la potestà conceduta loro per la salute comune, si fanno, o per poca prudenza o per troppa ambizione, autori di nuove turbazioni" (Guicciardini, 1970b, 110).

4 On paradoxes as a potential key for Machiavelli interpreters see Jurdjevic, 2007.

5 Machiavelli, 1965, 1:33-34. "[I] think I am right in bringing him forward in this way as worthy of imitation by all those through Fortune and by means of another's forces attain a ruler's position... Anyone, therefore, who thinks it necessary in his princedom newly won to secure himself against his enemies, to win friends, to conquer by force or by fraud, to make himself loved and feared by the people, followed and respected by the soldiers, to destroy those who can or are likely to injure you, to replace ancient customs with new ways, to be severe and agreeable, magnanimous and liberal, to destroy disloyal armies, to raise new ones, to keep the friendship of kings and of princes in such a way that they are compelled either to aid you with a good grace or to harm you with reluctance, cannot find more recent instances than this man's actions."

6 For examples of the former see Skinner, 2019, 10–15; McCormick, 2018, 21–44; Black, 2013, 55–66; Anselmi, 2006, 221–30; Marchand, 1969, 327–55; Sasso, 1966; Mattingly, 1958, 182–91; Ward, 2011; Benner, 2013; Baron, 1961, 223–4; Scott and Sullivan, 1994, 887–900; Dietz, 1986, 777–99.

7 Najemy, 2013, 544.

8 Najemy, 545.

9 The same conclusion is reached by Mattingly and Benner.

10 This runs contrary to a prominent view that Cesare's chief innovation was the conscription of a native militia, on which see Larner, 1966, 17, 253–68; Woodward, 1913; Alvisi, 1878.

11 See Ward, 2011, for a discussion of esoteric reading of *The Prince.*

12 Najemy, 2013, 545.

13 Najemy, 545–7; following Bradford, 2011; Pepe, 1945; Larner, 1966.
14 Machiavelli, 1965, 1:30. "[O]nde che il duca deliberò non dependere più dalle arme e fortuna di altri" (Machiavelli, 1971, 267.
15 Machiavelli, 1965, 1:30. "E la prima cosa, indebolì le parti Orsine e Colonnese in Roma; perché tutti gli aderenti loro che fussino gentili uomini, se li guadagnò, faccendoli suoi gentili uomini e dando loro grandi provvisioni; e onorolli, secondo le loro qualità, di condotte e di governi; in modo che in pochi mesi negli animi loro l'affezione delle parti si spense, e tutta si volse nel duca" (Machiavelli, 1971, 267).
16 My emphasis on Borgia's uniquely positive role in *The Prince* thus follows Quentin Skinner, whose various analyses of *The Prince* and Machiavelli's legations also stress Borgia's exceptional status as a positive model. See Skinner, 1978, 38. Najemy, by contrast, concludes that Borgia was no different than the many other failed princes condemned by Machiavelli in *The Prince*, exceptional only in that his failure was "particularly egregious"; see Najemy, 2013, 555. That conclusion, however, begs the unanswered question of why Machiavelli would devote so much more attention to Borgia than to any of the other failed princes and why he condemns the latter in blunt, accusatory language but criticizes the former via ironic praise.
17 Machiavelli, 1965, 1:31. "Spenti, adunque, questi capi, e ridotti li partigiani loro amici sua, aveva il duca gittati assai buoni fondamenti alla potenzia sua" (Machiavelli, 1971, 267).
18 Machiavelli, 1965, 1:29. "Se, adunque, si considerrà tutti e' progressi del duca, si vedrà lui aversi fatti gran fondamenti alla futura potenzia; li quali non iudico superfluo discorrere, perché io non saprei quali precetti mi dare migliori a uno principe nuovo, che lo esemplo delle azioni sua: e se gli ordini suoi non li profittorono" (Machiavelli, 1971, 267).
19 Machiavelli, 1965, 1:31. "Aveva il duca gittati assai buoni fondamenti alla potenzia sua, avendo tutta la Romagna con il ducato di Urbino, parendogli, massime, aversi acquistata amica la Romagna e guadagnatosi tutti quelli popoli, per avere cominciato a gustare el bene essere loro" (Machiavelli, 1971, 267).
20 Machiavelli, 1965, 1:31. "Preso che ebbe il duca la Romagna, e trovandola suta comandata da signori impotenti, li quali più presto avevano spogliato e' loro sudditi che corretti, e dato loro materia di disunione, non di unione, tanto che quella provincia era tutta piena di latrocinii, di brighe e di ogni altra ragione di insolenzia, iudicò fussi necessario, a volerla ridurre pacifica e obèdiente al braccio regio, darli buon governo" (Machiavelli, 1971, 267).
21 Machiavelli, 1965, 1:31. "[E] preposevi uno iudicio civile nel mezzo della provincia, con uno presidente eccellentissimo, dove ogni città vi aveva lo avvocato suo" (Machiavelli, 1971, 267). On the Rota see Mallett, 1969.
22 On Cesare's government in Cesena see Fabbri 1987; Fabbri, 1990.

23 Machiavelli, 1965, 1:31. "[A] guadagnarseli in tutto, volle mostrare che, se crudeltà alcuna era seguita, non era nata da lui, ma dalla acerba natura del ministro" (Machiavelli, 1971, 267).
24 Machiavelli, 1965, 1:33 "Il che se li fusse riuscito (che gli riusciva l'anno medesimo che Alessandro morì), si acquistava tante forze e tanta reputazione, che per se stesso si sarebbe retto, e non sarebbe più dependuto dalla fortuna e forze di altri, ma dalla potenzia e virtù sua" (Machiavelli, 1971, 268).
25 Najemy, 2013, 545.
26 Najemy, 544.
27 My translation and my emphasis. The original reads: "Le rigorosità passate averli generato qualche odio" (Machiavelli, 1971, 267).
28 Machiavelli, 1965, 1:31. "Per purgare gli animi di quelli populi e guadagnarseli in tuttoLa ferocità del quale spettaculo fece quelli populi in uno tempo rimanere satisfatti e stupidi" (Machiavelli, 1971, 267).
29 Machiavelli, 1965, 1:31. "Preso che ebbe il duca la Romagna, e trovandola suta comandata da signori impotenti, li quali più presto avevano spogliato e' loro sudditi che corretti" (Machiavelli, 1971, 267).
30 On the coherence of chapter 7 see Sasso, 1988, 119–63. For his detailed study of the evolution of Machiavelli's utterances on Borgia see Sasso, 1966.
31 Machiavelli, 1965, 1:38. "Bene usate si possono chiamare quelle ... che si fanno a uno tratto, per la necessità dello assicurarsi, e di poi non vi si insiste drento, ma si convertiscono in più utilità de' sudditi che si può" (Machiavelli, 1971, 270).
32 Machiavelli, 1965, 1:40. "E consumate che furono le vivande e tutti gli altri intrattenimenti che in simili conviti si usano, Liverotto, ad arte, mosse certi ragionamenti gravi, parlando della grandezza di papa Alessandro e di Cesare suo figliuolo, e delle imprese loro" (Machiavelli, 1971, 270).
33 Machiavelli, 1965, 1:61–2. "Era tenuto Cesare Borgia crudele; nondimanco quella sua crudeltà aveva racconcia la Romagna, unitola, ridottola in pace e fede. Il che se si considerrà bene, si vedrà quello essere stato molto più pietoso che il populo fiorentino, il quale, per fuggire el nome del crudele, lasciò destruggere Pistoia. Debbe, pertanto, uno principe non si curare della infamia di crudele, per tenere li sudditi suoi uniti e in fede; perché, con pochissimi esempli, sarà più pietoso che quelli e' quali, per troppa pietà, lasciono seguire e' disordini, di che ne nasca occisioni o rapine; perché queste sogliono offendere una universalità intera, e quelle esecuzioni che vengono dal principe offendere uno particulare" (Machiavelli, 1971, 281–2).
34 Machiavelli, 1965, 1:40. "Praeterea del populo inimico uno principe non si può mai assicurare, per essere troppi; de' grandi si può assicurare, per essere pochi" (Machiavelli, 1971, 271).

35 Machiavelli quoted in McCormick, 2018, 24.

36 McCormick, 2018, 21–44. McCormick locates the unity between Machiavelli and Cesare in the virtually identical language that Machiavelli uses to describe himself in the dedication to *The Prince* – "And if from the summit of your highness, Your Magnificence sometimes turns your eyes to these low places, you will understand how much I bear an unmerited great and continuous malignity of fortune [*una grande e continua malignità di fortuna*]" – and to narrate Cesare's downfall, who experienced "an extraordinary and extreme malignity of fortune" (*una estraordinaria ed estrema malignità di fortuna*). The word *malignità* occurs only twice in *The Prince*: to refer first to Machiavelli and second to Cesare.

37 See Machiavelli, 1996a, 313. "[I]l duca Valentino, l'opere del quale io imiterei sempre quando io fossi principe nuovo." Note also that Machiavelli invokes Cesare as a model on the grounds of his governing style alone (not a word about "one's own arms"). Machiavelli, 1971, 1191.

38 Machiavelli, 1996a, 313. "[S]enza sua riputazione, et senza potere portare al principe riverenza o timore" (Machiavelli, 1971, 1191).

39 Machiavelli, 1996a, 313. "Il duca Valentino, l'opere del quale io imiterei sempre quando io fossi principe nuovo, conosciuta questa necessità, fece messer Rimirro presidente in Romagna; la quale deliberazione fece quelli popoli uniti, timorosi dell'autorità sua, affectionati alla sua potenza, confidenti di quella; et tutto lo amore gli portavono, che era grande, considerata la novità sua, naccque da questa deliberazione" (Machiavelli, 1971, 1191).

40 Najemy, 1993, 332–3. Robert Black offers additional arguments against an ironic reading of this letter; see Black, 2013, 122–3.

41 Machiavelli, 1965, 1:33. "E ch'e' fondamenti sua fussino buoni, si vidde: che la Romagna lo aspettò più di uno mese" (Machiavelli, 1971, 268).

42 Najemy, 2013, 548.

43 Najemy, 549.

44 Mattingly, 1958, 487.

45 Benner, 2013, 107.

46 The humanist and historian Raffaele Maffei in his 1506 *Commentaria* also discussed Cesare's good government in the Romagna; see Hilgarth, 1996, 120. On Maffei see Paschini, 1953, 337–76; Ullman, 1955, 378–82; D'Amico, 1987, 468–89. According to Larner, "papal control of the province remained ineffectual until the advent of Cesare Borgia and Julius II" (Larner, 1965, 91).

47 Machiavelli, 1965, 1:157. "[E] poiché gli è preso, o vivo o morto che sia, si può fare senza pensare più al caso suo ... Del quale Duca io non verifico in tutto quanto per la alligata si scrive, solo che gli è ad Ostia ad stanza del Papa" (Machiavelli, 1971, 548–9).

48 Machiavelli, 1965, 1:157–8. "Tornò ieri un uomo di quelli che nel principio el Papa aveva mandato in Romagna, e referisce la Chiesa avere in Imola e in Furlì poca parte, perché dubitano non essere rimessi sotto Madonna, e che 'l Duca è desiderato in Imola, e che 'l castello di Furlì è per tenersi forte, e tenere fede al Duca fino a che sa che viva. È dispiaciuta questa relazione al Papa" (Machiavelli, 1971, 550).

49 Machiavelli, 1965, 1:158. "Ragionorono dipoi del duca Valentino, e in summa si vede ch'el Papa non lo tratta ancora come prigione per la vita, e lo ha fatto andare ad Magliana, dove è guardato, ed è un luogo discosto qui sette miglia. E così lo va el Papa agevolando, e cerca avere e contrassegni da lui per via d'accordo, perché non s'intenda che lo abbi sforzato ad farli dare, acciocché quelli castellani su tale opinione ch'el Duca fussi forzato, non facessino qualche sdrucito di dare quelle rocche ad ogni altro che ad el Papa" (Machiavelli, 1971, 554). Machiavelli's wording here is likely mistaken: he suggests the castellan's loyalty is to the pope rather than to Cesare. He must have meant Cesare, the only reading of this paragraph that makes sense (also consistent with his previous dispatch and Guicciardini's account, discussed next).

50 Machiavelli, 1965, 1:132. "Terzo, quanto alla sua condotta, io gli dissi, parlando sempre come da me, che l'Eccellenza di questo duca non si aveva a misurare come gli altri Signori, che non hanno se non la corazza, rispetto allo stato che tiene; ma ragionare di lui come di un nuovo potentato in Italia, con il quale sta meglio fare una lega e un'amicizia, che una condotta" (Machiavelli, 1971, 441).

51 Machiavelli, 1965, 1:137. "Due dì sono venne qui il presidente della Ruota, che questo Signore ha ordinata in questo stato, che si chiama messer Antonio da Monte a San Sovino, uòmo dottissimo, e di ottima vita, e tiene la residenza sua a Cesena" (Machiavelli, 1971, 458).

52 On the dating of this text see Black, 2013, 57–8.

53 Machiavelli, 1965, 1:169. "Ma e soldati del duca, non sendo contenti del sacco delle gente di Liverotto, cominciorno ad sacheggiare Sinigagla; et, se non fussi che il duca con la morte di molti represse la insolentia loro, l'harebbono sacheggiata tucta" (Machiavelli, 1971, 11).

54 Najemy, 2013, 551.

55 For the Last Supper parallel and an analysis of related biblical allusions in chapter 7, see McCormick, 2018, 21–44.

56 Machiavelli, 1989, 1:166. "Al quale rispose el duca che in Toscana non voleva muover guerra, per essergli e Fiorentini amici, ma che era bene contento andassino ad Sinigaglia" (Machiavelli, 1971, 9).

57 Machiavelli, 1989, 1:166. "Donde nacque che, non molti dì poi, venne adviso come la terra si era loro arresa, ma che la rocca non si era voluta arrendere loro, perché il castellano la voleva dare alla persona del duca

et non ad altro; et però lo confortavono ad venire innanzi" (Machiavelli, 1971, 9).

58 Mallett, 1969, 182.

59 Bradford, 2011, 127–9.

60 Machiavelli, 1989, 1. "Al duca parve la occasione buona et da non dare ombra, sendo chiamato da loro et non andando da sé" (Machiavelli, 1971, 9).

61 Machiavelli, 1989, 1:166. "Et, partito intorno ad mezo dicembre da Cesena, se ne andò ad Fano, dove, contucte quelle astutie et sagacità possé, persuase a' Vitegli et ad gli Orsini che l'aspectassino in Sinigaglia … Et benché Vitellozo stessi assai renitente, et che la morte del fratello gli havessi insegnato come e' non si debba offendere un principe et dipoi fidarsi di lui, nondimancho, persuaso da Paulo Orsino, suro con doni et con promesse corropto da el duca, consentì ad aspectarlo" (Machiavelli, 1971, 9).

62 Guicciardini, 1970a, 243–4. "Solo gli stati di Romagna stavano fermi, ne' quali certo, se fussi stato sano, si sarebbe conservato, perche gli aveva messo a governo di quegli popoli, uomini che gli avevano governate con tanta giustizia e integrita, che era sommamente amato da loro" (Guicciardini, 1970c, 212–13).

63 "The fortress held out for a while in the name of a Spanish castellan, who was trying to gain some personal advantage from its surrender" (Guicciardini, 1970a, 244). "[B]enchè la rocca fussi un pezzo tenuta in nome di uno castellano Spagnuolo che vi era drento, che cercava darla con suo vantaggio" (Guicciardini, 1970c, 213).

64 Guicciardini, 1969, 166. "[A]veva al presente molto Maggiore difficoltà che prima non s'era immaginato a questo e a tutti gli altri disegni, per la sua pericolosissima infermità" (Guicciardini, 2013, 732).

65 Machiavelli, 1965, 1:33. "E lui mi disse, ne' dì che fu creato Iulio II, che aveva pensato a ciò che potessi nascere, morendo el padre, e a tutto aveva trovato remedio, eccetto che non pensò mai, in su la sua morte, di stare ancora lui per morire" (Machiavelli, 1971, 268).

66 Guicciardini, 1969, 166. "Per il che si querelava con grandissima indegnazione che, avendo pensato molte volte in altri tempi a tutti gli accidenti che nella morte del padre potessino sopravenire, e a tutti pensato i rimedi, non gli era mai caduto nella mente potere accadere che nel tempo medesimo avesse egli a essere impedito da sì pericolosa infermità" (Guicciardini, 2013, 732).

67 Guicciardini, 1969, 169. "Solamente la Romagna … stava quieta, e inclinata alla divozione del Valentino; avendo per esperienza conosciuto quanto fusse più stato tollerabile a quella regione il servire tutta insieme sotto un principe solo e potente che quando ciascuna di quelle città stave sotto un signore particolare, il quale né per la sua debolezza gli potesse difendere né

per la povertà beneficar, più tosto, non gli bastando le sue piccolo entrate a sostentarsi, fusse costretto a opprimergli" (Guicciardini, 2013, 734–5).

68 My translation; "gustare el bene essere loro." I quote from Machiavelli, 1971, 267.

69 Guicciardini, 1969, 168. "Ricordavansi ancora gli uomini che, per l'autorità e grandezza sua e per l'amministrazione sincera della giustizia, era stato tranquillo quell paese da' tumulti delle parti, da' quali prima soleva essere vessato continuamente con spesse uccisioni d'uomini" (Guicciardini, 2013, 735).

70 Guicciardini, 1969, 168–9. "Con le quali opera s'avea fatti benevoli gli animi de' popoli; e similmente co' benefici fatti a molti di loro, distribuendo soldi nelle persone armigere, uffici, per le terre sue e della Chiesa, nelle togate, e aiutando le ecclesiastiche nelle cose beneficiali appresso al padre: onde né l'esempio degli altri, che tutti si ribellavano, né la memoria degli antichi signori gli alienava dal Valentino" (Guicciardini, 2013, 735).

71 Guicciardini, 1969, 169. "Il quale benchè fusse oppressato da tante difficoltà, pure e gli spagnuoli e i franzesi facevano instanza grande, con molte promesse e offerte, di congiugnerselo" (Guicciardini, 2013, 735).

72 Guicciardini, 1969, 175. "Valentino per mare se n'andasse alla Spezie e di quivi, per terra, a Ferrara e dipoi a Imola, ove si conducessino cento uomini d'arme e cento cinquanta cavalli leggieri che ancora seguitavano le sue bandiere" (Guicciardini, 2013, 751).

73 Guicciardini, 1969, 175. "[I] pontefice sdegnato lo fece ritenere in sulle galee in sulle quali era già montato, e dipoi con onesto modo menare alla Magliana; donde giubilando tutta la corte et tutta Roma della sua retenzione" (Guicciardini, 2013, 751).

74 Guicciardini, 1969, 175. "Fu condotto in palazzo, ma onorato e carezzato, benchè con diligente guardia; perchè il pontefice, temendo che i castellani, disperati della salute sua, non vendessino le fortezze a' viniziani, cercava d'avere da lui i contrasegni con umanità e con piacevolezza" (Guicciardini, 2013, 751–2).

75 "Machiavelli knew that Borgia had no chance of becoming 'lord of Tuscany'" (Najemy, 2013, 550).

76 Machiavelli, 1965, 1:32–3.

77 Guicciardini, 1970a, 211–12. "Concernevano più tosto le facultá de' cittadini e la ritornata di Piero con la ribellione di quegli che l'avevano cacciato, che la perdita della libertá e diminuzione di quello dominio ci era restato; qui, perduto Arezzo e quasi tutto lo stato nostro, si vedeva ridotta in termini la cittá, che, se el re non riparava, bisognava cedere alle condizioni che volessino gli avversari, le quali si mostravano si dure, che per meno male si sarebbe desiderata la ritornata di Piero, perché si dubitava non avere a pigliare el giogo del papa e Valentino" (Guicciardini, 1931, 231).

78 Guicciardini, 1965, 130. "Ma accelerò el mandarmi per essere le cose di Firenze in grandi travagli: per avere, quando nascessi qualche revoluzione di stato nella città, o di fuori qualche movimento pericoloso alla libertà, uno refugio dove mandare sua miglioramenti" (Guicciardini, 1961, 6).

79 Guicciardini, 1965, 130. "E per detta cagione quando mi partì' da Firenze mi dètte ducati cinquecento d'oro, e di poi a pochi giorni riscaldando le cose di Firenze me ne mandò altri cinquecento, e di quivi a non molto tempo me ne mandò mille: e di tutto benché io fussi giovane e sanza freno di persona gli rendei diligente conto" (Guicciardini, 1961, 6).

80 Machiavelli, 1965, 1:18. "Né si accorse, con questa deliberazione, che faceva sé debole, togliendosi gli amici e quelli che se gli erano gittati in grembo, e la Chiesa grande, aggiugnendo allo spirituale, che gli dà tanta autorità, tanto temporale. E fatto uno primo errore, fu costretto a seguitare; in tanto che, per porre fine alla ambizione di Alessandro e perché non divenissi signore di Toscana, fu costretto venire in Italia" (Machiavelli, 1971, 261).

81 Mallett, 1969, 190.

82 Mallett, 190; emphasis mine.

83 Mallett, 190.

84 For a discussion of the posthumous, *damnatio memoriae* portraits of the Borgia see Hilgarth, 1996, 119–29. Most sources for contemporary verdicts on Cesare's government in the Romagna are diplomatic, hence composed by ambassadors – by definition members of elite families – of hostile powers. A pair of popular poems about Cesare, however, composed shortly after his death and intended for street performances in Venice (an audience of the many rather than the few) invoke Cesare's good government and suggest that the many Romagnoli looked forward to the potential restoration of his rule. See Garnett, 1886, 138–41.

85 Soranzo, 1954, 513–45.

86 Guicciardini, 1970a, 93–4, 197.

87 Reflecting on the staggering contrast between Alexander's exceptional good fortune and equally exceptional moral turpitude, Guicciardini draws a distinctly Protestant conclusion about the limited efficacy of good works and the mysteries of predestination: "And nevertheless he had been exalted by the most unusual and almost perpetual good fortune from early youth up to the last days of his life, always desiring the greatest things and always obtaining more than he desired. A powerful example to confound the arrogance of those who, presuming to discern with the weakness of human eyes the depth of divine judgments, affirm that the prosperity or adversity of men proceeds from their own merits or demerits: as if one may not see every day many good men unjustly vexed and many depraved souls unworthily exalted; or as if, interpreting it in another way, one were to derogate from the justice and power of God, whose boundless might cannot

be contained within the narrow limits of the present, and who – at another time and in another place – will recognize with a broad sweep, with rewards and eternal punishments, the just from the unjust" (Guicciardini, 1969, 166).

88 Ridolfi, 1968, 122–36.

89 Ridolfi, 122. On the Romagnol basis for Guicciardini's analysis of the papacy's temporal power in his *History of Italy* see Fournel 2008, 41–55.

90 Quoted in Ridolfi, 1968, 125.

91 Ridolfi, 129.

92 Machiavelli, 1965, 1:10. "[U]na lunga esperienzia delle cose moderne e una continua lezione delle antique" (Machiavelli, 1971, 257).

93 Machiavelli, 1965, 1:24. "Perché, camminando gli uomini quasi sempre per le vie battute da altri, e procedendo nelle azioni loro con le imitazioni, né si potendo le vie di altri al tutto tenere, né alla virtù di quelli che tu imiti aggiugnere, debbe uno uomo prudente intrare sempre per vie battute da uomini grandi, e quelli che sono stati eccellentissimi imitare, acciò che, se la sua virtù non vi arriva, almeno ne renda qualche odore" (Machiavelli, 1971, 263–4).

94 Machiavelli, 1965, 1:134. "E el modo del mantenere è stare armato d'arme sue, vezzeggiare e sudditi e farsi amici e vicini; il che è il disegno suo" (Machiavelli, 1971, 444).

95 See Machiavelli's *Memorandum to the Medici* in Jurdjevic, Piano, and McCormick, 2019, 211–13.

Conclusion

1 Pocock, 2003; Skinner, 1978; Skinner 2012, 39–93, 118–59.

2 I use the term *republican tradition* here because it is ubiquitous in the related scholarship. James Hankins, however, has thoroughly demonstrated the inherent anachronism of that expression. The term has exclusivist connotations—the denial of legitimacy to any non-elective monarchy—that only began circulating during the Enlightenment. In most Renaissance political thought, the term *republic* was used to describe both princely rule and the power-sharing arrangements of Florence and Venice because any regime that responsibly stewarded the common good qualified as a "res publica." Aristotle and the Italian humanists all took for granted as natural the existence of a wide variety of legitimate constitutions, loosely conceptualized around the one, the few, and the many. Humanists in Florence and Venice began to use the term *res publica* in an exclusivist sense in the mid-fifteenth century but did so to accommodate the particular context that saw the two republics of Florence and Venice allied against ducal Milan and monarchic Naples (and in Florence to accommodate the

wealthy oligarchy's defeat of the popular guild regime). See Hankins, 2019, 71–85. Neither Machiavelli nor Guicciardini was a republican exclusivist. Although both certainly preferred republican rule in Florence to the Medici and championed versions of the Polybian mixed constitution, they had no difficulty accommodating to the Medici triumph in Florence and no difficulty seamlessly navigating their own republican context and the monarchical world that surrounded them during the early years of the Italian wars. Throughout his writings Guicciardini consistently argued that moral distinctions between regime types were false and that the legitimacy of any regime should be based entirely on its practical results; equally consistently, Machiavelli praised the republics and princes throughout history that empowered the people to discipline wealthy elites.

3 In his classic *Machiavelli and Guicciardini*, Felix Gilbert also treated the two thinkers as fundamentally similar in method, assumptions, and political outlook, though he was less interested in the tradition than in their creation of political realism and modern historical analysis and its connections to the world view of the Florentine ruling elite. Gilbert, 1965.

4 McCormick, 2011; McCormick, 2018; Winter, 2018.

5 Gilbert, 1965, 278.

6 Najemy, 2022, 321.

7 Strauss quoted in McCormick, 2018, 146.

Bibliography

Alvisi, Edoardo. 1878[ST1] . *Cesare Borgia: Duca di Romagna.* Imola, Italy: Tipografo d'Ignazio Galeati e figlio.

Anselmi, Gian Mario. 2006. "Machiavelli, i Borgia, e le Romagne." In *Machiavelli senza i Medici (1498–1512): Scrittura del potere / potere della scrittura,* edited by Jean-Jacques Marchand, 221–30. Rome: Salerno Editrice.

Arrighi, Vanna. 1990. "Bernardo del Nero." In *Dizionario Biografico degli Italiani,* vol. 38 (1990). Accessed online.

Ascoli, Albert Russell. 2013. "Vox Populi: Machiavelli, *Opinione,* and the *Popolo,* from the *Principe* to the *Istorie Fiorentine.*" *California Italian Studies* 4, no. 2 (2013): 1–23. https://doi.org/10.5070/c342015903

Baron, Hans. 1961. "Machiavelli: The Republican Citizen and the Author of *The Prince.*" *English Historical Review* 76 (1961): 217–53. https://doi.org/10.1093/ehr/lxxvi.ccxcix.217

Bausi, Francesco. 2005. *Machiavelli.* Rome: Salerno.

Benner, Erica. 2013. *Machiavelli's Prince: A New Reading.* Oxford: Oxford University Press.

Black, Robert. 2013. *Machiavelli.* London: Routledge.

Black, Robert. 2014. "Machiavelli and the Militia: New Thoughts." *Italian Studies* 69 (2014): 41–50. https://doi.org/10.1179/0075163413z.00000000058

Black, Robert. 2022. *Machiavelli: From Radical to Reactionary.* London: Reaktion.

Bradford, Sarah. 1976. *Cesare Borgia: His Life and Times.* New York: Macmillan.2

Brucker, Gene. 2010. "Niccolo Machiavelli, His Lineage, and the Tuscan Church." *I Tatti Studies in the Italian Renaissance* 13 (2010): 79–90. https://doi.org/10.1086/its.13.41419715

Bullard, Melissa Meriam. 1980. *Filippo Strozzi and the Medici: Favor and Finance in Sixteenth-Century Florence and Rome.* Cambridge: Cambridge University Press.

Butters, Humfrey. 2010. "Machiavelli and the Medici." In *The Cambridge Companion to Machiavelli,* edited by John M. Najemy, 64–79. Cambridge: Cambridge University Press.

Cadoni, Giorgio. 1983. “Per l’interpretazione del *Dialogo del reggimento di Firenze di* Francesco Guicciardini.” *Storia e politica* 23 (1983): 625–63.

Cadoni, Giorgio. 1994. *Crisi della mediazione politica e conflitti sociali: Niccolò Machiavelli, Francesco Guicciardini, e Donato Giannotti di fronte al tramonto della Florentina Libertas.* Rome: Jouvence.

Cadoni, Giorgio. 1999. *Un governo immaginato: L’universo politico di Francesco Guicciardini.* Rome: Jouvence.

Carta, Paolo. 2008. *Francesco Guicciardini tra diritto e politica.* Padua: Cedam.

Celli, Carlo. 2019. *The Defeat of a Renaissance Intellectual: Selected Writings of Francesco Guicciardini.* University Park: Penn State University Press.

Chiappelli, Fredi. 1984. “Guicciardini, Machiavelli, e il caso di Paolo.” *Annali d’Italianistica* 2 (1984): 53–63.

D’Amico, John. 1987. “The Raffaele Maffei Monument in Volterra.” In *Supplementum Festivum: Studies in Honor of Paul Oskar Kristeller,* edited by James Hankins, John Monfasani, and Frederick Purnell, 468–89. Binghamton, NY: MRTS.

Dietz, Mary. 1986. “Trapping the Prince: Machiavelli and the Politics of Deception.” *American Political Science Review* 80, no. 3 (1987): 777–99.3

Dionisotti, Carlo. 1980. *Machiavellerie.* Turin: Einaudi.

Fabbri, Piero Giovanni. 1987. *La conquista di Cesena da parte di Cesare Borgia, nella storiografia cesenate del Cinquecento (1500–1576). Nuova rivista storica* 81 (1987): 357–76.

Fabbri, Piero Giovanni. 1990. “Cesare Borgia a Cesena: Istituzioni, vita politica e società nella cronaca di Giuliano Fantaguzzi dal 1486–1500.” 1990. *Archivio storico italiano* 148, no. 1 (1990): 69–102.

Focher, Ferruccio. 1996. “Il *Dialogo del Reggimento* di Firenze di Francesco Guicciardini.” *Critica storica* 5 (1996): 504–38.

Focher, Ferruccio. 2000. “Francesco Guicciardini e il reggimento di Firenze: Dalle *Storie fiorentine* al *Dialogo.*” In *Libertà e teoria dell’ordine politico: Machiavelli, Guicciardini, e altri studi.* Milan: Franco Angeli.

Fournel, Jean-Louis. 2000. “L’unico dialogo di Francesco Guicciardini o la lingua della nuova repubblica.” *Giornale storico della letteratura italiana* 579 (2000): 321–36.

Fournel, Jean-Louis. 2008. “Una digressione romagnola? Il potere temporale dei papi nel IV libro della *Storia d’Italia* di Francesco Guicciardini.” In *Città in Guerra: Esperienze e riflessioni nel primo ’500,* edited by Gian Mario Anselmi and Angela De Benedictis, 41–55. Bologna: Minerva.

Fournel, Jean-Louis, and Jean-Claude Zancarini. 2009. *La grammaire de la république: Langages de la politique chez Francesco Guicciardini (1483–1540).* Geneva: Droz.

Garnett, Richard. 1886. “Contemporary Poems on Caesar Borgia.” *English Historical Review* 1, no. 1 (1886): 138–41. https://doi.org/10.1093/ehr/i.i.138

Gilbert, Felix. 1939. "Machiavelli and Guicciardini." *Journal of the Warburg Institute* 2, no. 3 (1939): 263–6. https://doi.org/10.2307/750104

Gilbert, Felix. 1965. *Machiavelli and Guicciardini: Politics and History in Sixteenth-Century Florence.* Princeton, NJ: Princeton University Press.

Gilbert, Felix. 1968. "The Venetian Constitution in Florentine Political Thought,]." In *Florentine Studies: Politics and Society in Renaissance Florence,* edited by Nicolai Rubinstein, 463–500. Evanston, IL: Northwestern University Press.

Guicciardini, Francesco. 1931. *Storie fiorentine dal 1378 al 1509.* Edited by Roberto Palmarocchi. Bari, Italy: Laterza e figli.4

Guicciardini, Francesco. 1932. *Dialogo e discorsi del reggimento di Firenze.* Edited by Roberto Palmarocchi. Bari, Italy: Laterza & Figli.

Guicciardini, Francesco. 1961. *Opera.* Edited by Vittorio de Caprariis. Milan and Naples: Riccardo Ricciardi. https://doi.org/10.1086/ahr/59.2.367

Guicciardini, Francesco. 1965. *Francesco Guicciardini: Selected Writings.* Edited by Cecil Grayson and translated by Margaret Grayson. Oxford: Oxford University Press.

Guicciardini, Francesco. 1969. *History of Italy.* Edited and translated by Sidney Alexander. Princeton, NJ: Princeton University Press.

Guicciardini, Francesco. 1970a. *The History of Florence.* Edited and translated by Mario Domandi. New York: Harper Torchbooks.

Guicciardini, Francesco. 1970b. *Maxims and Reflections of a Renaissance Statesman.* Edited and translated by Mario Domandi. Gloucester, MA: Peter Smith.

Guicciardini, Francesco. 1970c. *Opere.* Edited by Emanuella Lugnani Scarano. Turin: Unione Tipografico-Editrice Torinese.5

Guicciardini, Francesco. 1994a. *Dialogue on the Government of Florence.* Edited and translated by Alison Brown. Cambridge: Cambridge University Press.

Guicciardini, Francesco. 1994b. *Ricordi.* Edited by Giorgio Masi. Milan: Mursia.

Guicciardini, Francesco. 1997. "How the Popular Government Should Be Reformed." In *Political Philosophy,* edited by Jill Kraye and translated by Russell Price, 201–31. Vol. 2 of *Cambridge Translations of Renaissance Philosophical Texts.* Cambridge: Cambridge University Press.

Guicciardini, Francesco. 1999. *Francesco Guicciardini.* Edited by Giuseppe Pontiggia. Rome: Istituto Poligrafico e Zecca dello Stato.6

Guicciardini, Francesco. 2013. *Storia d'Italia.* Edited by Emmanuela Scarano. Turin: Unione Tipografico Editrice Torinese.

Guicciardini, Francesco. 2019. "On the Method of Electing Offices in the Great Council." In *Florentine Political Writings from Petrarch to Machiavelli,* edited by Mark Jurdjevic, John P. McCormick, and Natasha Piano. Philadelphia: University of Pennsylvania Press.

Hankins, James. 2017. "Leonardo Bruni and Machiavelli on the Lessons of Florentine History." In *Le cronache volgari in Italia,* edited by Giampaolo

Francesconi and Massimo Miglio, 373–95. Rome: Istituto storico italiano per il Medio Evo.

Hankins, James. 2019. *Virtue Politics: Soulcraft and Statecraft in Renaissance Italy.* Cambridge, MA: Harvard University Press.

Hilgarth, Jocelyn N. 1996. "The Image of Alexander VI and Cesare Borgia in the Sixteenth and Seventeenth Centuries." *Journal of the Warburg and Courtauld Institutes* 59 (1996): 119–29. https://doi.org/10.2307/751400

Jurdjevic, Mark. 2007. "Machiavelli's Hybrid Republicanism." *English Historical Review* 122 (2007): 1189–227. https://doi.org/10.1093/ehr/cem351

Jurdjevic, Mark. 2014. *A Great and Wretched City: Promise and Failure in Machiavelli's Florentine Political Thought.* Cambridge, MA: Harvard University Press.

Jurdjevic, Mark, Natasha Piano, and John McCormick. 2019. *Florentine Political Writings from Petrarch to Machiavelli.* Philadelphia: University of Pennsylvania Press.

Larner, John. 1965. *The Lords of Romagna: Romagnol Society and the Origins of the Signoria.* Ithaca, NY: Cornell University Press, 1965.

Larner, John. 1966. "Cesare Borgia, Machiavelli, and the Romagnol Militia," *Studi romagnoli* 17 (1966): 253–68. https://doi.org/10.3726/978-3-653-04463-8/21

Luciani, Vincent. 1950. "Recent Guicciardini Studies (1945–1948). *Italica* 27, no. 2 (1950): 109–27. https://doi.org/10.2307/475471

Machiavelli, Niccolò. 1965. *The Chief Works and Others.* 3 vols. Edited and translated by Allan Gilbert. Durham, NC: Duke University Press.

Machiavelli, Niccolò. 1971. *Tutte le opere.* Edited by Mario Martelli. Florence: Sansoni.

Machiavelli, Niccolò. 1988. *Florentine Histories.* Edited and translated by Harvey Mansfield. Princeton, NJ: Princeton University Press.

Machiavelli, Niccolò. 1996a. *Machiavelli and His Friends: Their Personal Correspondence.* Edited and translated by James Atkinson and David Sices. DeKalb: Northern Illinois University Press.

Machiavelli, Niccolò. 1996b. *The Discourses on Livy.* Edited and translated by Harvey Mansfield and Nathan Tarcov. Chicago: University of Chicago Press.

Machiavelli, Niccolò. 1997. *Opere.* Vol. 1, edited by Corrado Vivanti. Turin: Einaudi.

Machiavelli, Niccolò. 1998. *The Prince.* Edited and translated by Harvey Mansfield. Chicago: Chicago University Press.

Machiavelli, Niccolò. 1999. *Opere.* Vol. 2, edited by Corrado Vivanti. Turin: Einaudi.

Machiavelli, Niccolò. 2005a. *Opere.* Vol. 3, edited by Corrado Vivanti. Turin: Einaudi.

Machiavelli, Niccolò. 2005b. *The Prince.* Edited and translated by Peter Bondanella. Oxford: Oxford University Press.

Machiavelli, Niccolò. 2007. *The Essential Writings of Machiavelli.* Edited and translated by Peter Constantine. New York: Random House.

Machiavelli, Niccolò. 2019. *Machiavelli: Political, Historical, and Literary Writings.* Philadelphia: University of Pennsylvania Press.7

Mallett, Michael. 1969. *The Borgias: The Rise and Fall of a Renaissance Dynasty.* London: Paladin.

Marchand, Jean-Jacques. 1969. "L'évolution de la figure de César Borgia dans la pensée de Machiavel." *Schweizerische Zeitschrift für Geschichte* 19 (1969): 327–55.

Martinez, Ronald. 2010. "Comedian, Tragedian: Machiavelli and the Traditions of Renaissance Theater." In *The Cambridge Companion to Machiavelli,* edited by John M. Najemy, 206–22. Cambridge: Cambridge University Press.

Mattingly, Garrett. 1958. "Machiavelli's 'Prince': Political Science or Political Satire?" *American Scholar* 27, no. 4 (1958): 482–91.8

McCormick, John. 2001. "Machiavellian Democracy: Controlling Elites with Ferocious Populism." *American Political Science Review* 95, no. 2 (2001): 297–313. https://doi.org/10.1017/s0003055401002027

McCormick, John. 2011. *Machiavellian Democracy.* Cambridge: Cambridge University Press.

McCormick, John. 2015. "Machiavelli's Inglorious Tyrants: On Agathocles, Scipio, and Unmerited Glory." *History of Political Thought* 36, no. 1 (2015): 29–52.

McCormick, John. 2016. "Machiavelli's Greek Tyrant as Republican Reformer." In *The Radical Machiavelli: Politics, Philosophy, and Language,* edited by Filippo del Lucchese, Fabio Frosini, and Vittorio Morfino, 337–48. Leiden: Brill.

McCormick, John. 2017. "On the Myth of the Conservative Turn in Machiavelli's *Florentine Histories.*" In *Machiavelli on Liberty and Conflict: Commemorating the 500th Anniversary of the Composition of "The Prince,"* edited by Nadia Urbinati, David Johnston, and Camila Vergara. Chicago: University of Chicago Press.

McCormick, John. 2018. *Reading Machiavelli: Scandalous Books, Suspect Engagements, and the Virtues of Populist Politics.* Princeton, NJ: Princeton University Press.

McCormick, John. 2022. "Class Warfare in Guicciardini's Considerations on Machiavelli: Alibis, Evasions, and Counter-Provocations. " In *Republicanism and Democracy: Close Friends?,* edited by Skadi Siiri Krause and Dirk Jörke, 15–25. Berlin: Springer.

Moulakis, Athanasios. 2000. "Civic Humanism, Realist Constitutionalism, and Francesco Guicciardini's *Discorso di Logrogno.*" In *Renaissance Civic Humanism: Reappraisals and Reflections,* edited by James Hankins, 200–22. Cambridge: Cambridge University Press.

Najemy, John M. 1982. "Machiavelli and the Medici: The Lessons of Florentine History." *Renaissance Quarterly* 35, no. 4 (1982): 551–76. https://doi.org/10.2307/2861371

Najemy, John M. 1990. "The Controversy Surrounding Machiavelli's Service to the Republic." In *Machiavelli and Republicanism*, edited by Gisela Bock, Quentin Skinner, and Maurizio Viroli, 101–18. Cambridge: Cambridge University Press.

Najemy, John M. 1993. *Between Friends: Discourses of Desire in the Machiavelli-Vettori Correspondence of 1513–1515.* Princeton, NJ: Princeton University Press.

Najemy, John M. 1996. "Baron's Machiavelli and Renaissance Republicanism." *American Historical Review* 101, no. 1 (1996): 119–29. https://doi.org/10.2307/2169227

Najemy, John M. 2006. *A History of Florence, 1200–1575.* Oxford: Blackwell.

Najemy, John M. 2007. "Occupare la tirannide": Machiavelli, the Militia, and Guicciardini's Accusation of Tyranny." In *Della Tirannia: Machiavelli con Bartolo*, edited by Jérémie Barthas. Florence: Olschki.

Najemy, John M. 2009. "Civic Humanism and Florentine Politics." In *Renaissance Civic Humanism: Reappraisals and Reflections*, edited by James Hankins, 75–104. Cambridge: Cambridge University Press.

Najemy, John M. ed. 2010. *The Cambridge Companion to Machiavelli.* Cambridge: Cambridge University Press.

Najemy, John M. 2013. "Machiavelli and Cesare Borgia: A Reconsideration of Chapter 7 of *The Prince.*" *Review of Politics* 75 (2013): 539–56. https://doi.org/10.1017/s0034670513000570

Najemy, John M. 2022. *Machiavelli's Broken World.* Oxford: Oxford University Press.

Palumbo, Matteo. 2007. "L'inattualità del dialogo: Guicciardini tra Savonarola e Machiavelli." In *Governare a Firenze. Savonarola, Machiavelli, Guicciardini*, edited by Jean-Louis Fournel and Paolo Grossi, 109–24. Paris: Quaderni dell'hôtel de Galliffet.

*Paschini, Pio. 1953. "Una famiglia di curiali: I Maffei di Volterra." *RSCI* 7 (1953): 337–76. https://doi.org/10.5840/agstm196662207

Pepe, Gabriele. 1945. *La politica di Borgia.* Naples: Ricciardi.

Pocock, J.G.A. 2003. *The Machiavellian Moment: Florentine Political Thought and the Atlantic Republican Tradition.* Princeton, NJ: Princeton University Press.

Polizzotto, Lorenzo. 1994. *The Elect Nation: The Savonarolan Movement in Florence, 1494–1545.* Oxford: Oxford University Press.

Ridolfi, Roberto. 1960. *La vita di Francesco Guicciardini.* Rome: Belardetti.

Ridolfi, Roberto. 1963. *The Life of Niccolò Machiavelli.* Translated by Cecil Grayson. Chicago: University of Chicago Press.

Ridolfi, Roberto. 1968. *The Life of Francesco Guicciardini.* Translated by Cecil Grayson. New York: Alfred A. Knopf.

Roth, Cecil. 1925. *The Last Florentine Republic.* London: Methuen.

Rubinstein, Nicolai. 1954. "I primi anni del Consiglio Maggiore di Firenze (1494–99)." *Archivio storico italiano* 112 (1954): 151–94.

Rubinstein, Nicolai. 1960. "Politics and Constitution in Florence at the End of the Fifteenth Century." In *Italian Renaissance Studies: A Tribute to the Late Cecilia M. Ady*, edited by E.F. Jacob, 148–83. London.

Sasso, Gennaro. 1966. *Machiavelli e Cesare Borgia: Storia di un giudizio.* Rome: Edizione dell'Ateneo.

Sasso, Gennaro. 1984. *Per Francesco Guicciardini: Quattro studi.* Rome: Istituto Storico Italiano per il Medio Evo.

Sasso, Gennaro. 1988. "Coerenza o incoerenza del settimo capitolo del *Principe*." In *Machiavelli e gli antichi e altri saggi*, vol. 2, 119–63. Milan and Naples: Ricciardini.

Scott, John T., and Vickie Sullivan. 1994. "Patricide and the Plot of the *Prince*: Cesare Borgia and Machiavelli's Italy." *American Political Science Review* 88, no. 4 (1994): 887–900. https://doi.org/10.2307/2082714

Silvano, Giovanni. 1990. "Gli 'uomini da bene' di Francesco Guicciardini: Coscienza aristocratica e repubblica a Firenze nel primo '500." *Archivio storico italiano* 4 (1990): 845–92.

Skinner, Quentin. 1978. *The Foundations of Modern Political Thought.* Vol. 1, *The Renaissance.* Cambridge: Cambridge University Press.

Skinner, Quentin. 2012. *Visions of Politics: Renaissance Virtues.* Cambridge: Cambridge University Press.

Skinner, Quentin. 2019. *Machiavelli: A Very Short Introduction.* Oxford: Oxford University Press.

Soranzo, Giovanni. 1954. "Il clima storico della politica veneziana in Romagna e nelle Marche nel 1503." *Studi romagnoli* v (1954): 513–45.

Tafuro, Antonio. 2005. *Il reggimento di Firenze secondo Francesco Guicciardini: Condizioni politiche. Vicende personali; Scelte istituzionali.* Naples: Dante & Descartes.

Ullman, Berthold Louis. 1955. "The Maffei Codices." *Studies in the Renaissance* (1955): 373–82.

Ward, James O. 2011. "Reading Machiavelli Rhetorically: *The Prince* as Covert Criticism of the Renaissance Prince." *California Italian Studies* 2 (2011). https://escholarship.org/uc/item/4sc5s550 https://doi.org/10.5070/c322008931

Wilcox, Donald. 1984. "Guicciardini and the Humanist Historians." *Annali d'Italianistica* 2 (1984): 19–33. https://doi.org/10.5040/9781350237100.0008

Winter, Yves. 2018. *Machiavelli and the Orders of Violence.* Cambridge: Cambridge University Press.

Woodward, William Harrison. 1913. *Cesare Borgia: A Biography.* London: Chapman and Hall.

Index